Acting on Principles

Acting on Principles

A Thomistic Perspective in Making Moral Decisions

JANKO ZAGAR, O.P.

WIPF & STOCK · Eugene, Oregon

ACTING ON PRINCIPLES
A Thomistic Perspective in Making Moral Decisions

Copyright © 2010 Janko Zagar, O.P. All rights reserved. Except for brief quotations in critical publications or reviews, no part of this book may be reproduced in any manner without prior written permission from the publisher. Write: Permissions, Wipf and Stock Publishers, 199 W. 8th Ave., Suite 3, Eugene, OR 97401.

Wipf & Stock
An Imprint of Wipf and Stock Publishers
199 W. 8th Ave., Suite 3
Eugene, OR 97401
www.wipfandstock.com

ISBN 13: 978-1-60899-804-3

Originally published © 1984:
University Press of America, Inc.

NIHIL OBSTAT
R. P. Bryan Kromholtz, O.P., S.T.D.
Censor ad hoc

IMPRIMI POTEST
R. P. Emmericus Vogt, O.P., M.A.
Prior Provincialis
Die 22 Maii 2010

Manufactured in the U.S.A.

Contents

Foreword vii
Acknowledgments ix
Introduction: Moral Continuity and Change xi

PART I THE MEANING OF HUMAN LIFE
1. Acting for a Purpose 3
2. Happiness as Basic Motivation 13
3. Christian Perspective on Happiness 24

PART II CONDITIONS OF RESPONSIBILITY
4. The Nature of Voluntariness 45
5. Structure of Human Acts 55

PART III MORAL GOOD AND EVIL
6. The Nature of the Distinction 73
7. Situation Morality 94
8. Conscience 104
9. Social and Spiritual Dimension of Human Activity 127

PART IV EMOTIONS
10. Nature and Morality of Emotions in General 151
11. Love, Pleasure, and Pain 168

PART V MORAL FORMATION
12. Dispositions 183
13. Human Virtue 196
14. The Supernatural Dimension of Morality 214

Bibliography 221

Foreword

THE PURPOSE OF THIS BOOK IS TO PRESENT AQUINAS' FUNDAMENTAL moral theology, not as a historical study of a medieval theologian, but as an evaluation of his input from the perspective of our own contemporary changes and trends. Since Aquinas is both a part of the Christian moral tradition and yet different from what sometimes passes for and is criticized as this tradition, our study fills a gap in contemporary moral literature by expounding Aquinas' authentic principles of moral decisions, not as an antiquarian interest, but as a workable reference in making them.

The book is the result of some twenty years of teaching and can be used profitably for the same purpose in seminaries and colleges. Beginning with an introductory survey on moral continuity and change, the book is divided into five parts, subdivided into chapters and sections, covering the basic moral themes from the meaning of human life to the spiritual formation of the human person. Some moral cases used as illustrations are adapted from case studies in *The Hastings Center Report*, a bimonthly publication of The Hastings Center. We use the McGraw-Hill edition of the *Summa*, which has the advantage of the accompanying Latin original, although the translation sometimes lacks consistency in terminology, being the work of different translators. A bibliography of the works quoted in the text concludes our presentation.

Acknowledgments

THIS BOOK IS THE RESULT OF OVER TWENTY YEARS OF TEACHING; YEARS which have seen not only radical changes in moral attitudes and new challenges to moral norms, but also some tense moments between what became known as the old and new morality. In publishing it, I want to thank my students, who during these years stimulated my research and encouraged its publication. Since English is not my native language, this would have been impossible without substantial help from many other persons. I want to mention in particular Fr. Fabian S. Parmisano, O.P., who patiently and at the expense of his own time smoothed the rough ways of my writing and made many other valuable suggestions.

Introduction

Moral Continuity and Change

PEOPLE WHO ACT ON PRINCIPLES INVITE RESPECT AND ADMIRATION. But acting on principles has become difficult, even questionable, in our changing society, if by principles we mean universally binding norms. Moral absolutes are not in fashion, even as a matter of study. There are valuable discussions on particular moral problems, but little is being done by way of systematic preparation to help in their solution. The reason may be the suspicion generated by the traditional moral manuals which are, in fact, too legalistic and outdated for the modern world. A second reason may be the general feeling that human situations are so personal and unique that they can never be conceptualized into principles and norms.

Yet a study of moral principles imposes itself by the fact that moral decisions cannot be made in a vacuum. How do we make a moral decision? In seeking answers to moral dilemmas, we can do several things: we can guess; we can pray; we can consult; we can follow an established practice or obey the existing law; and finally, we can try to form our own conscience.

Guessing is risky, especially in grave matters; prayer is good, but it does not dispense one from personal knowledge and responsibility; the laws and customs may not cover new problems, and, being historically conditioned, people may question their current value. Consequently, while all these sources are helpful, they do not dispense one from personal learning and the formation of one's own conscience in making moral decisions. But conscience, to which and for which we are ultimately responsible, is not an isolated, self-centered criterion of everything that comes our way. Its judgment must reflect the reality in which we exist, the authenticity of the good we seek, and respect for the society in which we live. Moral decisions, personal as they are, must, therefore, take into consideration the existential human condition which is not only one of natural desire for personal happiness, but also one of human fellowship. Consequently, the search for common values or moral principles remains a moral imperative.

What a study of moral principles, or a discipline such as moral theology, aims at are not some ready-made answers or blueprints for every situation; it is rather a framework or perimeter of actions which will help us to make the right decision at the right time. In a sense, therefore, moral theology, or fundamental moral theology, if it deals with fundamental principles, is a "science," albeit of its own kind, which can be shared. Since it deals with the contingent area of human activity, it can never provide a mathematical certainty, but this does not diminish its rational reliability and practical usefulness.

The term "moral" comes from the Latin word *mos*, which can mean two things: "custom," or the way people live, and "disposition," or the way a person is inclined to act. Both meanings are related to and identical with human activity, so that human acts and moral acts are the same. The term is not always used in this way. "Moral" is often identified with good and "immoral" with bad conduct. "Moral" or morality can also mean a norm or system, as when we say "Christian morality" or "secular morality." In the plural form, "morals" usually means moral science, and "morale," as in "good morale," indicates a person's good spirit and disposition. It may be useful to remember these meanings as they occur in various texts or in our own use.

Because human life and moral life are the same, every study of human conduct must take into consideration the realities which constitute human nature and environment. One such reality is the active human mind, intelligent and free, or the human person as a subject. The other reality is the world as its object: the order of things as related to each other and to a common goal. One particular area of this reality is the moral order, or human acts as they are related among themselves and to a common goal. Thus, the mind can perceive tenderness as a value in relation to another person, and both tenderness and relationship as a mutual human need and fulfillment. The third reality is the naturalness of social relations, Aristotle's *naturaliter sociale*, as the normal condition of human existence and progress.

The fact that we are all born in time and space, i.e., in a given social environment, is of utmost moral significance. Since societies and cultures ordinarily outlive their individual members, moral science needs to consider the present in relation to the past and the future. We are historical beings. This must particularly be recognized in moral theology. As a framework of present moral decisions, moral theology draws from the past and must look to the future, because its ultimate foundation is Christ "who is the same yesterday, today and forever." The gospel, as the Vatican II *Document on Divine Revelation* states, "is the source of all saving truth and moral teaching." Yet there is a historical unfolding of the good news of Jesus Christ. If the roots are the same, the tree grows with human insights and experience past and present.

It is in the perspective of continuity and change that we propose to examine Aquinas' fundamental moral principles, testing their value in the light of contemporary developments, especially the moral teaching of the Second Vatican Council. The greatness of a Catholic theologian consists of two main qualities: his fidelity to the gospel and his relevance to the concrete human situation. We believe that Aquinas meets these requirements. He is important, not only because of his unique position in the Catholic tradition, but also because of his method and the contemporariness of his statements relative to many current issues.

Since moral principles are not a blueprint but a framework of moral decisions, the kind of method we use in formulating such principles to achieve the maximum of intelligibility, acceptance, and application becomes important. Because moral life and human life are the same, the best beginning of moral study is the common human experience itself. This seems to be man's continuous preoccupation: the meaning of his existence, "for man will always yearn to know, at least in an obscure way, what is the meaning of his life, of his activity, of his death."[1] In a like manner, Aquinas begins his moral section of the *Summa*.[2] Assuming that the human person

---

1. Vatican Council II: *The Church Today*, n. 41.

2. *Summa Theologiae* consists of three Parts: Part I treats of God in himself and of creation as proceeding from God. Part II treats the human beings as returning to God by their free response to his calling. This is the moral section which is itself divided into two parts indicated as I-II (*Prima-Secundae*) and II-II (*Secunda-Secundae*). I-II deals with general principles, both intrinsic (powers and dispositions) and extrinsic, such as

is a knowing and willing agent, the two most fundamental questions are: "What do I live for?" and "How do I achieve it?" These existential questions underlie the first basic division of the study of moral principles: the question of a human goal *(de fine ultimo)* and the question of human acts *(de actibus humanis)* as leading to or departing from such a goal.

In regard to the goal, it is important to investigate not only the facts and kinds of goals people have, but also to evaluate such goals from both a human and a Christian perspective: do people have any common goals, should they have them, is there an ultimate goal for all of us, etc.

In regard to human activity we must first inquire what we "can" do or how free we are in our moral choices. This comes under the heading of the "pre-moral condition" of human acts. Secondly, we must inquire what we "ought" to do in view of our human goals and destiny, which is the moral evaluation of human acts. This, in fact, is the central issue under which we shall discuss moral specificants, norms and conscience, situation ethics, internal and external acts and their consequences. Once this is done we shall go back to have a second in-depth look at human activity and character formation. Here we shall discuss the nature and morality of emotions, the origin and growth of moral disposition, natural and supernatural virtues, and God's special help, found in the gifts of the Spirit.

Since human beings are moral in virtue of being acting human persons, the history of morals is as old as the history of man himself. Both are subject to growth and change. Moral theology takes into consideration these changes and the way various generations and cultures formulate their ethical codes. But this is not its only consideration. Even more important is the revealed word of God. Both the Old and the New Testaments abound with moral insights, inspirations, and commandments. In fact, the permeating principle of all Christian moral teaching has always been the law of love as promulgated by Christ and continued by his disciples.

The first encounter between a specifically Christian and secular or pagan morality is revealing. The first Christians, beginning with the apos-

---

the law and grace. II–II deals with particular virtues and their ramifications. The third (III) Part of the Summa is devoted to Christ as the mediator of our salvation and to the sacraments. Each part consists of questions and articles. Each article opens with a set of objections and concludes with responses to them. Our references to the Summa follow the established practice indicating the Part, question, article, and objection or response as the case may be, e.g., III Q. 5 a. 3 ad 3.

tles themselves, were confronted not only with the pagan moral tradition, but in the case of Greeks, even with a systematic moral science. The first reaction was a suspicion not only about pagan morality, but also about the pagan attempt to formulate a moral science. Morality for the Christians was not a matter of science, but of living and loving. For a long time, therefore, what we call moral theology existed on the margin of the systematic body of the Christian dogma formulated by the early councils. This is not to say that morality was ignored and neglected: the early patristic period is rich in treatises, homilies, and exhortations often more human and perceptive than in some later periods. A more systematic treatment of moral questions was slow to come, but it has some early beginnings.

One such beginning is the *Didache* (first cent.), probably the oldest attempt at a more systematic presentation of Christian morality. Its outline of the "two ways," the way of good and the way of evil, anticipates the later structure of moral theology of virtues and vices. An even more systematic presentation may be found in Clement of Alexandria's *Stromata* ("Miscellanies") and in Origen's *Peri Archon* ("On Principles"). It is interesting that Clement referred to the Hebrew Bible and the Greek philosophy as the "two Old Testaments of Christianity," a thought which subsequently had both its supporters and its opponents. As a supporter of it, Reinhold Niebuhr observes that all modern views on human nature are variations of these two sources and that the perfect expression of this union is to be found in the Thomistic synthesis of Augustinian and Aristotelian thought.

The centuries which followed the early Christian period were marked by two currents or approaches to morality, which continued to be characteristic of moral theology throughout its history. Although such history of morals is a complex subject, as the plurality of ethical systems testifies, there are nevertheless two polarizing currents: one follows a personal, internal, and spiritual response to values, a morality of virtues; the other one consists of the observance of norms, commands, and rituals, a morality of law. The early Fathers, St. Basil and St. John Chrysostom in the East, and Augustine, Ambrose, and Gregory the Great in the West, belong to the first current; although they were concerned also with practical instruction of their clergy. Ambrose introduced from the classical pagan literature the classification of the cardinal virtues. Augustine is undoubtedly the most original and influential thinker of this period. His treatises on original sin, grace, eternal law, beatitudes, virtues, and sacraments remain a permanent contribution to the Christian theological teaching, laying the ground for future moral studies. Aquinas himself made a great use of them.

The pendulum turned around the sixth century, as the Iro-Scottish missionaries devoted themselves to the evangelization of Europe. Their missionary commitment did not allow time for other creative work; it was the administration of sacraments and implementation of the Church's discipline that preoccupied their minds. History has preserved for us a number of pastoral manuals, known as *Libri penitentiales,* which served as a help to confessors.

A revival of a more creative moral theology began in the twelfth century with the so-called "Books of Sentences," treating moral questions within general theological studies, often along the familiar patterns of the articles of faith. The best known was the *Book of Sentences* by Peter Lombard. One of Aquinas' early works was a commentary on this book. But on the whole, moral theology continued to be mainly pietistic. Neither Peter Lombard, nor even St. Bonaventure and St. Albert the Great, devised a plan that could compare to Aristotle's Ethics. Yet the Aristotelian Ethics emerged about this time as a serious challenge when the old and familiar questions were raised in the new universities: can love, happiness, and human conduct ever be the subject of a systematic knowledge?

Aquinas took the challenge. It meant a risk, as it always does, not only from a spiritual perspective but also from human consideration, to take a divine content of love and grace on the one hand and the contingent human activity on the other and submit them, so it may seem, to rational arguments and systematic treatments. But this was not really a submission. It was rather an opening of the mind to the totality of God's creative presence on a natural as well as supernatural level. The Scripture retained its spiritual and theological primacy. Its moral teaching was not only expounded by the method of the *Nichomachean Ethics,* but also enriched by Christian tradition, historical references, and the individual person's psychological and sociological experience, to the extent that these data were critically available at that time. What mattered was the principle of such an opening, and the principle was that God who speaks through Scripture speaks also through human experience and we must listen to both. The two sources of instruction are complementary in one undivided science of God: theology, of which moral theology is an integral part.

The question was this: can we think, contemplate, reason, and argue about God as he is in himself? The dogmatic definitions of the traditional theology already gave a positive answer; yes, we can. Can we think, contemplate, reason, and argue about God as he is in his creation, especially in the human person, his image? St. Thomas says: yes, we can. He has two brief and important statements in this regard: one from the beginning of the *Summa Theologiae*, and the other from the prologue to its moral part.

> Because the chief aim of the sacred doctrine is to teach the knowledge of God not only as he is in himself, but also as he is the beginning of things and their last end, and especially of rational creatures, in our endeavor to expound this science we shall treat first of God, secondly of the rational creature's movement toward God and thirdly of Christ who as man is our way to God.[3]

These are the three parts of the *Summa*. By integrating man as he is in his human and historical condition into this *totum*, theology is given a new dimension. The prologue to I–II states this in the following way:

> Because, as Damascene says, man is made in the image of God in so far as he is patterned after God through intellectuality, freedom of will and self-determination; after the discussion on the exemplar, namely God, and those things which come forth from the power of the divine will, there remains to be studied his image, namely man, in so far as he too through his free will is the principle of his own works.[4]

These introductory statements contain several important characteristics for moral theology and its study. Let us notice the following:

1. Inseparability between the human person in the world and the "image of God," which is reflected also in the inseparability between the soul and body, an important assumption of Aquinas' psychology. The human person is one; natural and supernatural values, though distinct, are nonetheless interwoven. Every human person is "the image of God," and in every human person we study, so to speak, the destiny of God in the rational creature, which is not just a part of the universe, but something very unique in the universe.

---

3. S.T. I, Q. 2, Prologus.
4. S.T. I, Q. 1, a. 1 ad 2.

2. Morality or the moral order is man's creation and distinct from the rest of nature, e.g., the physical order and laws. The image of God, as St. Thomas sees it, consists of the human person being "the principle of his works," as God is the principle of all things. Principle here means the cause or creator. As God is the creator of the entire universe, so man also is the creator of his moral universe, the moral order, the world of free human activity.

3. Moral theology is a reflection, but not an abstract reflection. It is a systematic study of human conduct proceeding from the data of reason and faith, aiming at giving a total vision of life. The term "systematic" is always a little suspect when it comes to morals and human life. We already noticed it in the case of early Christians and find it in contemporary existentialist criticism of systematic morality. The, question, however, may simply be whether we want to live our lives making moral decisions on the basis of consistent principles or merely to use a hit-and-miss method. A philosopher once insightfully remarked that the devil would gladly sacrifice the sins of an entire century for one false theory. The socialist movements of the nineteenth century, especially Marxism, seem to have had such an ideological advantage over the initial Catholic approach to social issues, which was mainly charitable. The social encyclicals of the last hundred years corrected this gap by providing a social doctrine to inspire action.

4. Moral theology is a practical science; it studies the human person in action, what he ought to do in virtue of what he is (the image of God). In regard to the works of God, theology accomplishes its work when it knows them; in regard to the works of man, its task just begins. The aim of moral theology, as we said, is not to make once and for all particular moral decisions, but to gain understanding by which such decisions are made. The task of moral theology is to show the way to a total conformity with the divine exemplar. The actual doing belongs to the individual person as well as to the community of persons; a doing that we call moral growth and maturity.

5. A final but no less important characteristic of such an understanding of moral theology is the unity of theology. Today

we have a variety of theologies: dogmatic, systematic, functional (moral), pastoral, biblical, liturgical, mystical, ecumenical, theologies of work, liberation, even the death of God theology. We live in an era of specialization and, at least academically speaking, there is a practical and legitimate reason for such specialization.

But with all due respect to specialization, there is also a danger to it. Theology is one science and moral theology in particular is not an isolated subject. All ancient and great theologians—Alexander of Hales, St. Albert, St. Bonaventure, and St. Thomas—thought of theology as one science: *scientia de Deo et aliis rebus in ordine ad Deum*, a discourse on God and of all the rest as related to God. This is what differentiates theology from other sciences of man such as psychology, sociology, economics, etc. The term "moral theology" is itself of a later development; Aquinas never uses the term. The practical implication of this is very important; it tells us that one cannot really be a moral theologian without being a total theologian; that there is no true moral knowledge without the knowledge of the Christian truth (dogma), and that there is no separation between contemplation and action, but action reflects contemplation and contemplation flows into action.

The unity of theology as envisioned by the great scholastics did not last for very long. The first attack came from the nominalism of William Ockham (1285-1359). With his emphasis on the particular as the only reality, he also separated the will from reason, freedom from knowledge, and action from contemplation. The result was a total particularization of every human act with obligation to one's own will as the central moral theme; a theme brought to its pedestal in Kant's categorical imperative some centuries later. But there were less drastic breaks. A Dominican, St. Antoninus of Florence (1389-1459), bishop of a rich and corrupt city and pressed by moral cases, published in 1454 a separate moral treatise: *Summa Moralis*. Later, in the sixteenth century, a Jesuit theologian, Gabriel Vasquez, argued that the second Part of Aquinas' *Summa* should not be treated as a theological work because it deals too much with the natural and positive laws which are not theological subjects. Both the Dominicans and the Jesuits protested against such separation on the grounds of Aquinas' own argument that there is no reason why one and the same thing could not be looked upon from both natural reason and supernatural revelation: "there is nothing to stop the same things from being treated by the philosophical sciences when they can be looked at in the light of natural reason and by another science when they are looked at in the light of divine revelation."

The sixteenth-century neo-scholastics defended the unity of theology, but not for very long. The desire to purify theology from what was called the stains of scholasticism, together with the new, post-tridentine missionary needs and new catechetical methods, brought about the disunity and separation that we still feel today. Moral theology began to lose its dogmatic (and biblical) foundation and became practical instruction. Torn away from its roots in contemplation, it ended in casuistry and legalism. Its focus was not God and things related to God, nor the human person's free return to God, the ultimate end, but how to make a good confession and a valid marriage. This was the time of the discovery of the new world, with great pastoral demands and little time for study. Moral manuals and *vademecum*s replaced the great summas.

The spirit of the Renaissance has something to do with the new development, although in a different way. With the revival of Greek art, philosophy, and anthropology, the Renaissance man emerged as a self-sufficient being in much greater degree than the scholastics would allow. St. Thomas makes a distinction between the natural and the supernatural; he grants man's autonomy in the realm of the natural, cultural, and social possibilities, but he always adds that even in this order there is no progress without God's help (*non tamen sine adjutorio divino*). The efficient presence of the first mover is always there. The Renaissance, as did our modern time, lost this insight into the divine presence. In contrast to this humanism, the Reformation went to another extreme, denying any efficiency to the natural man and his works and emphasizing "faith alone." It is against this Protestant position that the Catholic moralists of this time, in the spirit of the Renaissance, reacted by emphasizing—perhaps just a little too much—"works alone," the *opus operatum* or *finis operis* of objective morality. As confidence in reason declined through philosophical skepticism following Descartes' universal doubt and British empiricism, the exclusive role of the will grew: the will of God with his commandments and the will of isolated individuals seeking their conformity to it. This is what prepared the way for our contemporary situation.

Contemporary moral theology suffers in two of its basic, traditional assumptions: goal or meaning to human life and the means to it, namely human activity or human freedom and responsibility.

There is today what we may call a "goal crisis," especially of an ultimate goal or purpose of human life. Individuals are confused about any ultimate meaning of their lives; married couples don't know what their happiness is; religious communities argue about their purpose and relevance; and citizens doubt the common good of their countries. Human energy is still there, but having no long-range objective, it ends in immediate gratification as the only reality.

There is also a "responsibility crisis." Contemporary mentality does not face freedom and responsibility; it rather suppresses it by suppressing personal moral guilt, attributing it to psychological disorder or social environment.

In evaluating contemporary moral theology, two observations should be made. One is that what came to us under the name of "tradition" is mainly the post-tridentine, legalistic morality with its emphasis on acts rather than agents. This obscured and sometimes actually distorted the authentic mind of Aquinas and, for that matter, of the early Christian and patristic theology. The second observation is that the world has indeed changed since the thirteenth century. There are new psychological and sociological factors to be taken into consideration: cultural and religious pluralism; mobility of the population; greater technological control of human life and death; birth control technique and availability, which put sexuality and family into a different perspective; economic and political relations with new liberation movements; plus the internal problems of the Church, the question of authority and infallibility, biblical criticism, etc. Such developments seem to challenge moral theology in its two basic sources of information: reason, by doubts about the moral value of the natural law in a technological age, and revelation by new hermeneutics and critical attitudes of the Church's magisterium.

Contemporary moral theology has some of its own challenges and perplexities. As human progress and experience sharpen the conflicts of values, doubt of their absoluteness increases. If telling the truth is an absolute value, how does one reconcile it with the value of saving life by "lying" about the identity or hiding place of an innocent person in time of persecution, as the examples of the Second World War still bring to memory? Or, if life is an absolute value, how much must a family spend, a doctor do, or a society pay to keep one alive, perhaps in a vegetative state or against the patient's own will? A more welcome challenge is the return of the scientific and public world to moral questions. For a long time in the modern world, the standard approach to political, legal, economic, and international areas of life has been analytical, not moral: a bloodless data analysis, not moral concern. This is changing, we may say, by popular demand, as the political scandals (Watergate, Vietnam War), legal shortcomings in questions of death, transplants, abortion, and economic and international situations call for moral assessment of human rights and priorities beyond and above the abstract knowledge of facts. While the challenge is welcome, the partnership between science and morals is not easy. It is a give-and-take partnership in which the Catholic moral theology seeks a greater flexibility in comparison with the traditional legalistic attitude, and the Protestant theology, traditionally subjectivist and existentialist, searches for a more systematic framework.

In its *Decree on Priestly Formation*, the Second Vatican Council calls for an updating of moral theology: "a special attention needs to be given to the development of moral theology." In response to this call, as well as to the new social and scientific challenge, attempts are being made to formulate and bring about such a renewal. Among the tendencies which have emerged, the following merit mention, although not necessarily endorsement: a) the rejection of the natural law approach of the manuals and replacing it with positive, especially psychological and sociological science; b) the revision of a more authentic, Thomistic concept of the natural law, not as a static, biological function but as a dynamic and empirical understanding of human nature; c) the shift of emphasis from object and physical effects to the knowing human subject and his perceptions, or what Karl Rahner calls "the discernment of the Spirit in decision making;" d) inter-subjectivity ethics, which views morality as a relationship or the way of living with one another; e) love-ethics, which relies on empirical evaluation of the consequences of actions in terms of love or a total human benefit; and f) fundamental option morality, which stresses the role of a person's ultimate goal of life. This is not an exhaustive list of contemporary currents, but it is sufficient perhaps to indicate the underlying concern and trend.

In general, there is a reorientation from the traditional emphasis on objective order and moral act in itself to the human person and his call in Christ; a reorientation from commandments and sin to a call and response in love.

Our own study of moral principles will be in view of preparing ourselves to deal with concrete, situational problems of our time.

Consequently, we must keep an open mind: if the tradition can answer our question, we thank the tradition; if it cannot, we seek another answer. Again, what we are seeking is not a list of ready-made answers, a code, but a framework of reference to escape confusion.

In this context, an updating of moral theology and its liberation from legalism is imperative, but concessions and popularity contests are not valid substitutes. If Christian morality is a call to perfection and our free response to it, it must be taken seriously, and the formation of personal conscience must be its central concern. It is important that as Christians we emphasize our specifically Christian vision of the world and values. But attention must also be paid to the pluralistic nature of our society. What is the basis of our dialogue: is it to be Christian or to be human? Are we opposed to abortion as Christians or as human beings? The natural law morality may still hold an important place, as the Christian vision of eternity must be tested in time and space. For these reasons, our moral theology cannot be only scriptural; it must also be scientific (with all the limitations of a moral science). In this context, the suggestion of the *Decree on Priestly Formation* concerning moral theology, in particular the contribution of Thomas Aquinas, may not be just lip service. It says that "by way of making the mysteries of salvation known as thoroughly as they can be, students should learn to penetrate them more deeply with the help of speculative reason under the tutelage of St. Thomas."[5] This is what we shall try to do.

---

5. Vatican Council II, *Decree on Priestly Formation*, n. 16.

Part I

The Meaning of Human Life

1

Acting for a Purpose

IN OUR STUDY OF MORAL PRINCIPLES, WE HAVE TO USE CERTAIN TERMS which will be fully explained as we proceed. One such term is "human act," which is defined as an act done with knowledge and will, or a deliberate and responsible act. This does not say all about a human act, but it gives us a beginning. This beginning is rather important. Aquinas writes that "human acts and moral acts are the same." This means that morality and human living are the same and that a study of morality must begin with ordinary human experience. Now the most fundamental and obvious experiential facts in human life are the facts of motivation or purpose, and the search for happiness. Victor E. Frankl, a survivor of the World War II concentration camps, writes in *Man's Search for Meaning*: "There is nothing in the world, I venture to say, that would so effectively help one to survive even in the worst conditions, as the knowledge that there is a meaning in one's life."[1] Frankl's psychological tenet is that therapy comes from meaning, not meaning from therapy.

Reflecting on the same phenomenon, Erich Fromm says that unless a person belonged somewhere, "unless his life had some meaning and direction, he would feel like a particle of dust and be overcome by his individual insignificance. He would not be able to relate himself to any system which would give meaning and direction to his life. He would be filled with doubt, and this doubt eventually would paralyze his ability to act—that is to live."[2]

---

1. Frankl, *Man's Search for Meaning*, 105–106.
2. Fromm, *Escape from Freedom*, 36.

4 Acting on Principles

Moral theology begins with and remains centered on the fact of motivation and the search for meaning and happiness. Both motivation and the search for happiness are not only a common psychological experience; they are also supported scripturally, especially by the eschatological character of the gospel. The law of nature accords with the law of revelation: "For this law that I enjoin on you today is not beyond your strength or beyond your reach. It is not in heaven, so that you need to wonder, 'Who will go up to heaven for us and bring it down to us, so that we may hear it and keep it?' No, the Word is very near to you, it is in your mouth and in your heart for your observance. See, today I set before you life and prosperity, death and disaster" (Deut. 31: 11–15).

Aquinas therefore begins his treatise on morality with what seems to be self-evident: the fact of motivation and the desire for happiness. Both are a common psychological experience. Explicitly or implicitly, they contain a series of morally significant propositions which may be useful to summarize at this point. They are:

1. All human (i.e., deliberate) activity is always for an end or purpose.

2. In all subordinated (related) human acts, there is always an ultimate end or purpose.

3. At least implicitly, there is an ultimate end of the entire human life in which formally, although not necessarily materially, all people agree. Happiness is considered to be such an ultimate end.

4. End or purpose is the cause of every human act, and as such it gives to the act its first moral specification.

5. Only a common ultimate end, not only formally but also materially common, can unite collective and individual human efforts into a social harmony and cooperation; only a supreme ultimate good which satisfies all human aspirations can qualify for such an ultimate end.

The first two theses, "acting for an end" and the existence of an "ultimate end in each subordinate series of actions," are experiential facts. "Acting for an end" or having a motive pertains to the definition of human acts which are always done with knowledge and will or else they are not properly human. It seems obvious also that there must be an ultimate end or purpose in every series of related human activity, since it makes no sense to enroll in a college, to pay tuition, attend classes, etc., unless one hopes to learn something, to graduate and make use of it in life. And if someone enrolls just to have something to do, then that is his end.

It is less obvious that a person's entire life (all actions combined) is ordained to a determined ultimate end; in other words, that every person has a constant and systematic vision of his or her life. John Dewey explicitly rejects the idea of "fixed ends" as contrary to change and progress. The fact is that the conceptions of happiness fluctuate and that an ultimate end can only be specified by demonstration or accepted on faith. It is even less obvious that there is a common ultimate end for all human persons and all generations, as the national and international differences and conflicts concerning a common goal of humanity sorrowfully prove. We must say, therefore, that the true concern of moral study is not so much the fact of motivation or of an ultimate purpose in related activity, but rather and primarily the existence and meaning of an ultimate goal of human life, the *finis vitae humanae* as Aquinas keeps repeating, and the way to achieve it.

TERMINOLOGY

Moral theology, like every other science, uses certain terminology which becomes its technical language. One such term or expression concerning the question of end is that "end specifies the act." This means that the purpose for which an act is done determines the moral value of the act. Some acts seem to have a built-in finality, with which a personal purpose or motive may or may not agree. Thus, the end of stealing is stealing (taking what belongs to another against his will), although the thief may steal because of an emergency (stealing a boat to escape captivity in a war), or because he is a compulsive gambler and needs money. Such personal motivation makes a moral difference, but there is a considerable disagreement as to what extent, if at all, such motivation can change the built-in purpose of an act, particularly if the act is evil in itself. This is a central issue of morality to which we shall return in due course.

Another technical expression along the same line says that "the end is first in intention and last in execution" *(primum in intentione et ultimum in executione)*. This means that the agent first perceives and intends his goal and then proceeds to achieve it. This also is morally significant, because it raises the question as to what extent a pure desire or intention of an end, without its materialization, affects the moral goodness or badness of a person.

Aquinas takes up this relationship between the end and the act to point out something that will remain fundamental to his own conception of morality and moral study, namely that it is the end which determines the goodness or badness of a human act: end as known and specified by the reason, or as perceived by the agent, and presented to the will for realization. Here is his statement:

> An act done but once is not directed except to one immediate end, and from this it gets its specific character, but it can be meant for several further ends, of which one is designed for another. All the same it is possible for an act of one physical kind to be willed for diverse ends; for instance the taking of human life considered as a physical event is generically always the same, yet considered as a moral act it can be of specifically different kinds when the purpose is upholding justice or when satisfying anger: one is an act of virtue, the other an act of vice. Now an action receives its specific character from a term that is essential to it, not incidental. Moral purposes lie outside merely natural processes, and conversely the purpose there does not constitute moral situations. And so there is nothing to stop acts of the same physical category from belonging to diverse moral categories, and vice versa.[3]

The relationship between a built-in end or "the end of the act," as we call it, and "the end of the agent," or the subjective perception of a built-in end of an act will be the focus of our analysis of Aquinas' understanding of objective morality. Such subjective perception of the end still differs from subjective motives of the agent, as an erroneous conscience differs from intentional choice of what one knows to be wrong.

CLASSIFICATION OF ENDS

It is obvious that in our daily life we have many and different ends, although in view of an ultimate goal which keeps us moving. Certain ends as certain things are desired for themselves, e.g., life and health; other things are desired for something else, e.g., medicine or diet for health. This introduces a useful distinction between the primary and secondary ends, with an *ultimate end* always in the background. The role of an ultimate end must itself be explained by another distinction between related

3. S.T. I–II, Q. 1, a. 3 ad 3.

and unrelated ends. This means that in the variety of purposes some are related (vertically), e.g., working, saving money, buying property, building a house, living in it; while other ends relate only horizontally, as we want money, then changing our mind we want land, or power, etc. It is only in the related ends (*fines ordinati per se*) that there must be an ultimate end; in other words, a series of causally related purposes cannot proceed indefinitely (*non datur processus ad infinitum*). The argument is reminiscent of the *Prima Via*, Aquinas' argument from motion for the existence of God as the first mover. On the horizontal level or in unrelated ends, we can keep changing our preferences indefinitely. There is a moral significance in this classification of ends, too. Although the primary ends and especially an ultimate end are the most important, in practice we must not underestimate the role of the secondary ends: a good grade or a better-paying job are valid motivations.

ULTIMATE END

There are many questions which we can and will be asking about the meaning of an ultimate end, particularly the end or meaning of human life as a whole. Two such questions must be asked now. Assuming, as we do, that there is purpose in nature and in human activity, the first question Aquinas asked is "what it signifies" or how important is the conception itself of an ultimate goal in human life. The other question is "what it is when achieved," or in what, specifically, does such an ultimate end consist: what is our true happiness? Let us elaborate a little further on these two questions.

END: WHAT IT SIGNIFIES

Some kind of an ultimate purpose or fulfillment within the limits of our own experience seems to be structured in nature itself. There is always a beginning and an end of life: birth and death as two mysterious principles governing our human existence. However, the meaning of the end in our present context is not the end in a physical sense, death, but *finis* as a fulfillment, an achievement; *telos* in Greek and hence the term "teleological ethics." Vatican II's *Declaration on the Relationship of the Church to Non-Christian Religions* echoes this teleological basis of morality when it states: "Men look to the various religions for answers to those profound mysteries of the human condition which, today, as even in olden times, deeply stir the human heart: What is man? What is the meaning and the purpose of his life? What is goodness and what is sin? What gives rise to our sorrows and to what intent? Where lies the path to true happiness? What is the truth about death, judgment and retribution beyond the grave? What, finally, is that ultimate and unutterable mystery which engulfs our being, and whence we take our rise and whither our journey leads us?"[4] It is in the context of such existential and perennial questions that the treatise of the ultimate end must be viewed; it is these questions that moral theology makes its own.

A special reason why the question of an ultimate end is important is the fact that, from a Christian and Catholic position, we already have an answer to what an ultimate end is: God is our ultimate end. The answer, however, is only the beginning of another question: what does it mean to have God as the ultimate goal in our present, human condition: what does it mean socially and politically; to a worker, a physician, a teacher, a husband and wife, etc.?

The significance of ultimate end is further seen in regard to the point of departure or the point of reference in morality. It suggests a morality of vision rather than a morality of obedience to nature. It is of capital importance for our study and understanding of morality that the point of departure is, as we already stated, the human person in his or her perception of a life vision.

A careful reading of Aquinas' text reveals such a point of departure. We must not be misled by his frequent references to the Aristotelian physics or even metaphysics; to the purpose in nature as the exemplar of the purposeness in human life. The analogy is there, but there is also a profound difference so that the teleological principle in nature must not lead to a naturalistic and biological conception of human life.

It is important to note that Aquinas begins his moral treatise not by identifying man with the rest of nature and its cosmic laws, but by differentiating him from it. There is a distinction between the physical and the moral order; between the function of nature (including biological functions of the human body) and the free, contingent, and responsible human activity. This is why the subject matter of morals is not finality in a cosmic sense, but a human end: *finis vitae humanae*. We look at man not as a part of nature, but rather that he is not. The human person alone is "the

---

4. Vatican Council II, *Declaration on the Relationship of the Church to Non-Christian Religions*, n. 1.

image of God;" the rest of nature is only his trace, *vestigium Dei*. Hence the familiar distinctions which we find in this opening text: distinction between "a human act" and "an act of man" (*actus humanus* and *actus hominis*); "natural activity" and "rational activity" (*agere per naturam et agere per intellectum*); "natural appetite" and "rational appetite" *(appetitus naturalis et appetitus rationalis)*, etc. There is a finality (*telos*) in nature, but it is only in the human person that such finality becomes a free and conscious motivation.

Finally, the significance of the ultimate end, "what it signifies," implies that moral life, and especially Christian moral life, is not only or primarily a life of obligation (obedience to laws), but also and primarily a life of vision in which obligation (ought) is in fact a free response to value (is).

END: WHAT IT IS WHEN ACHIEVED

The term which we use to describe the content of an ultimate end when realized is *happiness*; a term inherited from Aristotle, and frequently used as a value concept in ethics. The term, however, seems to beg the question. We shall discuss "happiness as the basic motivation" in our next chapter. Let us conclude this section with a few additional introductory remarks and with reference to a contemporary moral current related to the idea of an ultimate end known as the fundamental option.

The most important remark we can make is that instead of beginning his moral theology with the Decalogue, or the Precepts of the Church, or some other extrinsic norms, Aquinas begins with man's natural drive for happiness. We all want to be happy: *homo naturaliter desiderat beatitudinem*.[5] People must not be blamed for wanting to stay alive, to prosper and feel good, to advance socially, etc. Life, liberty, and happiness are the self-evident truths of the modern "Declarations of Human Rights." "To be good and to be desirable signify the same," writes Aquinas in another place, "and since evil is the opposite of good, it is out of the question that any evil as such can be directly wanted, either by natural appetite, or by animal appetite or by intelligent appetite which is will."[6] We cannot have a more optimistic beginning of moral study. But what is good, what is happiness, and why people go wrong, are different questions.

5. S.T. I, Q. 2, a. 1 ad 1.
6. S.T. I, Q. 19, a. 9.

FUNDAMENTAL OPTION

One contemporary theological current blending with the traditional concept of an ultimate end is the so-called "fundamental option." The term comes from Karl Rahner, although the idea under such terms as "basic freedom," "basic moral decision," and "basic self-determination" is not new. Joseph Fuchs follows Rahner in this, and Bernard Häring has a lengthy chapter (V) on "Fundamental Option" in Vol. I. of his *Free and Faithful in Christ*.

What fundamental option basically means is that people have and ought to have a sound life orientation, as when one chooses to be a Catholic. When such life direction is made seriously, it is expected that, failures notwithstanding, all other acts and aspirations will fall in line with it. Karl Rahner argues that freedom is not mere choice between objects and acts as they occur in life. Life itself, he says, is a choice: a choice of self in a total perspective of one's existence. In the Christian context, this becomes a choice between a self-realization in the direction of God, or a radical refusal of self to God. To be true, the choice of such basic freedom is worked out through human acts, but it is achieved over the period of man's entire lifetime. Consequently, morality shifts from its traditional emphasis on individual and particular acts and objects to the perduring intentionality of a person's "fundamental option."[7]

Fundamental option is a response to what seems to be a shortcoming in the traditional ultimate-end morality, namely its overemphasis on moral determination through object, motive and circumstances of each particular act without due attention to the long-range life vision and character development. The perspective of the ultimate is lost in the casuistry of the particular. This may have adverse effects on a person's moral growth. Individual acts are often imperfect and sinful, a fact of human weakness. An overemphasis on such particular acts, full of failures and frustrations, may be psychologically and morally destructive of the total person whose total orientation toward good and God still persists. In the words of Karl Rahner, "there is a basic act of freedom which embraces and shapes the whole of human existence. This act is indeed realized and can be exercised only by means of those individual acts of man which can be localized in space and time and which can be objectified with regard to their motives. Yet this basic act cannot be simply identified by

---

7. McCool, *A Rahner Reader*, 255–62.

an objective reflection with such individual acts; it does not represent either the merely moral sum total of these individual acts, nor can it be simply identified with the moral quality of the last of the free individual acts exercised (before death). The concrete freedom of man by which he decides about himself as a whole by effecting his own finality before God, is the unity in difference of the formal *option fondamentale* and the free individual acts of man no longer attainable by reflection, a unity which is the concrete being of the subject of freedom having-achieved-itself."[8]

Joseph Fuchs, who follows Rahner in this regard, may be somewhat clearer on this subject. In his view, the fundamental option for Christians is Christ. "The following of Christ means simply to be a Christian . . . The following of Christ is basically not this or that categorical act of Christian behavior, but the transcendental commitment of the self. All true morality, then, is the following of Christ, because it is sustained by this transcendental commitment; not this or that way of behavior in certain circumstances, but that true moral behavior which is in harmony with the spirit of Christ and thereby 'imitates' the attitude of Christ."[9]

Like Rahner, Fuchs also does not want to deny the importance of the individual, "categorical" acts and "philosophical reflection." But in their moral evaluation, he relies on what Rahner calls "faith instinct," an assumption that good people will somehow feel instinctively what is good and right.

Fundamental option is an attempt to deal with the dialectic of the total and particulars in the existence and psychological and moral development of the human character. For this reason, Häring points out in his analysis of the subject, that fundamental option is both supporting and supported by those contemporary psychologists who, like Eric Erikson, Abraham Maslow, Victor Frankl, and Erich Fromm, stress the importance and capacity of integral personal growth in the formation of character. In this regard, too, the fundamental option is not such a new conception of morality. To quote Fr. Häring again, "the traditional moral theology, especially the Thomist branch, gave proper attention to the basic decision for the ultimate end (*finis ultimus*). All the individual decisions and the quality of one's freedom depend on this choice."[10]

---

8. Ibid., pp. 259–60.
9. Fuchs, *Human Values and Christian Morality*, 161–62.
10. Häring, *Free and Faithful in Christ*, 1: 164.

So what is the difference? To the extent that fundamental option does not become a mere justification of whatever a person does, a "faith alone" principle, the difference may be one of emphasis and pedagogy. What is more important, the person or his acts? A person-oriented morality or an act-oriented morality? Vatican II's "Pastoral Constitution on the Church" (*Gaudium et Spes*) deals with the same issue in regard to conscience: is conscience a person- or an act-oriented reality? This, of course, will be a central issue of our own study of morality, which we cannot anticipate at this time.

For Aquinas, as we shall see, morality must be total and it must be specific, personal (in the sense of total person), and particular (in this or that act). In the words of St. Paul: "If I speak with human tongues and angelic . . . if I give everything I have to feed the poor and hand over my body to be burned, but have no love, I gain nothing" (1 Cor. 13). Yet what is love if such particular acts do not matter, and how do we determine that they are in the line of such love? Fundamental option theologians do not reject the importance of such individual "categorical" acts, but it is not clear how "the person" and "the act" morality can be successfully harmonized without the traditional (Thomistic) schema of moral specification through object, motive, and circumstance.

2

Happiness as Basic Motivation

MORALITY IS HUMAN LIFE ITSELF; MORE PRECISELY, FREE HUMAN activity. Whatever pertains to this activity has a moral significance. For this reason we take the fact of "acting for a purpose" as our starting premise, since it is the most obvious and most fundamental human experience. For the same reason, we take the "search for happiness" as an integral part of this premise since this, too, is an obvious psychological and sociological phenomenon. In fact, the end and happiness are practically the same reality because acting for an end implies acting for some good or happiness, whether true or apparent. Evil, like pain, is never an object of desire; if it seems to be, it is only under the aspect of some good.

Unlike physical realities, such as water or air, happiness cannot be scientifically defined. It is, nevertheless, experienced and described as "that which all desire." Yet it is not uncommon either in popular estimation or ethical studies to identify happiness with a particular satisfaction. In this regard happiness can mean anything from an evening cocktail to listening to music or contemplating truth. Consequently, the question is not whether people seek enjoyment, but whether what they enjoy is the best enjoyment. The old adage *de gustibus non disputatur* holds only to a certain point, since most of the time our tastes and our gratifications have to be adjusted both to our own long-range interests and to the interests of others. The result is that our understanding of happiness as our basic motivation calls for a realistic view of ourselves as human persons. This view, in turn, includes two important facts: one is that we must view ourselves in the total perspective of our existence, which means to keep in mind not only the present and immediate gratification, but also the future consequences; the other fact is our human fellowship or our social interdependence, which limits individual claims.

PERSPECTIVES ON HAPPINESS

If happiness or good is a natural and legitimate moral motivation, what are the possibilities open to us?

St. Augustine writes in *The City of God* (Book 8) that there are basically two perspectives on the extrinsic search for happiness: one is natural or philosophical; the other, supernatural or theological. The natural or philosophical perspective concentrates on temporary and worldly possibilities of happiness; the supernatural or theological perspective directs our attention to God and the other-worldly realities as the ultimate happiness.

Those who limit their search for happiness to the natural or philosophical possibilities may seek happiness of the body, the soul, or a humanistic harmony of both.

Human search for happiness is more complex than any classification can describe. In I–II, Q. 2, aa. 1–8, Aquinas takes some of the most common human aspirations and examines their credentials for an authentic human fulfillment. There is no doubt that people have always been motivated by riches, honors, fame, power, bodily health, and pleasure, as well as by intellectual and moral excellence. The emphasis on one or another of these values colors not only a person's character, but very often the mentality of entire societies. Thus, nineteenth-century individualistic capitalism and its counterpart, Marxist materialism, are both based on the primacy of material and bodily interests, which still permeate the contemporary social mentality and plight. There are always persons who react against such materialism by emphasizing religious and spiritual values and seeking happiness in personal withdrawal, mystical experience, religious communes and conversion, and similar phenomena, not uncommon in the modern world. While all these values may have a legitimate place in human aspirations, and some more than others, the point is that none provides the complete satisfaction to the human heart, and most of them are unreliable. As an eighteenth-century French writer, Mme. de Puisieux, puts it: "Happiness is like a ball we run after when it rolls and kick when it stops." The century was famous for its concern for happiness, an immediate and total happiness, and literally hundreds of books and pamphlets were published under the same title: happiness.

Secular human experience is not the only witness to such universal search for happiness. There is, as St. Augustine writes, the theological perspective as well, or what we shall call the Christian perspective on happiness. This, however, is an issue by itself, which we shall discuss later.

SUMMA AND THE BASIC DISTINCTIONS

In the treatise on the ultimate end with which the I–II of the *Summa* opens, Aquinas devotes the first question to the end in general and the four subsequent questions to the subject of happiness. On the surface, these questions may appear to be a kind of ethical cliché, which may be the reason why there is such a conspicuous absence of similar discussion in most of contemporary moral theology, as if we have to shun our natural drives and our human and Christian aspirations.

It is true that in a certain sense, and theologically speaking, we begin with a preconceived idea, namely that God is our ultimate happiness. But there is a lot for a moralist and a theologian to learn and to explain what precisely this means in concrete terms, in the present human condition. As *Lumen Gentium* states: "We must give an answer to those who seek an account of that hope of eternal life which is in us."

This is what Aquinas, as a theologian, offers to do: to give an account of a specifically Christian hope of happiness. But this hope is offered in time and space of our human existence and in a competitive world of different and more immediate alternatives. Consequently, our understanding and evaluation of happiness in general must be pursued in greater depth. In order to do this, Aquinas offers a series of distinctions and clarifications, which put things and values into a better perspective and order.

The treatise on happiness or *beatitudo* unfolds along two main questions: *What constitutes happiness* or what person or thing can make us happy (I–II, QQ. 2–4); and *How do we attain it* or how do we appropriate it to ourselves (I–II, Q. 5). Assuming that we are talking about an ultimate all-comprehensive happiness, the first question gradually eliminates, one after another, all temporary possibilities and leads to a theological conclusion that if there is such a thing as an absolute happiness, it can only be God. Once this is said (and in Christian faith accepted) the second question—how do we attain happiness—becomes an intriguing theological speculation about what the eternal life, promised by Christ, is all about. We shall return to this question.

On the basis of our two sources of information, human experience (reason) and revelation (faith), and parallel to St. Augustine's double perspective on happiness, Aquinas can introduce his first distinction between a *natural* or *imperfect* and a *supernatural* or perfect happiness. Natural happiness is possible in and belongs to this world. But whatever we choose as our happiness in this world, it is confined by it and by our own existential limitations and thus imperfect, considering our unlimited desires. The fact is that by our natural skill and powers we can obtain many good things in life; health, knowledge, peace, a high standard of living, etc. But we know their limitations. Supernatural happiness, as the word says, is beyond this world, a gratuitous gift of God to those who believe. It is a perfect happiness which cannot be achieved without grace, and ultimately it is reserved for life in heaven.

A second important distinction is between *objective* and *subjective* happiness. By objective happiness, we mean the person or thing that makes us happy, e.g., wealth, other people, God in himself; by subjective happiness, we mean the way we are happy, e.g., seeing our vast possessions, feeling healthy, touching, hearing, contemplating, etc. Synonymous terms for the same distinction are material and formal happiness. Thus, money may be our material happiness and our use and enjoyment of it our formal happiness. A point should be made here: only God is both objective and subjective happiness in himself (his being is his happiness); everything else and specifically all human beings have some relationship and dependence on something or somebody for their happiness. A few additional distinctions should be mentioned as a help in reading the *Summa* on this matter. Aquinas speaks of *beatitudo per se* and *beatitudo per participationem*. Happiness *per se* or by itself is once again self-sufficiency, which Aquinas attributes only to God. In his estimation, everything else is happiness by participation. Along the same line, he speaks of *created* and *uncreated happiness*. Finally, because we may and often are wrong in choosing our happiness, there is a true (*vera*) and a false (*falsa*) happiness. So much for the distinctions and terminology.

OBJECTIVE HAPPINESS

In examining a theological and moral issue such as we are presently discussing in regard to an ultimate end and our human happiness, there are two things to be kept in mind as a test for the validity of our argument:

one is how true and authentic is our assumption in relation to the revealed word of God (Scripture and tradition); the second one is how true and convincing such an assumption is to the existential individual and social human experience. Thus, when we argue that God is our ultimate happiness, we must have a foundation for this in Scripture and the faith of the Church, and the argument must have a meaning for human needs and aspirations; in other words, we must be able to work out a reasonable program of life on the basis of faith and experience, a program which will be both Christian and human.

Such a program is not always easy: throughout the history of Christianity there has always been a tension between the "here" and "hereafter," between the kingdom of the world and the kingdom of heaven, between a social and political commitment to "liberation" and the spiritual primacy of salvation. With regard to this tension, Aquinas' discussion of happiness in these questions and articles (I–II, QQ. 1–5) is significant not only theologically and morally, but also sociologically and politically. The order of values which he outlines as the conditions of happiness includes pleasure, knowledge, rightness of the will, bodily health and perfection, external goods and companionship, but in a balanced order of priorities judged according to their need for our present life and our eternal happiness in heaven. Some are required absolutely for the present well-being or "imperfect happiness," like bodily existence and some perfection of it. Some are required conditionally "as tools to serve happiness" like external goods, or as an addition to it like good friends. The perfect happiness in heaven, being a spiritual reality, does not require material support. Nevertheless, it still presupposes such "tools" as a preparation to it and entitles human persons to their rightful use. The closer they relate to perfect human happiness, the more important they are even in the present life. Thus, personal freedom is more important than property. Contemporary social encyclicals are in step with the same order of priorities, as their teaching aims to produce the same balance between the temporal and the transcendental values in human life and social relations.

Our present question continues to be about an objective happiness: a person or a thing on whom or on which we depend for our happiness, a *beatitudo qua beati sumus*, a happiness by which we are happy.

There are many things which are valuable to us, and some may in fact be indispensable to our human existence. People have always been motivated by money, by pleasure, by power, by virtue and social status.

So if an analysis of these values is a cliché, then the analysis of human life and history are clichés as well.

People have also been misled, divided, and frustrated by the same motivations, in the words of Ecclesiastes: "All man's toil is for his mouth, yet his desire is not fulfilled." Victor Frankl summarizes a psychological reflection in this regard when he says that neither Freud's "will to pleasure" nor Adler's "will to power" but rather the "will to meaning" is our deepest motivational force. If the will to meaning is repressed or ignored, an inner emptiness (the existential vacuum) opens up in us which cannot be filled with material wealth, power, fun, alcohol, drugs, sex, or thrills. It may be important to stress once again that the subject of an ultimate happiness is linked to the question of whether we can and ought to have a vision and meaning of life, and what happens if we don't. In Paul Tillich's words, the lack of such vision is the cause of "the anxiety of meaninglessness . . . the loss of an ultimate concern, of a meaning which gives meaning to the meanings. This anxiety is aroused by the loss of a spiritual center of an answer, however symbolic and indirect to the question of the meaning of existence."[1] Moral theology aims at providing such a meaning and vision. Aquinas' own method in analyzing the nature of happiness is interesting on several accounts. First, assuming as he does, that God alone is the ultimate happiness, it will be easier for us to say what happiness is not than what it is, since it is easier also to say what God is not than to say what he is, as dogmatic theology asserts. Second, in dismissing, not as unnecessary and useless, but as man's ultimate fulfillment, things like wealth, power, pleasure, etc., St. Thomas had behind him the entire Christian tradition and an abundant secular literature and experience. Consequently, a sound, logical argument may be more appropriate than another sermon. The summary of the argument is this: ultimate happiness must be specifically human; it must exclude all evil; it must include all good. Since no created good nor the sum total of creation meets this requirement, no created good nor man himself is his ultimate objective happiness. The result is that either there is no such thing as an ultimate happiness and we are condemned to frustration and "nothingness," or else we must look for it beyond creation and beyond ourselves. Contemporary existentialism makes this issue its own: its atheistic branch (Sartre) leading indeed to an existential absurd, and its Christian branch (Kierkegaard) to a submission to God.

---

1. Tillich, *The Courage to Be*, 47.

One may object, of course, that most of us do not think in terms of an absolute, but take what comes, working for the "better" not for the "best." Such a pragmatic attitude may indeed be very common, but it is true only to a point. The "better" is an implicit search for the "best" and a tacit admission that the best cannot be found if we look for it only in this world. No one has ever been fully satisfied with what he has, except perhaps the one who, in the spirit of the gospel, had the grace to give up everything for the treasure that does not fail.

SUBJECTIVE HAPPINESS

From what people enjoy, we turn now to how they enjoy it. This, too, calls for a similar analysis, since there may be beautiful things which we can never afford and things we can enjoy in a variety of ways corresponding to the variety of our senses and faculties. There are joys of touching, seeing, hearing, or reading a good book. Our own theological perspective on happiness must take us even deeper. If the objective happiness—*res beatificans*—is not only an external good, but God himself, the question is how do (or shall) I enjoy God.

It is interesting to note that this is not an exclusively Christian question. Other religions, especially the Oriental religions, and some philosophies, are preoccupied with the same question. It is interesting also that the most common tendency in giving an answer is to propose some kind of self-effacement and identification with a universal, cosmic being and reality. A similar phenomenon is present in mysticism, including the Christian mystics (giving oneself to God), and one may find an echo of the same tendency in people seeking their identity in their class, peer group, family, nation, religion, etc.

The scholastic theologians had their own method of inquiry. They used Aristotle's categories of substance, accident, quality, quantity, relation, action, passion, *habitus*, etc., to describe the subjective or formal happiness. St. Bonaventure thought that happiness consisted in a special quality or disposition of the soul, such as being perfect or being holy; some thought that it was a *passio* or a continuous reception of God's grace poured into our hearts, and others that it was a relationship, a mutual possession of God and soul, or a friendship with God. All these are serious theological opinions which are still reflected in modern theology and spirituality. For instance, relation is a very important contemporary philosophical and theological concept of happiness. Aquinas would have only one problem with relation (or friendship) as the formal basis of happiness, and this is if God's happiness is made dependent on human friendship and relationship.

Like his other scholastic contemporaries, Aquinas also employs the Aristotelian categories in discussing the question. An important factor in his discussion is the assumption of his psychology: the substantial union of soul and body in one human person; the distinction between the soul and its powers and faculties, and of the faculties among themselves, without destroying the unity of the person. With such understanding of the human person and of subjective happiness as something personal, Aquinas makes two initial statements: one is that subjective happiness must be something created, since we, its bearers, are created beings; second, it must be an operation (*actio*), since action or activity is the ultimate perfection of a being, as the perfection of an eye comes out in its actual seeing.

The term "activity," as the source of subjective happiness, may need explanation. There is a distinction between "being active" as we understand the meaning and Aquinas' "being *actu*," or actualized. To be *actu* means that a given potential has been fully developed. A child and an adult are both "active" in their respective ways, but the human potential is fully developed (biologically and intellectually) only in an adult. Consequently, and unlike our modern understanding of activity as a transitory, extrinsic performance of something, Aquinas understands it as first of all the perfection of the agent himself: an expansion of his inner actuality. Of course, it may not always be possible to know when a being is fully actualized. This is particularly true in the case of man and his intellectual faculties of reason and will. Because of this, subjective happiness also is an open-ended activity. Since we are psychologically aware of this openness, of the gap or "nothingness" between what we are and what we can be, to use J.-P. Sartre's words, the result will be a continuous human unfulfillment or else finding one's perfection and happiness in God alone. The following passage from the *Summa* may be appropriately quoted in this regard:

> Each thing is perfect inasmuch as it is actual, for what is potential is still imperfect. Happiness, therefore, must go with man's culminating actuality. Clearly this means his being active; indeed Aristotle speaks of activity as *second actuality*. For what already is actually a being by having a form may yet be only potentially

active, thus a man of science when not engaged with his field of study. That is why, in other things too, Aristotle says that each is for its activity. Therefore man's happiness has to be an activity.[2]

A more spiritual reflection on the same subject is found in the answer to the objection that "happiness remains in the person, whereas activity does not, but passes into another." Aquinas answers:

> Happiness denotes a certain ultimate completeness, and since different kinds of things mount to various degrees of perfection, the term admits variations of meaning. God's is essential happiness; his very existing is his acting, and thereby he enjoys no other than himself. Final perfection for men in their present life is their cleaving to God by activity which, however, cannot be continuous or consequently single, for activity becomes multiple when interrupted. That is why we cannot possess perfect happiness now, as Aristotle admits; after a long discussion of the sort of happiness men can reach, he concludes, "we call them happy, but only as men." God, however, promises us complete happiness, when we shall be as the angels in heaven.[3]

These reflections already indicate which human activity, among a variety of them, holds a primacy in regard to happiness. A perfect happiness cannot formally consist in activities which are neither permanent nor perfect. Naturally, this applies to all biological functions and sense operations like touching, hearing, seeing, etc. The issue, once again, is not how important, strong, and pleasurable such operations are, but their proper place and value in the total existence and vision of one's life. In this regard, even if we abstract from our assumption of an eternal life after death, one does not need to be a mystic to see that there is something more to human activity than eating and drinking.

CONCLUDING REMARKS

Before we turn to the Christian perspective on happiness as the basis of morality, it may be useful to summarize the main points so far developed. The terms and distinctions which we have been using may appear somewhat technical and antiquated, but most of them are still current in moral-theological language and a useful tool of communication. Moreover,

2. S.T. I–II, Q. 3, a. 2.
3. S.T. I–II, Q. 3, a. 2 ad 4.

underneath such technicalities there is a simple yet important content. We can make the following points:

- On the basis of ordinary human experience, we accept as self-evident two facts: one is that people are motivated in their lives or that they always act for an end or goal (speaking, of course, of the acts done knowingly and willingly); the other one is that such an end or goal is, at least formally or in principle, identical with good or happiness, since happiness is what everyone desires.

- On the same basis of experience, we accept the fact that people have different and sometimes conflicting desires, and that consequently happiness can mean different things to different people.

- Respecting the rights of everyone to his / her own taste, we must, nevertheless, ask some specific questions. Once such question is whether a person can or ought to have a more persistent vision of himself in his search for happiness. The other question is whether such a vision can be held in isolation and indifference to other people. The answer to the first question must be a "yes"; the answer to the second a "no." It is not only prudent but psychologically important to have a long-term vision of one's life; people do not really marry because of the honeymoon, they must have a larger vision of marriage or else it will not last. It is obvious also, although sometimes we have to learn by experience, that as human beings we cannot pursue our visions in isolation: we live in fellowship, normally in organized societies. Consequently our motivations affect other people as we are affected by them, all calling for a harmonization of our interests.

- The conclusion of these experiences is that if we want to be serious about our lives and actions, we must have a vision of ourselves and a vision which can be shared with those with whom we live. History is full of such visions: from hedonism to utilitarianism, capitalism and socialism, universal brotherhood and monastic peace to mystical disappearance in the absolute.

- It is in response to such conflicting aspirations as well as to a natural openness of the human heart to new and greater things that our inquiry must become more specific: what is happiness? where can it be found? in money? in power? in pleasure? in death?

- Philosophical reasoning comes to one conclusion: happiness, worthy of that name, must be all-inclusive, self-sufficient, with no danger attached, a common good satisfying all and each. But the philosophical reasoning cannot give a proper name to such happiness, because there is none such in this world.
- Turning to subjective happiness, we reached a similar conclusion: it has to consist in an operation because operation makes a being perfect; it has to be a specifically human, reliable, and lasting operation, of the mind in its act of knowing and loving.

Taking stock of these conclusions, we may say that we are a part of the world but not totally submerged in it; that we are individual persons but socially dependent; that we have our senses, stimuli, and reflexes, but they do not determine our whole being, we also have a free and open mind in search for the meaning of things, events, and especially our own existence.

3

Christian Perspective on Happiness

OUR CONSCIOUS ACTIVITY IS ALWAYS FOR SOME PURPOSE; MOST OF THE time for an immediate or proximate purpose, like having dinner to satisfy hunger or enjoy company, but ultimately we have and should have a more lasting and unifying vision of our activities and of our entire life. Such vision gives meaning to our existence and determines our particular choices and lifestyle. It is within our power and our human privilege as we mature to determine our own visions of ourselves, but living in fellowship, the society also exercises its influence and often forms our visions with its own conceptions of values.

The Church also offers a vision of life with its own promises for and demands upon our conduct. What is this vision, and what is its significance in the context of our basic assumptions of "acting for an end" and a natural "search for happiness"?

A current question discussed in contemporary moral theology is how distinctive and specifically Christian/Catholic is "Christian Ethics."[1] Although the question is not new in the history of Christian morality—it goes back to the beginnings of Christianity—it has received, nevertheless, a new impetus, as we experience a greater awareness and acceptance of cultural and religious pluralism. It is obvious that from a practical perspective there are agreements and disagreements on particular issues: one doesn't need to be a Catholic to condemn genocide, racism, torture, slavery, etc., but Catholic morality still holds its own specific views on abortion, divorce, birth control, and similar issues. These agreements and disagreements are,

---

1. See: Curran, *Readings in Moral Theology No. 2*. Almost the entire volume is devoted to this subject.

however, a superstructure to a more fundamental question, which is that of an ultimate vision or goal of life. Christians and Marxists may agree on identical social reforms, but their ultimate reasons are still different as they view human fulfillment, one in a transcendental union with God, and the other in a communistic order of the world. Assuming, as we do, that there is a specifically Christian vision of life based on the good news of Jesus Christ, the next question is whether such a vision is limited to being a Christian or Catholic or a vision to be shared with all mankind. Our position is that it is a vision offered to all; in other words, that moral theology as a science of this vision is not a sectarian ethical system, but an authentic answer to the natural human desire for happiness. But at this point, as we know, things become debatable and moral theology a *scientia argumentativa*. The Christian perspective on happiness is public knowledge: it points to heaven rather than to the earth, "for here we have no lasting city, but we seek the city which is to come" (Heb. 13: 14).

The position thus taken is both radical and mysterious. The first question which comes to mind is: what is heaven? This question is followed by a second: how does heaven relate to our natural and social aspirations bound up with our earthly human condition? The first question is strictly a theological one, although it fascinates anyone's imagination. Its sources of information are not experience and science, but Scripture and the tradition and teaching of the Church. The second question is both theological and sociological, as we inquire what "the pie in the sky" does for people on earth. Our discussion will proceed according to these two questions.

THE KINGDOM OF HEAVEN

The "kingdom of heaven" in Matthew, or the "kingdom of God" in Mark and Luke, is the central theme of Jesus' good news. Although a humanitarian ethical significance is not alien to the term as the "kingdom is already in us" through Christ's victory over sin and our rebirth in him, nevertheless, the constant teaching of the magisterium, the Christian faith, and theological understanding identify the kingdom with the eschatological expectation of the world to come. It is in the sense of such a transcendental fulfillment that the kingdom of heaven, as "not yet" and perhaps never fully to be realized on this earth, becomes morally challenging. Since in this sense, the kingdom of heaven is beyond our natural comprehension and description, its reality can only be asserted by our inner openness to it and the frustration of the existential emptiness of our life without it. This is how the Pastoral Constitution on the Church in the Modern World sees the issue:

> It is in the face of death that the riddle of human existence becomes most acute. Not only is man tormented by pain and by the advancing deterioration of his body, but even more so by a dread of perpetual extinction. He rightly follows the intuition of his heart when he abhors and repudiates the absolute ruin and total disappearance of his own person.
>
> Man rebels against death because he bears in himself an eternal seed which cannot be reduced to sheer matter. All the endeavors of technology, though useful in the extreme, cannot calm his anxiety, for a prolongation of biological life is unable to satisfy that desire for a higher life which is inescapably lodged in his breast.
>
> Although the mystery of death utterly beggars the imagination, the Church has been taught by divine revelation, and herself firmly teaches, that man has been created by God for a blissful purpose beyond the reach of earthly misery. In addition, that bodily death from which man would have been immune, had he not sinned will be vanquished, according to the Christian faith, when man who was ruined by his own doing is restored to wholeness by an almighty and merciful Savior.
>
> For God has called man and still calls him so that with his entire being he might be joined to Him in an endless sharing of a divine life beyond all corruption. Christ won this victory when He rose to life, since by His death He freed man from death. Hence to every thoughtful man a solidly established faith provides the answer to his anxiety about what the future holds for him. At the same time faith gives him the power to be united in Christ with his loved ones who have already been snatched away by death. Faith arouses the hope that they have found true life with God.[2]

This statement of Vatican II has behind it a sound scriptural and a constant magisterial, theological, and liturgical tradition and an uninterrupted faith of the Christian people. Although, as Aquinas writes in *Commentary on Ethics* (n. 113), "happiness in a future life is entirely beyond the investigation of reason," our curiosity and language are trying their best to express the mystery.

Scriptural and liturgical language most frequently used to describe heaven is as follows: *Life*, ("if you wish to enter into life keep the com-

---

2. Vatican Council II: *The Church Today*, 18.

mandments"); *Eternal life* ("everyone who has left house, brothers, sisters, father, mother . . . for the sake of my name will be repaid a hundred times over, and also inherit eternal life"); *Treasure* ("Get yourselves purses that do not wear out, treasure that will not fail you, in heaven where no thief can reach"); *Paradise* ("today you will be with me in paradise"); *Glory* ("what we suffer in this life can never be compared to the glory . . . which is waiting for us"); *Vision* ("Now we see in a dim reflection . . . but then face to face"); *Everlasting light*; *Bliss*, etc.

The teaching of the Church (magisterium) on the subject of eternal happiness aims to emphasize those aspects which are doctrinally sound and morally significant. Three specific pronouncements must be mentioned since they have been repeatedly emphasized by various councils, to mention only this branch of the magisterium. They are: 1. God is the perfect happiness of man; 2. Such perfect happiness is a gratuitous gift of God; 3. By divine Providence good works are required to obtain beatitude.

Since this is not historical or dogmatic research, there is no need to multiply references. We need consider only a few statements. The first pronouncement, which also implies that it is only in heaven that God is our perfect happiness, is a standing tenet of the Christian faith. The council of Toledo in the seventh century and of Vienne in the fourteenth century anticipated the statement of Vatican II, saying that, "the Church truly knows that only God whom she serves meets the deepest longing of the human heart which is never fully satisfied by what this world has to offer."[3] The same Council of Vienne and Vatican I may be quoted on the gratuitousness of supernatural happiness affirmed by Vatican II, saying that "Christ directs and guides the people of the New Testament in its pilgrimage toward eternal happiness"[4] and that "God is with us to free us from darkness of sin and death and to raise us up to life eternal."[5]

In regard to the necessity of good works, the most significant is the Council of Trent, which dealt with the Reformation. Session 6, can. 26 (Denz. 1260) is devoted to this issue. The constant and explicit reference to human responsibility in personal conduct and social relations in the Vatican II documents is an obvious endorsement of this pronouncement.

---

3. Ibid., n. 41.
4. Vatican Council II, *Dogmatic Constitution on the Church*, 21.
5. Vatican Council II, *Divine Revelation*, n. 4.

The second and third pronouncements contain important theological ramifications and an apparent conflict which divided the Reformation theology of "justification by faith alone" and the Catholic emphasis on the necessity of good works. We shall say a little more about this later on.

"VISION"

Most of the theological terminology describing the kingdom of heaven or perfect beatitude is posterior to Aquinas. The expressions used are *vision, intuitive vision, seeing directly God Triune and One, everlasting bliss,* etc. Having reached the conclusion that only God can be the ultimate objective happiness of man and that subjectively such happiness must consist in the highest and most specifically human operation, Aquinas links such happiness with contemplation of God, which he calls "vision": "there can be no complete and final happiness for us save in the vision of God." The argument he uses is the curiosity and insatiability of the human mind, the hunger to know, which may remind us of our own space programs exploring the universe because it is there. The text must be quoted in full. Using the words of St. John, "when he shall appear, we shall be like him and see him as he is" (1 Jn 3: 2), as his biblical support, Aquinas proceeds:

> There can be no complete and final happiness for us save in the vision of God. The evidence? Consider first, that man is not perfectly happy so long as something remains for him to desire and seek; and secondly, that a power's full development comes only from its shaping object. Now we agree with the *De Anima*, the object of mind is what really is, that is, the essence of a thing. And so the mind's expansion into perfection is proportionate to its possession of what really is.
>
> If, then, the essence of an effect is known through which, however, the essence of its cause cannot be known, namely what it really is, then quite simply the mind does not reach to the cause, though it may be able to gather from the effect that a cause is really there. Accordingly when a man knows an effect and also that it has a cause then the desire still stirs in him to know also what the cause really is. This is part of his constitution, and full of wonder, which, as noticed at the opening of the *Metaphysics*, sets us out to explore. For instance, on seeing a solar eclipse, we reflect that there must be a cause for it, yet because this is not known we start to wonder and so go on to investigate, nor shall we rest until we come to see the cause for what it really is.

Well then, were the human mind, from knowing what the created effects about us were, to have reached the position of knowing no more about God than that he exists, then not yet would it have come to the point of perfection by knowing the first cause unreservedly, and a natural desire to find it would remain. Not yet would a man be in perfect bliss. Complete happiness requires the mind to come through to the essence itself of the first cause. And so it will have its fulfillment by union with God as its object, for we have already explained that in him alone our happiness lies.[6]

Aquinas' argument in this article aims at one thing: to show that the beatific vision—the Christian eschatology—relates to the most fundamental desire of the human person. In order for such a vision or contemplation of God to make sense to us, we must take for granted the continuity of our personal identity before and after death; an identity which is assured by the immortality of the soul, and ultimately, by the resurrection of the body. In this regard, Aquinas offers another argument based on the nature of the human soul. "Because the soul is directly created by God, it cannot be blessed unless in immediate vision of God . . . [and] . . . As man received his first perfection, namely the soul, from an action of God, so also his ultimate perfection, which is his supreme happiness, comes immediately from God and rests in him."[7] Vision is the "spiritual" possession by love of the loved one, God; a possession in which our true meaning is finally confirmed and given back to us. Such vision of love or loving vision is something active, complete, but never ending.

The vision of God, we already indicated, is beyond natural human comprehension. Consequently, we must be on guard against any excessive anthropomorphism. As Dante writes: "Where God governeth without medium, the law of nature has no relevance."[8] Imagination runs into its own problems: contemplation of God for all eternity? What can this mean? A medieval legend relates that a monk once asked himself how this can be. Bemused by his speculation on the matter, he wandered into a forest and heard a nightingale singing. Everything was so beautiful as he was listening, enchanted. Remaining there for a while, he returned to his monastery. But when he came back to the house, no one knew him and he did not recognize anyone. He gave his name and the name of his

---

6. S.T. I-II, Q. 3, a. 8.
7. Thomas Aquinas, *Quodlibetales*, Q. 8, a. 1; idem, *De Virtibus in Communi*, Q. 1, a. 10.
8. Dante, *Paradiso*, Cant. 30, l. 43.

abbot, but this did not help; there was no abbot of that name. Finally, they looked into the annals of the abbey and there they saw what happened. A thousand years before, a monk had left the abbey; a thousand years had passed, but for the monk it was only a moment: time stood still. A legend, but not alien, to the experiences of rapture, love, admiration, when time no longer counts. It is a taste of eternity. "When we've been there ten thousand years | Bright shining as the sun | We've no less days to sing God's praise | Than when we first begun" (*Amazing Grace*).

St. Augustine's reflection on the first letter by St. John may appropriately be quoted:

> We have been promised that we shall be like him, for we shall see him as he is. By these words, the tongue has done its best; now we must apply the meditation of the heart. Although they are the words of St. John, what are they in comparison with the divine reality? And how can we, so greatly inferior to John in merit, add anything of our own? Yet, we have received, as John has told us, an anointing by the Holy One which teaches us inwardly more than our tongue can speak. Let us turn to this source of knowledge, and because at present you cannot see, make it your business to desire the divine vision. The entire life of a good Christian is in fact an exercise of holy desire. You do not yet see what you long for, but the very act of desiring prepares you, so that when he comes you may see and be utterly satisfied . . .[9]

THEOLOGICAL AND SOCIOLOGICAL RAMIFICATIONS

We must now examine some practical ramifications of the position that the beatific vision is our supreme and ultimate happiness. Some of these ramifications are primarily theological, others are both theological and sociological, and some only sociological.

Among the theological issues we may mention the historical debate on the primacy of vision and truth versus love and good as the *formale* or essence of beatitude, or what also became known as the Dominican and Franciscan theological schools and spirituality. The difference, sometimes hotly debated in the past, is less inflammatory today. The point to be made is, first, that vision and love, like truth and good, are not exclusive but inclusive, and second, that an undue emphasis on one or the other may, indeed, influence a person's lifestyle and set priorities on either

---

9. *Liturgy of the Hours*, Second reading for Friday of the sixth week.

knowledge, study, contemplation, or on commitment and action in religious and apostolic endeavor. It may also result in an over-rationalistic versus voluntaristic morality, although such modern currents have had other causes. Reason and will, like contemplation and action, have their proper role in beatitude and should have it in the present life. Beatitude, in the words of St. Augustine, is *gaudium de veritate* ("joy in truth"), and Aquinas explains his understanding in the following way: "The vision of God as a seeing is an act of mind, as being a good and ultimate end it is the object of the will. Such also it is as an enjoying. The mind indeed is the power laying hold of this end; yet the will it is which sets us in motion towards it and enjoys it when attained"[10] and again "there are two moments in pleasure, namely the awareness of a seemly object, which is for the cognitive power, and the delighting in it, and this, which is for appetitive power, is its culminating meaning."[11]

DESIDERIUM NATURALE

Another theological issue, which raised occasional storms in the past and continues to hold our attention at the present, is the meaning of "natural desire" to see God. In order to affirm that the vision of God is man's perfect happiness Aquinas argues, in the article quoted above, that there is a natural desire in man for such perfection and that without it, "a natural desire to find it would remain." The argument implies another of Aquinas' assumptions, namely that such natural desire cannot be in vain.

The argument, as we mentioned above, rests on the assumption that the human mind is by nature inquisitive and restless until it finds the causes and essences of things. This means that given the beauty and mystery of creation, the mind naturally seeks to know the Creator and remains unfulfilled until it finds him, in the words of St. Augustine: "You have made us for yourself and our hearts are restless until they rest in you."

This could be the end of a harmless theological reflection, if it weren't for a few rather sensitive consequences. How natural is our "natural desire" to see God? If it is not natural, then the argument loses its force. If it is natural, then it may have too much force; it may mean what some writers held before and some others concluded after Aquinas, that the attainment of such happiness is also natural and the vision of God "due" to us in

---

10. S.T. I–II, Q. 11, a. 1 ad 1.
11. S.T. I–II, Q. 11, a. 1 ad 3.

virtue of our humanity. Historically the Church opposed both extremes, maintaining a natural openness of the human spirit to the Infinite, and condemning theologies such as Pelagianism and Jansenism, which either denied the necessity of grace or claimed that grace is due to us.

There is a contemporary version of the same problem. In a general search of how to become more "relevant" to the world, some theologians believe that in order to cope with modern naturalism and secularism, it is necessary to make the faith more natural and secular; to place the supernatural at the very heart of nature, so that Christ and salvation are not an option but a necessity for man to become fully human. Teilhard de Chardin is the underlying source of this thinking, but there are other sources as well, such as the need for Christians to be politically and socially involved in the world's affairs, and fear that if grace and salvation are an addition or an accident to human nature, the Church also will continue to be accidental to the world.[12]

Karl Rahner is sensitive to this problem, both in its traditional controversy and contemporary significance. He feels the need to preserve the supernatural in religion, but he is also critical of an entirely "extrinsicist" view of grace. There is, he writes, an intrinsic (immanent) natural openness of the human spirit to its "ultimate horizons," even before actual justification. He argues that creation and Incarnation are not separate, but one divine decree, and that God offers himself to his creation from the beginning of human history. Accordingly, there is a built-in longing of the soul for God, or a capability of human nature to accept God's gift of himself when he actually gives himself in the Incarnation. For Rahner, therefore, all men are in the supernatural order, yet the actual gift of God is still gratuitous. The soul may refuse it and this will be its own condemnation.[13]

It is obvious that this kind of theological reflection is one of the most difficult subjects and likely to remain with us as a continuing problem of how to reconcile the gratuitousness of the beatific vision (salvation) with man's natural openness to it and the need of his good works to achieve it. Once again let us state briefly what we think is the meaning of Aquinas' argument concerning the "natural desire" to see God. To say that all men naturally desire to see the essence of God is not convincing. Many people not only do not think about the essence of God, but actually deny his

---

12. See: Baltazar: *Teilhard and the Supernatural.*
13. McCool, *A Rahner Reader*, Chapter 9, on moral theology.

existence. What Aquinas is saying is not that people actually desire God, but that it is natural to do so given our openness to an infinite, unknown finality. We naturally desire to be loved and to be absolutely loved. But to be absolutely loved we must be aware of an absolute love. The gospel tells us that "God is love."

The beatific vision cannot be natural in the sense that, e.g., justice or marriage are natural, even if not everyone is just or married. This would destroy the distinction between the natural and the supernatural order and imply that we can understand the mystery of the Holy Trinity in the same way that we can understand the value and meaning of justice. Since we are not perfect, we are not by nature lovable or deserving of perfect love. God loved us when we were still sinners. We may say, moreover, that man is not even curious about the essence of God. But what we can safely say is that man is curious about everything and thus open to the Infinite. We want to be loved and to know that we are loved, absolutely. To deny this is to deceive ourselves. As Simone Weil writes: "The danger is not lest the soul should doubt whether there is any bread in waiting for God: but lest, by a lie, it should persuade itself that it is not hungry. It can only persuade itself of this by lying, for the reality of its hunger is not a belief, it is a certainty."[14] Consequently, it is the fact that we are continuously hungry for something greater and better that we can say to be naturally open to God. To be so open does not mean to be capable of attainment by ourselves. There are many things we cannot do by ourselves, even if they are natural to us. So man is "naturally" open to God, but only God can fulfill this openness, and this "supernaturally." There is in man what the theologians call "obediential potency" (*potentia obedientialis*) for anything God wants. God can change the stones into the children of Abraham. However, here is a significant difference. To change stones into human beings is totally against ordinary nature: it is "un-natural" for stones to become humans. It is not so unnatural for human beings to see God, because by their intellectuality they are already on the level of spiritual beings. The human soul is immortal not by a special grace, but by its God-given immateriality.

Implicit in this argument is another principle which Aquinas ordinarily uses in support of the immortality of human soul. (S.T. I, Q. 75 a. 6; *Contra Gentiles* II, 55.) "Natural desire," he writes, "cannot be in vain."

---

14. Weil, *Waiting for God*, 210.

This statement rests on Aristotle's assertion that nature is not aimless and does not produce things in vain. Once again the idea could be misconstrued as a "human right" to divine vision, which is not what it implies. It only means that if there is a natural desire for ultimate happiness there must be a way of achieving it, as a wolf's instinct is fulfilled by catching its prey. Of course, there is frustration in nature: the wolf does not always catch its prey. To say, therefore, that our natural desire to see God and to attain our happiness in him cannot be in vain does not mean that we cannot frustrate such a possibility in our present, pilgrim state, which is our way to it, or that the vision of God is due to us unconditionally. It only means that God who created us for himself has also made himself available to us through the Incarnation; it means that if we put our hope in God we shall not be disappointed. But it is our human responsibility to put our hope in him.

TEMPORARY HUMAN SIGNIFICANCE

It is time now to see what significance such a conception of ultimate happiness has for our temporary human needs and rights. But before doing so, a summary of our preceding analysis may be in order. On the basis of an ordinary human experience of motivated activity (acting for an end) and a natural drive for happiness seldom fulfilled and often frustrated; on the basis also of a more in-depth rational analysis and finally supported by the revealed word of God (faith), we are able, by combining this information, to formulate a concept of happiness as one of total goodness and self-sufficiency and identify it with our notion of God. From our own subjective point of view, we conclude that such happiness can consist only in our life with and in God, by seeing and loving him. A certain anticipation of this happiness—imperfect happiness—may be achieved in the present life in the contemplation and love of God, applying the mysteries of faith to the practice of virtues. But its fullness is reserved for after death, in the kingdom of heaven. This is the essence of our Christian hope and our vision of life.

The implication of this is that at the beginning of our moral study we give to human existence an entirely transcendental orientation: fixing our eyes on heaven rather than on the earth, on the absoluteness of God rather than on the potentialities of man. This is what Karl Marx calls the highest form of alienation, and characterizes religion as "the opium of the people." It transfers, he says, the rights and greatness of man to the right and greatness of God, diverting our attention from material happiness on earth to a utopian happiness in heaven. Marxism is not the only secular eschatology, and, as we indicated earlier, it is not without influence on contemporary theological thinking and on people in general, especially the socially oppressed. The Vatican II *Pastoral Constitution on the Church in the Modern World* speaks with great concern about this problem (see especially nos. 7, 10, 19–21, 37, etc.). Most of the ideas expressed in this document, as well as in other social encyclicals on this subject, reflect Aquinas' thought on the relationship of faith to such human values as the care for the body, the right to property and pleasure, equal rights, education, freedom, etc., all of them a valuable ground for a reasonable dialogue between the Church and the world on the human condition and social relations. Aquinas himself further develops these themes in his special morality in the treatises on particular virtues, the relationship between the individual and society, human rights and laws, the nature of the common good, and other related subjects.

In this section of I–II of the *Summa*, Q. 4, is an evaluation of selected worldly and human values: an existential evaluation of Christian hope. Q. 5 concludes the treatise on a more theological note by examining the chances we, as humans, have to see God.

Having concluded that the vision of God (beatific vision, eternal life, the kingdom of heaven, etc.), is our ultimate goal and happiness, we need to flash back on our temporal condition: what does it mean to be a Christian in the world? The Christian attitude toward worldly values such as pleasure, wealth, the body in general, or even toward the higher values of the mind, such as knowledge and wisdom, often vacillates between a "renunciation of the world" and a greater or lesser submission to or indulgence in it. As in every other vacillation, a right balance seems to be the proper solution. In Q. 4, Aquinas lays the ground for such a balance; a balance which he subsequently develops in greater depth in his treatises on emotions and moral virtues.

Aquinas' basic position is this: given the entirely spiritual and transcendent nature of the beatific vision—the perfect happiness in heaven— none of the temporary values can add anything to it and thus are not absolutely necessary for it.

A second point which Aquinas makes is this: we live in the world and we need and want some happiness in it. But since the world in which we live is limited and imperfect, our happiness in it will always be limited and imperfect. However, such imperfect happiness is still desirable, and imperfect as it is in itself, it may still be a condition for greater and ultimate happiness.

A third point related to this is a clarification of what and how much we have and need in this world as a condition for eternal happiness. To clarify this, Aquinas examines possible relations or the manner in which something may be required: "Things may be required in four manners: First, as a preliminary or preparation, thus science requires discipline. Second, as its completion, thus living body requires soul. Third, as an outside help, thus an enterprise requires friends. Fourth, as an accompaniment, thus we may say fire requires heat."[15]

Taking a different example for the same purpose we may say that to be a "happy" doctor one needs a preliminary training; actual working as a completion; clients or patients as an outside help (condition); and one's own fitness, such as good health, as an accompaniment. With this in mind and the vision of God presupposed as our perfect happiness, we examine what and how indispensably something is required for its attainment and final enjoyment. In I–II, Q. 4, aa. 1–8, Aquinas examines the requirements of pleasure, comprehension or knowledge, rightness of the will, body, health, external goods and friends, a well-selected area of values commonly considered as valid condition of our happiness. Their examination is interesting, not only as they may or may not be a true condition of our perfect happiness, but also as they are in themselves, their priorities and importance: e.g., are friends more important than pleasure and wealth? We shall depart somewhat from following Aquinas' order in this case, so that we may put a greater emphasis on more controversial values, such as pleasure, body, and external goods.

Since the vision of God is a spiritual reality, it is obvious that our mental faculties of reason and will and their perfection and function are required in some way. But how much do we need to know and how well do we have to will? Some comprehension or understanding of a beatifying object is necessary in order to enjoy it, but such comprehension does not need to be exhaustive. This is particularly true in regard to God, whom we shall enjoy perfectly when we comprehend him perfectly ("face to face"), a perfection we cannot attain in this world. Consequently, our Christian

---

15. S.T. I–II, Q. 4, a. 1.

joy in the present world is only partial, a time of "joyful hope" of a future happiness, a "situation of hope" in which "the love-relation sets us questing for the end." But comprehension as a condition for happiness and joy on all levels has a practical implication. It lays a theological ground for a series of human rights and duties: to knowledge and education; to truth and information; to leisure and reflection, etc.

Rightness of the will or moral integrity is required as a condition of happiness in the present life and will be an accompaniment in the life to come. This means that in the present life we must will and love what God wills and loves; in heaven this will come naturally from our knowledge of God's goodness. Applied to practice, the idea implies the right and duty to proper moral and spiritual formation.

We touch upon a more sensitive issue when we ask the same question in regard to the body, the frequent "underdog" of Christian piety. Body and some bodily perfection are an integral part of the human person and thus an indispensable condition of any happiness in the present life. The same cannot be said for the perfect happiness in the vision of God, since this is not a physical operation. But let us not draw any wrong conclusions. The idea, as Aquinas observes, has led some to hold that the soul should be quite detached from the body. Aquinas rejects such a conclusion: "How odd this is (separating mind from the body). For since it is natural for the soul to be united to the body, how is it credible that the perfection of the one should exclude the perfection of the other? Let us declare, then, that happiness complete and entire requires the well being of the body, both before and during its activity."[16]

Aquinas escaped the occupational hazard not only of the mystics, but often of ordinary believers and their spiritual directors. The body is, first of all, a preliminary condition; our bodies are our lives; it is a consequent condition as well, since given the unity of the human person and our faith in the resurrection, the happiness of the soul overflows into the risen body. How healthy one needs to be is a somewhat different question, but we must take notice that sickness and ill disposition affect the activity of the mind. Once again we find sound theological argument for rights and duties concerning growth, health, and protection of the human body and its sacredness. The *Pastoral Constitution of the Church* echoes this theology when it states:

16. S.T. I–II, Q. 4, a. 6.

Though made of body and soul, man is one. Through his bodily composition he gathers to himself the elements of the material world. Thus they reach their crown through him, and through him they raise their voice in free praise of the Creator. For this reason man is not allowed to despise his bodily life. Rather, he is obliged to regard his body as good and honorable since God has created it and will raise it up on the last day. Nevertheless, wounded by sin, man experiences rebellious stirrings in his body. But the very dignity of man postulates that man glorify God in his body and forbid it to serve the evil inclinations of his heart.[17]

Pleasure is another controversial topic, not as a spiritual joy but as the erotic in human life. For Aquinas "pleasure is bound up with happiness as its accompaniment, as the repose of desire in a good that is held." Of course, there are different pleasures and some, e.g., sensuous pleasure, are neither a condition nor a consequence of heavenly joy. But even sensuous pleasure calls for a balanced evaluation. As long as we desire the right thing, we may also enjoy its possession: it is human and natural to do so. Even the sensuous, the erotic, if it is not obviously contrary to reason, is not a hindrance, but an incentive: "what we do pleasurably we do with more attention and perseverance." The case is different with pleasures which distract us from our true purpose. "Extraneous pleasure can hold up activity, sometimes by distracting us from its purpose, sometimes by setting up a conflict. We are more intent on the things we take pleasure in, and strong counter-action can deflect us from what we propose to do. Also, a sensuous pleasure contrary to reason blocks the judgment of practical wisdom more than does that of theoretical understanding."[18] Such conception of pleasure is far from any excessive puritanism. This Aquinas affirms in a later section when he speaks of the emotion of pleasure, saying: "No one can live entirely without any sensual or physical pleasure: the very man who teaches that all pleasure is evil is bound to be caught taking some pleasure; then people will be disposed towards pleasure more than ever by the example of what he does, ignoring what he says. For in matters of human activity and passion, where experience counts for so much, example carries more weight than words."[19] This, too,

---

17. Vatican Council II, *The Church Today*, 14.
18. S.T. I–II, Q. 4, a. 1 ad 3.
19. S.T. I–II, Q. 34, a. 1.

lays the ground for the rights and duties to maintain the emotional balance needed for mental and bodily health.

"External goods are required for the imperfect happiness open to us in this life, not that they lie at the heart of happiness, yet they are tools to serve happiness which lies in the activity of virtue. Ownership of them is required in order to lead a life of contemplative virtue, and of active virtue as well."[20] External goods are not needed for the perfect happiness of seeing God. We need them now to support our animal bodies or to exercise the physical functions proper to our condition. "Perfect happiness, however, is for a soul without a body or a soul united to a body which is no longer animal but spiritual." One does not need to be rich to enter the kingdom of heaven and the poor do not need to despair, but our present physical condition requires means of sustenance and human persons have the right to possession of material goods without putting their whole heart into them.

A final example that Aquinas gives in this regard is that of friends and fellowship. In the present life happiness calls for friends, "not to make use of them" since a happy man is self-contained, but to share one's goodness and happiness, to give support and be supported in both the active and contemplative life. "If, however, we speak of perfect happiness in our heavenly home, then companionship with other human beings is not strictly necessary, since a man is wholly and completely fulfilled in God. Nevertheless, friends add a well-being to happiness. And so Augustine reflects that spiritual creatures receive no other interior aid to happiness than the eternity, truth and friendship of the Creator. And if they can be said to be helped from without, perhaps it is only because they see one another, and rejoice in God at their companionship together."[21] Such companionship, or the communion of saints, is an article of our Christian faith.

If we prudently discern and use the external goods and have a realistic appreciation of our physical rights and needs, the principles expounded in these reflections promise a healthy personal and social life in the world and do not conflict with our expectation in the world to come.

---

20. S.T. I–II, Q. 4, a. 7.
21. S.T. I–II, Q. 4, a. 8.

ATTAINMENT

The attainment or the possibility of our happiness in heaven (the vision of God) is a matter of Christian faith founded on human openness to the absolute and God's redemptive action. Through the grace of God and our own response in love we can obtain our perfect supernatural happiness in heaven: "For God has called man and still calls him so that with his entire being he might be joined to him in an endless sharing of a divine life beyond all corruption."[22] This is the good news of the New Testament and the foundation of the entire Christian life.

In conclusion to the treatise of the ultimate end and happiness with which we began our study of moral theology, we may summarize our analysis with the following statements:

1. In all our human activities (acts done with knowledge and will) we always act for an end and, at least implicitly, for an ultimate end of our life.

2. This ultimate end must be (objectively or in itself) an absolute and supreme good (happiness), which can only be what we call God.

3. Formal or subjective happiness ultimately consists in our union with God through knowledge (vision) and concomitant love.

4. Such perfect happiness is possible only in the eternal union with God in heaven. Only imperfect happiness is possible in the present life, and we have a right to it and to the bodily and material means to it.

5. Perfect happiness in heaven cannot be obtained by our natural powers, but only by the supernatural grace of God, which is sufficiently given to all.

6. Good acts or moral integrity are required by God's providence, and they are meritorious even for our supernatural happiness.

7. Thus, with God's help, we are capable of obtaining our supernatural happiness in God.

The rest of this conclusion, as developed by Aquinas (I–II, Q. 5, aa. 1–8), offers some valuable moral and spiritual reflections. Reaffirming once again that we can obtain our perfect happiness because of our open-

---

22. Vatican Council II, *The Church Today*, 18.

ness to the absolute and God's grace to fulfill it, Aquinas asks several related questions.

"Can one person be happier than another?" The answer lies in the distinction between objective and subjective happiness. Since God is objective happiness, "there is no variation in blessedness, for there is but one supreme good, namely God, and men are in bliss by their joy with him. As for the second, one can be more blessed than another, for the deeper his joy, the more blessed he is. And in point of fact, his joy can be deeper because he is more open and adapted to receive it."

"Can anyone be happy in this world?" The same distinction applies here. Perfect happiness (the vision of God) cannot be obtained in this life, because of the contingent human condition and because the vision of God is not a matter of sense experience. But we can obtain some happiness in this world and should work for it. Men are called blessed in this life either because of their hope of gaining happiness in the future life—by hope we are saved—or because of some snatch of happiness—anticipating our joy in the supreme good.

"Can happiness be lost?" Imperfect happiness in the world, yes; perfect happiness in heaven, no. The reasons are logical: any happiness in danger of being lost is not a true happiness. Moreover, once the supreme happiness is attained, there is no change in the will for anything else. God will not change his gift and no other creature or agent can endanger it.

"Can one obtain happiness by natural powers?" Imperfect happiness, yes; we can improve our human condition, increase our standard of living, and grow in knowledge and virtue. Perfect happiness, no; therefore we need the salvific work of the Church and sacraments as instituted by Christ for this purpose.

"Can a superior creature help us?" Not really; only by disposing us. The idea is important to put our apostolic work into proper perspective: we are not really "saving souls"; only preparing the way of the Lord by word, prayer, and example.

"Are good works required?" The necessity of good works or moral integrity has already been affirmed: it is implicit in the conception of a righteous will, as a principle of action. God could have given himself without demanding anything from us, but his divine wisdom decided otherwise. Created in his image, as we are, we act for our end; it is our privilege and our duty. Unlike the angels who by one act opted for or against God, "man reaches [his end] through many motions of activity, which are called his merits."

And a final reflection: "Does every human being desire happiness?" A distinction must be made again. "Beatitude can be considered in the abstract and in the concrete. Take it in its general meaning, then everybody is bound to wish for happiness. For it signifies, as we have said, complete goodness. Since the good is the object of the will, the perfect good is that which satisfies it altogether. To desire to be happy is nothing more than to wish for this satisfaction. And each and everyone wishes it. Take it, however, to the point where happiness lies, then all do not recognize it, for they are ignorant about the object which gathers all good together. And so, in this sense, not everybody wills happiness."

There are many ways in which we can study moral theology: decalogue, precepts of the Church, the Sermon on the Mount, moral cases, law, etc. Aquinas begins with man in his natural, human condition and experience. To him, every human person is in the image of God and called to restore this image in his life. Consequently, Aquinas' moral theology is profoundly humanistic; a morality not reserved to a few enthusiastic mystics, but accessible to all. It begins with intrinsic, connatural aspirations of man to be happy and builds from there. But it does not remain on a purely natural level; it takes into consideration revelation, since this, too, is believed as a historical fact.

The essence of morality is to act knowingly and willingly for an end. Aquinas searched and found this end on the basis of rational and scriptural evidence and information. The end is God. The question which now remains is which acts lead and which do not lead us to God.

Part II

Conditions of Responsibility

1

The Nature of Voluntariness

WE SAID IN OUR INTRODUCTION THAT THERE ARE TWO BASIC DIVISIONS of moral science: a study of the goal of human life and a study of the means to it. Our analysis of the human goal and the conclusion that only God can fulfill the ultimate meaning of human life led us to conclude also that although the vision of God is a gratuitous gift, nevertheless, "good acts are necessary" by God's providence as our human response in love to his gift. This response is what we call free and responsible human activity. "Since we cannot come to happiness save through some activity, we have now to attend to human acts, so that we may learn which of them will open the way and which of them will block it."[1] Our human acts are the means to our happiness: the rest of our moral study must, therefore, be devoted to human acts.

Although, as Aquinas will keep saying, all human acts are singular and must ultimately be evaluated on this level, nevertheless, no human act is ever an entirely isolated instance. Behind each human act there is a human person with all his psychological, sociological, religious, family, and educational background and conditioning. The extent of such conditioning is a difficult and often controversial issue in contemporary psychology. How much is a person molded by his biological and instinctual drives, his childhood and education, his family and society, or how conditioned he can be made by all these factors is a daily preoccupation not only of the psychiatrists, but of the lawyers and courts.

It is not our intention to explore the depth of this problem at this point, since it does involve another moral factor which we shall discuss

1. S.T. I-II, Q. 6, Prologus.

later, namely, moral dispositions. Presently, we must assume with Erich Fromm that "history seemed to be proving that it was possible for man to govern himself, to make decisions for himself, and to think and feel as he saw fit."[2] Even when we take for granted such personal freedom, there is still a dynamic psychological process in every moral decision, from an initial perception of a value to a full commitment to it. How and when is a moral decision really made? How responsible are we for what we do?

Some factors which determine the way people act are general characteristics of all human beings, e.g., that people are rational, that they can think and that they feel free at least to some extent; that they have similar emotional reactions of love, anger, fear, hope; similar drives for food, shelter, sex, friendship; that they can learn as well as forget, etc. Other characteristics are more specific or even individual, such as a particular religion, age, education, profession, etc. All these factors and characteristics must be taken into consideration as possible constructive or destructive variables in a person's character.

HUMAN ACT AND ACT OF MAN

Actus humanus and *actus hominis* is the first distinction which helps us to maintain an orderly procedure in the course of our analysis. *Actus humanus*, or a "human act," is "what proceeds from the will with the knowledge of the end," reason and will being specifically human powers. Such an act may be internal, e.g., to intend, or it may be externalized, e.g., telling a lie willingly and knowingly. *Actus hominis*, or an "act of man" designates not only such uncontrolled reflexes as sneezing or coughing, but also those sensory reactions to pain and pleasure which evade rational control, and which, to the extent that they do, we call emotions. We shall discuss emotions in a later chapter. One thing to be mentioned at this point is that at least some currents in contemporary psychology reject this distinction either because of their deterministic conception of the human mind, or their insistence on the unity of the human person. Christian morality cannot accept determinism as a viable psychological conception of man, a conception which, moreover, has no convincing scientific basis. The possibility of behavioristic determinism in laboratories is a threat to human freedom, not a description of it. As to the unity of the human person, the distinction between the vegetative, sensory, and intellectual

---

2. Fromm, *Escape from Freedom*, 17.

functions is not opposed to it. Emotions, in particular, are an integral part of a person's psychological and moral make-up. But the distinction still holds between those acts which we control, like a premeditated revenge, and those which, like a sudden outburst of anger, we may not. Since morality is a free response to values and a specifically human phenomenon, it seems a valid procedure to first examine human acts in their purity and then the emotions.

Human acts themselves must be considered under a double aspect: their psychological structure and their moral value. We already alluded to this as a distinction between what we can do and what we ought to do in regard to our ultimate end. We begin with the psychological structure of the human act, or what is sometimes called the "pre-moral condition" of human activity. The expression "pre-moral condition" of human activity calls for an explanation. Strictly speaking, there is no "pre-moral" condition of human acts, because all human acts are always moral acts. What the expression says is that before we differentiate moral acts into good or bad, we must determine their moral nature, that is to say that they are free and responsible. Freedom and responsibility are morally neither good nor bad; they are the ontological condition of morality, a fact of human nature, without which no moral structure of good and evil is possible. Such condition is, of course, ontologically good, giving human beings the dignity of persons. But how free and responsible a person is in a given situation is not always clear. It is from this perspective that we must examine the nature and evidence of freedom.

PSYCHOLOGICAL STRUCTURE OF THE HUMAN ACT

In acting for an end, especially when this end is our ultimate goal, the first question we ask is: what can we do? The answer must be that we feel we can do certain things. Freedom and responsibility are human experiences which we cannot deny in practice. However, we also experience that sometimes we are not as free as we would wish to be: there are things we choose to do, not because we really want them in themselves, but because of something else, like undergoing surgery because we want to stay alive. How free, independent, and, consequently, responsible we are in what we do is an important and somctimes complex question. Freedom is not always a matter of either/or, black and white, but of the gray areas of human contingencies.

Although every human act is always a particular event in time and space with no exact duplicate, such an act, nevertheless, is also the result of an individual and personal ambiance, reflecting the social, religious, and other formative factors in a person's character. Moreover, each particular human act is itself the result of a mental process, from a simple perception of a good (end) to a full commitment to its achievement. In moral theology this process is often called the "psycho-genesis" of the human act. Aquinas analyzes the psychological structure of the human act in S.T. I–II, QQ. 6–17. There are eleven questions on this subject, in comparison with only four questions on the moral evaluation of the human act (S.T. I–II, QQ. 18–21). The significance of this lengthy, psychological enquiry lies in Aquinas' position that the morality of the human act consists in the acting person or the intention of the agent (*finis operantis*) rather than in the act done (*finis operis*), making a person responsible more for what he intends than what he actually does. Since intention is an internal commitment to an end, which may or may not externally materialize, it is important to know what is going on in the mind itself.

Inspired by Aristotle's analysis of the same process but not limited to it, Aquinas suggests that there are two levels of human operation we must consider. One is the order of intention or the internal, immanent making of a decision; the other is the order of execution, the external, practical implementation of such a decision. In the order of intention we consider two things: the end and the means to it. In regard to the end there are four mental steps, interrelating the activity of the reason and the will. First there is a simple perception of a good (end), with corresponding simple desire of it. This results in the first judgment about possibility, impossibility, or advisability of the end, again a function of the reason, which is followed by the will's intention to pursue the course. Once an end is judged good and as such intended by the will, the mind sets on the means. There are four steps in the mental operation concerning the means: the reason deliberates about the means and the will consents; a decision is made on particular means to be chosen by the will. This completes the order of intention: "I am going to tell the truth by writing a personal letter to the President himself." The next level is the order of execution. There are four steps in this order as well. The first is the command, a rational order given to my hand to write, and the application of this order in actual writing, which is the performance of the command and its application. Once my letter is in the mailbox, all is accomplished and enjoyed.³

These twelve acts are not isolated compartments, but rather moments in the development of the same human action. Time is not necessarily a factor, although some acts like "judgment" or "deliberation" may and indeed ought to develop over time before an "intention" is made or "consent" given. Simple perception and wish are almost instinctive reflexes, and thus hardly free and responsible. When a doctor and a priest come upon the same victim of a car accident, it is most likely that the first thing the doctor will think about is stopping the bleeding, and the priest about giving absolution. It is only on "second thought" that each one may wonder what should be done first. The question of our initial perception of things is an important one. But before returning to it, we need to make a few additional distinctions regarding human acts.

KINDS OF HUMAN ACTS

Internal and external acts. This distinction is clear from our previous discussion. As the words suggest, the internal acts are of the mind, such as thinking, willing, desiring, intending, etc. External acts are physical, visible, and tangible in time and space, such as walking, talking, writing, etc. Naturally, all human acts must be internal (internally intended), and some are also external. A moral question in this regard will be to what extent, if at all, such externalization modifies the morality of the internal act.

Elicited and imperated acts. The purpose of this distinction is to explain how activities and functions of various faculties and organs are voluntary acts. To be "elicited" means to originate from and pertain to a particular faculty or organ. Thus to think, to deliberate, are elicited acts of the reason; to wish, to intend, are elicited acts of the will; to see is the act of the eye; to listen, the ear; to talk, the guttural organs; etc. Now all human acts must be voluntary, but only some are directly elicited by the will. The other acts become voluntary by being commanded by the will enlightened by intelligence. Unfortunately, our activities may be commanded by less reputable drives like passions and vices. Since we are made up of such a variety of powers and organs, from reason and will to sensuality and

---

3. Thomas Gilby gives a tabulation of this process in "Appendix I: Psychology of Human Acts," in his translation of *Summa Theologiae*, I–II, QQ. 6–17. It may be found after this chapter on page 54.

biological functions, it is important not only to insist that only the highest faculty of the mind must be in command, but also to find out which other powers and functions fall or do not fall under such command.

Moral theology makes special distinctions between natural and supernatural acts, as their effects are only natural, like the acts of moral virtues, or supernatural, i.e., directly ordained to God, like the acts of theological virtues. Another distinction is between valid and invalid acts, mainly because of the juridical conditions which are required for the validity of some acts, e.g., a valid marriage. Finally, there is the distinction between good and bad human acts, which will be discussed in depth later.

VOLUNTARINESS

Human or moral acts are a co-product of reason and will, with the will playing a very special role. The will is the moving or the executive power of the person, moving itself and other powers to action. Consequently, human acts are rightly called voluntary acts. Of course, the will does not operate in a vacuum; it moves when it has a reason to move and the reason is a good and end, which are its proper objects. The good and end are presented to or specified for the will by the cognitive power of reason. This introduces a further distinction in the process of human activity, which is significant for the conception of freedom. The distinction is between the *act of specification* and the *act of exercise*. In the act of specification (presentation of a good and end), the will depends on the cognitive powers, in the first place on reason; in the act of exercise to do or not to do, the will is autonomous. Since the will is a spiritual power open to the absolute good, it does not of necessity follow the goods and ends specified for it, because in our present life, all such goods and ends are contingent and limited. Consequently, we say that the will is free in regard to specification: to do this or that, which is called "freedom of specification" or alternatives. The will is also free in the act of exercise: to do or not to do, which is its proper autonomous act or "freedom of contradiction." With this understanding, we can now explain some other aspects of voluntariness.

INTENTION

Human acts, in order to be voluntary, must be intended. Such intention can be actual or virtual. Actual intention is direct and immediate, as when a person decides to marry. Virtual intention is an uninterrupted continuation of a previous actual intention without explicitly thinking of it, e.g., going to a destination without thinking of it at every step. A married couple does not need actual intention to express their love and have children each time they have sexual relations; a virtual intention suffices to make such acts voluntary.

KINDS OF VOLUNTARINESS

All we do is not equally voluntary. Some things we desire at all times; others we want only conditionally. It may be helpful, therefore, to mention a few different kinds of voluntariness as they are distinct among themselves. The first such distinction is between *necessary* and *free* voluntary. This is not a contradiction in terms. Like all appetitive powers, the will is ordained to a good as its proper object. The difference is that unlike the sensory appetite (*orexis*), the will is not determined to any particular good, but open to good as such or an absolute good which alone becomes its necessary object. If such an absolute good were presented to the will, the will would necessarily adhere to it, although the adherence would still be voluntary in the sense that it is still an act of the will. Theology argues, not without evidence from human psychology and experience, that only God in his absoluteness can qualify as such a necessary object of desire. Since we do not see God or any other absolute good in the present life, the distinction between necessary and free voluntary becomes somewhat theoretical. It is assumed, nevertheless, that some things are more necessarily voluntary than others. Aquinas suggests that by nature, a man "wills all that matches his entire ability, not just his will, for instance to know the truth, to be, to live, and so forth, indeed all that relates to the integrity he was born to have: the universal object of will embraces all these as so many particular goods."[4]

A second distinction is between perfect and imperfect, simply and partially voluntary. This distinction depends on how perfectly we know and how unreservedly we will a thing. "Perfect" and "imperfect" relate primarily to the side of knowledge present or absent in a decision; "simply" and "partially voluntary" regard the willing itself. To skip a meeting because we know it is going to be boring is a perfectly voluntary omission; to skip the meeting not knowing that an important decision is on the

---

4. S.T. I–II, Q. 10, a. 1.

agenda is imperfectly voluntary. Taking a vacation is simply voluntary for most people; taking a bitter medicine only partially.

The third distinction is between direct and indirect voluntary. Direct voluntary, or voluntary *in se*, as the term indicates, is a direct or immediate object of an action, like deception in lying, or stealing in robbery. Indirect voluntary, or voluntary *in causa*, is an unintended effect resulting from another voluntary action and related to it. However, what is or is not indirectly or *in causa* voluntary is not always easy to determine. To help an objective evaluation of voluntariness *in causa*, the following guidelines are proposed: 1) there must be an objective causal relation between the act and its effect, or something that ordinarily happens; 2) the effect must be subjectively foreseen or the causal relation known by the agent, which is presumed if it ordinarily happens and the presumption is rebuttable; 3) the effect could have been avoided; and 4) the effect should have been avoided as evil and damaging. Drunkenness is not ordinarily the cause of murder, should it happen; but a car accident due to drunken driving is indirectly voluntary, since statistically over 50 percent of traffic deaths in the United States, aside from other accidents, are attributed to drugs and alcohol. The accident could be foreseen and should be avoided. Other cases may not be so clear as the following examples may show.

One day in the winter of 1980, a gunman attacked an illegal gambling club on Mission Street in San Francisco, where some twenty people were playing. In the confusion, a shot was fired, which attracted the police. The gunman was quickly subdued, but in the process, a middle-aged man died of a heart attack. The gunman was charged with the attempted armed robbery, a direct voluntary act; should he also be charged with murder as indirectly voluntary?

In an outburst of anger, a husband threw a knife at his wife who, in panic, ran through the front door into the street and was run over by a passing car. Was the husband responsible for her death?

In treating S. for V.D. on several occasions, Dr. D. discovered that his patient was an active homosexual. Some months later, Miss B. came in for a routine medical check-up. Since Dr. D. happened to be a close family friend, the conversation turned to other matters. Thus he learned that Miss B. was engaged and about to be married. Being a friend, Dr. D. asked who her fiancé was. To his surprise, he learned it was S., his patient. He asked how long and how well she knew her fiancé. Not for very long, but well enough to be confident that the decision was right. They married.

Three months later they divorced. When Miss B. discovered that Dr. D. knew all about S. and did not tell her, she suffered a nervous breakdown. The family blamed the doctor for all that happened.

A Roman Catholic priest disagreed with the Church's position on birth control and avoided talking about it. A parishioner came for advice. The priest mentioned that the Church was not against planned parenthood, but failed to be more specific about the distinction between artificial and natural means. The parishioner began using the pill. A few years later, she suffered severe side effects and blamed the priest for bad advice.

Although the kinds of death which resulted in the first and the second cases were not foreseen and would not ordinarily happen, the risk of such a result or possibility of an accidental death would seem to be implied in both cases and thus indirectly voluntary. There is, therefore, a moral responsibility for these effects, although legally it may be argued differently in the courts.

The doctor in the third case cannot be blamed for the results of his action, because the effect could not have been avoided without violation of professional secrecy, although he might have tried some other means to prevent the marriage. The priest acted imprudently by avoiding the issue and not telling the Church's position as it stands, including the controversial aspect of it and his own disagreement. But he is not responsible for the medical side effects, which do not ordinarily happen and are not in the area of his knowledge and responsibility.

A final distinction, which sometimes occurs in Aquinas' text as well as in moral manuals, is between positive and negative voluntary action: positive when something is done, e.g., active euthanasia, negative when an action is omitted—as in the case of passive euthanasia. However, since every human act must be something willed, the negative voluntary is reducible to the will's positive decision not to act. This distinction seems to be adequately covered by the distinction between direct and indirect voluntariness.

STRUCTURE OF HUMAN ACTS*

MIND	HUMAN ACT	WILL
immanent activity in 'order of intention'		
about end		
1. perception		2. wish
3. judgement		4. intention
about means		
5. deliberation		6. consent
7. decision		8. choice
practical action in 'order of execution'		
9. command		10. application
	11. performance	
	12. completion	

* Gilby, *Summa Theologiae*, 17: 211.

5

Structure of Human Acts

SINCE VOLUNTARY ACTS ARE ACTS AND THEIR EFFECTS PROCEEDING from the intrinsic operating principle, which is the will under the light of rational knowledge, involuntary acts are those which lack such light of rational knowledge and/or the free exercise of the will. The factors which cause such defectiveness in either knowledge or will are called "moral impediments" (*hostes voluntarii*). They may diminish or even totally destroy voluntariness and consequently responsibility for an action and its effect. The principal moral impediments to be mentioned are: violence, fear, passion (concupiscence), ignorance, habit, and pathological mental or physical states. Other impediments known to modern psychology, such as anxiety, depression, brainwashing, peer group pressure, advertising, hypnosis, drugs, psycho-surgery, possible genetic engineering, etc., though important in themselves, may, nevertheless, fall under one or another of the above mentioned impediments for their moral significance. The underlying principle for all moral impediments of voluntariness is that any factor which takes away the use of reason renders the act involuntary, unless such deprivation of rationality was itself voluntary in cause. Let us examine some of the impediments individually.

VIOLENCE

Violence is an extrinsic, physical force contrary to the will of the agent. Thus, acts done under torture, beating, rape, and similar physical coercion are acts done under violence and must be differentiated from moral, social, economic, and other non-physical pressure on a person's mind. This does not mean that such moral "violence" is not important; it only means that it is of a different nature. Physical violence cannot be done to the internal acts of the will such as intention or consent; it can only be done to the external or imperated acts. The obvious example of physical violence is rape. Since violence is not without fear, it may be difficult to determine how much an act is due to violence and how much to fear. A girl may be forced under the threat of a gun to pick up the telephone to make an appointment with her fiancé which she knows is a trap to kill him. She may be forced to do the same by having a blazing iron pressed to her neck or her arms twisted. Physical violence is clearer in the second instance because of pain; it may not be so clear in the first instance. In neither case can she be forced to consent. If she does, the violence is no excuse: she becomes an accomplice. The moral principle concerning violence is, therefore, the following: acts done under violence or threat of violence are involuntary, if violence is external, physical and grave, and internally resisted. How much a person must resist externally is also a matter of situation, gravity of the act, and prudential judgment. To resist rape externally may not be the most prudential thing to do, if one's life is in danger.

FEAR

Fear is a mental disturbance caused by an imminent or future danger. This is somewhat different from the emotion of fear (*timor*), which is a sensory response to a dangerous, future evil. Fear (*metus*) in the present context, primarily affects the mind, and it may or may not involve emotional reaction. Thus, a doctor refusing a night home visit to a dying patient because he lives in a crime-infested section of town. This fear is real and mentally perceived as such; it must, therefore, be distinguished from "faceless fear" or anxiety, which is a different issue. There are a number of distinctions which must be made before determining the effect of fear on voluntariness of an act.

In regard to its *origin*, fear may be *intrinsic* or *extrinsic* to the agent: intrinsic fear originates in the agent himself, e.g., fear of death in serious illness; extrinsic fear is caused by another person or thing, e.g., fear of a storm, fear of hell, fear of God or superiors, etc.

In regard to its *intensity*, fear may be *grave* or *light*. Grave fear may be such absolutely, or serious for any person, such as the fear of death. It may also be relatively grave, scaring the inexperienced and children, but not adults and the experienced. Light fear, as the word suggests, is minor, as the fear of offending a friend. In regard to the act fear is *antecedent*, when an act is done "from fear" (*ex metu*), e.g., lying from fear of punishment, and *concomitant*, when an act is done "with fear" (*cum metu*), e.g., stealing with fear of being caught. The following practical guidelines may help in moral evaluation of fear:

1. Fear, as any other impediment which takes away the use of reason, renders the act involuntary.
2. Acts done with fear (concomitant fear—*cum metu*) are voluntary acts. I may be afraid to fly, but as long as I purchase my own ticket and board that plane, I am acting voluntarily.
3. Acts done from fear (antecedent fear—*ex metu*) are simply voluntary and only partly involuntary. Parachuting from a burning plane is voluntary, although not entirely. Such fear, therefore, diminishes voluntariness for the reason that a person would not act if it were not from fear.
4. Since fear does not entirely destroy voluntariness (unless it takes away the use of reason), it follows that the graver the matter involved, the less excusable is the fear. Thus, one must never commit a murder because of fear, even for his own life. The Christian martyrs are an example of the same principle in regard to faith, which must not be denied because of fear. On the other hand, with the positive laws in matters which are bad because prohibited, fear may be a legitimate excuse. Thus, one is not obliged to Sunday observance if his life or livelihood are in danger. Finally, the law may declare some acts, such as marriage contracts or religious vows, invalid if proved to be done from fear.

PASSION / CONCUPISCENCE

Passion (*passio*) is a term Aquinas uses for what in contemporary terminology we would call emotion. Sometimes "passion" indicates a stronger, less controllable emotion; a reason why, perhaps, the term passion may be more appropriate to use when we speak of emotions as impediments to voluntariness. Emotionality is an integral part of human personality; we are all emotional. It is only when a person's emotional state overpowers the rational judgment and free exercise of the will that we can speak of it as an impediment.

Passion, and especially the passion of concupiscence, is often identified with sexual drives and desires (lust); however, this is not the only passion to affect our rational deliberation and judgment. All passions are about a sensitive good or evil involving some bodily transmutation, e.g., becoming red in the face, pale, or physically shaking. Such passions can be love, desire, pleasure, hatred, aversion, sadness, hope, despair, aggression, fear (different from mental fear), or anger. We shall return to an analysis of the nature and moral significance of emotions; our present question is about their influence on voluntariness of a human act.

In regard to a human act, passion can be *antecedent* or *consequent*. Antecedent passion precedes the act, e.g., when a husband finds his wife in bed with another man and kills them both. Consequent passion may be twofold: "first it may take the form of a kind of overflow; the higher part of the soul is strongly bent upon some object that the lower part follows it. In that case, the presence of the emotion in the sensory *orexis* is a sign of the will's intensity, and hence an index of greater moral worth."[1] An example may be when people involved in the pursuit of social justice become angry at public and media indifference to it. Secondly, "it may be the outcome of choice: i.e., a man may make a deliberate decision to be affected by an emotion so that he may act more promptly,"[2] as when a father "builds up his anger" to throw it more effectively on his son's spending habits.

Antecedent passion diminishes perfect voluntariness. If it is so strong that it takes away the use of reason (heat of passion), it renders the act involuntary. The stronger and more natural a passion is, the less voluntary are the acts which follow. Thus, according to Aquinas, sins against chastity are more excusable than sins against justice, on the assumption that the emotional factor in the first is naturally stronger than in the latter.

Consequent passion, if it is the outcome of choice, increases voluntariness, because it was willed in the first place. Consequent passion in the form of overflow neither increases nor decreases voluntariness; it only shows the intensity of the will.

---

1. S.T., I–II, Q. 24, a. 3 ad 1. (The translator of this section of the Summa chose the word *orexis* instead of "sensitive appetite" for the Latin *appetitus sensitivus*.)
2. Ibidem.

IGNORANCE

Ignorance is a lack of due knowledge. In this sense it differs from a simple absence of knowledge (*non-scientia*), e.g., not knowing that to forge a check is punishable by law differs from a teacher of Spanish not knowing Chinese. In order to determine the influence of ignorance on the voluntariness or involuntariness of the human act, we must consider the following distinctions:

1. In regard to the object of knowledge, we distinguish the *ignorance of law* (or norm) and the *ignorance of fact* (application). One may not know that receiving stolen goods is against the law; and one may not know that what he received was stolen property.

2. In regard to the agent, ignorance may be *vincible* or *invincible*. Invincible ignorance is the lack of knowledge which cannot reasonably be expected in a person. This must be understood in concrete act, because it may be difficult to argue that any ignorance can remain invincible forever. Thus a teenager may be invincibly ignorant that sexual intercourse with his second cousin is also incest, punishable by law.

    Vincible ignorance is a lack of knowledge which it is possible to have and ordinarily expected in a person: e.g., a Catholic couple should know that a purely civil marriage is not recognized by the Church. Vincible ignorance admits degrees, according to the negligence and obligation involved. If the matter of the law or fact is minor and the negligence only light, then we can talk about a simply *vincible ignorance*, e.g., a husband not knowing that today is the birthday of his wife. Vincible ignorance can be crass when no effort is made to know the law or the fact in a serious matter, e.g., an attorney neglecting to study the evidence or a doctor to keep up with medical results. Vincible ignorance can also be "affected" (*affectata*) or intentional, which is a refusal of knowledge in order to cover up one's irresponsibility, e.g., refusing to answer the telephone, knowing that it is a creditor demanding his payment.

3. In regard to the act, ignorance may be *antecedent, concomitant,* and *consequent*. Antecedent ignorance is the cause of action

(acting from ignorance); concomitant ignorance is accidental to action (acting with ignorance); consequent ignorance is caused by previous negligence.

Invincible ignorance renders an act involuntary. Note, however, two things: one is that invincible ignorance makes sense only in an actual situation or a particular act, assuming that in the long run ignorance can be overcome; the other thing is that in important matters of public knowledge, the law may not admit such ignorance as a point for the defense, e.g., not knowing that to practice medicine without a license is a crime in the United States.

Vincible ignorance does not destroy voluntariness; however, it diminishes it, unless it is intentional (*affectata*). In other words, vincible ignorance is not a total excuse, because knowledge is possible. It is a partial excuse, on the assumption that if a person had full knowledge of all the facts, he would have acted differently. Thus, a person who misses an important appointment relying on his memory rather than his calendar is responsible, although not as much as if he did it on purpose. The degree of responsibility depends on the gravity of obligation. There are obligations binding everyone, e.g., that Catholics should know the basic teaching of the Church on important moral and doctrinal issues. But there are obligations which bind some people more than others in virtue of their professional status and expectations; e.g., a doctor ought to know more about medical treatment than his patient.

In regard to the act, only an antecedent ignorance renders the act involuntary, other things being equal. Consequent ignorance, being intentional, makes an act voluntary in cause. In consequent ignorance we are actually dealing with two acts of the will: the first act is to refuse to obtain knowledge, and its gravity depends on how obligatory such knowledge was; the second act is whatever is done as a result of such a refusal. The first act is presumed directly voluntary; the second is voluntary in cause. It is possible that in the psychological process between the original refusal to know and the second act, there may be a change of mind which would diminish voluntariness even in this case. But the principle of voluntariness in cause remains valid.

Concomitant ignorance is a special case, because it neither accuses nor excuses an act done with such ignorance. The act is said to be "non-voluntary," which is somewhat different from involuntary. Involuntary acts are contrary to the will and imply regret; non-voluntary acts are "without will." This may happen in a case of mistaken identity, as when in a hunting party, a jealous husband kills his wife's lover, thinking he was a deer. The killing was not voluntary, because he thought he was shooting a deer; it was not involuntary, either, because he had no regret for what happened.

Related to ignorance are oblivion and inadvertence, but their influence on voluntariness falls into the same category of principles as ignorance itself. To summarize the place of ignorance in voluntariness, we may say that: 1) invincible ignorance excuses; 2) vincible ignorance: a) if antecedent, excuses (if the ignorance is excusable); b) if consequent, accuses; c) if concomitant, neither accuses nor excuses.

HABIT

Habit is an operative, unthinking behavioral routine, which escapes ordinary rational control. Consequently, it differs from moral disposition (*habitus*), such as virtues, which are meant to be exercised "at will," i.e., knowingly and freely, as we shall see later. Here we are concerned with habits as impediments to freedom. The fact is that people become habituated to patterns of activity which are difficult to change, e.g., smoking and drinking habits, using bad language, masturbation, etc. An uncontrollable habit renders the act involuntary. However, some other factors must be kept in mind. One is how willingly and responsibly a habit was acquired; the other is how willing and serious the effort is to change a bad habit. Consequently, a person who willingly (or negligently) acquired a bad habit and does nothing to change it is responsible for the acts proceeding from it, even when the acts become, in a sense, automatic. On the other hand, the person who seriously struggles to change his habits bears less responsibility, and no responsibility if the habit is so strong that a person has no rational control over it. The power of habits on voluntariness may be a traumatic experience in practice, as many cases of adolescent and adult masturbation often indicate. A sound determination to change, striking the evil in its roots by contrary acts, strengthening the will in the direction of positive achievements and creativity, with patience and prayers, are the best moral remedies.

PATHOLOGICAL AND PSYCHOLOGICAL DISORDERS

Besides these commonly known impediments to voluntariness, there are others more subtle in their origin and more difficult to treat. The substantial union of soul and body in one human person accounts for continuous interaction between the mental (rational) and physical (organic) in a person's life and activity. This means that pathological (organic) malfunctions may affect the mind, and mental illness may cause disorders in physical functions of the body. Because of such interaction, it is not always easy in the case of abnormalities to determine what is a psychological and what is a pathological disorder. Some such disorders may be genetic; others may be due to brain damage through accidents, alcoholism, or drugs; but some are due also to the formative (or deformative) factors in early childhood, or even in later life. Not only heredity and physical constitution, but also environment, educational patterns, cultural and family background, interpersonal relationships, as well as religion, influence the emotional development and social adjustment of human beings. Consequently, it is difficult to produce a complete list and a clear classification of such organic and mental malfunctions. Their moral evaluation in regard to voluntariness is therefore bound to be somewhat general and uncertain. While the basic principle that every impediment which destroys the use of reason or the power of the will renders an act involuntary is clear and simple, its practical application to a concrete case is not easy. Some such disorders may be little more than ordinary character traits and differences, e.g., various "eccentricities," differing characteristics of persons of culture, science, or art. Other disorders are more serious.

A distinction is sometimes made between psychotic and neurotic malfunctions. The term psychosis applies to more serious illnesses of psychogenetic origin, such as schizophrenia, paranoia, and depression, which usually pervade the entire personality, distort the judgment of reality, and ordinarily require treatment and hospitalization. Neurosis (psychoneurosis) is less character-pervasive, leaving the person relatively free to maintain a normal perception of reality. Neurosis is a maladjustment rather than a psychic illness; its causes lie in an unfavorable milieu more than in a genetic condition. Anxiety, fear of responsibility, phobias, obsession, and a general failure to cope with situations are among common manifestations of neurosis. A particular kind of neurosis is hysteria: a state of mental disposition, sometimes permanent, sometimes transient, manifested both in psychic and physical disturbances. Mentally, a hysterical person is rather childish in character, dramatizing himself, complaining, and seeking attention. Physically, a hysteric may suffer in practically any organ, from blindness and amnesia to paralysis. The hysterical person is not necessarily a faker; he feels the symptoms of his illness. However, he is unaware of its true origin and the fact that it may serve only to allow him to escape the disagreeable issue he does not want to face.

From a moral point of view, it must be assumed that all psychotic malfunctions and many kinds of neurosis imply a loss of freedom and of the conscious mastery of activity. In such cases, psychiatric help must be sought. Neurotics seem to be more amenable to such help than psychotics, who seldom seek help or accept suggestions.

Among other examples of personality disorders, the most common are the psychopathic and sociopathic cases. Included here are various kinds of antisocial behavior, notably sexual deviation (perversion) and alcohol and/or drug addiction. The contemporary publicity about sex (the sexual revolution) and some new insights into the biological nature of sexuality make it difficult to distinguish between "normal" and "non-normal" (deviant) sexuality. The traditional standard was based on the external organic differences between male and female; consequently, any sexual activity contrary to such complementary difference (e.g., masturbation, homosexuality) was considered contrary to nature and deviant. As more is learned about the complexities of chromosomes, biology of sex, and such new treatments as transsexual operations, the standard has shifted, if not to a purely pleasure model of sexuality, at least to a greater variety of sexual expressions than were previously permissible. Consequently, a distinction must be made between a "moralo-social" and "psychopathological" sexual deviation. The first is a difference in value systems, because we deal with people not mentally insane but morally different. In this context, sexual promiscuity, homosexuality, or "anything between consenting adults" is not a psychopathological (or even sexual) deviation, but a moral one: voluntary, rather than an impediment to voluntariness.

It may be more difficult to detect and define a psychopathological sexual perversion. In fact, any uncontrollable compulsion to sex, even in a legitimate marriage, may be pathological and the cause of anxiety and divorce. However, there are more obvious sexual deviations, e.g., fetishism, masochism, sadism. Such psycho-pathological conditions diminish voluntariness, and if uncontrollable render the act involuntary, as in the case of passion. It should be kept in mind, nevertheless, that such deviant behavior is often the result of socio-moral factors, childhood milieu and abuse, indifference to and hatred of society, and later in life, a lack of voluntary self-control, which are all moral rather than pathological problems and should be treated as such.

Alcoholism is another problem. Here we must distinguish between drinking, habitual drinking, and alcoholism. In spite of various "temperance" movements, drinking is socially and morally acceptable when taken in moderation. Social events such as weddings, graduations, family reunions and similar "parties" take for granted some participants will get a little "high"; it is human. Such drinking, even when habitual (a regular evening cocktail), is not an impediment to voluntariness, since it is voluntary to begin with, unless someone, through inexperience, gets drunk by accident. Consequently, the attention must focus on the possible effects of intoxication, such as being a nuisance to others, danger of accidents (drunk driving), which, if they occur, are voluntary in cause.

The case of alcoholics is different. Most authorities and the civil courts now consider alcoholism as a disease; however, the view is by no means unanimous. Although the alcoholic might have been at fault when he first began to drink, the experience seems to indicate that once he became addicted or diseased, he no longer has freedom of choice: his drinking, the desperate resorting back to alcohol, as well as the acts which may follow (e.g., lying) must be considered involuntary. However, there is greater hope today of helping alcoholics, as well as psychopaths in general, if they can be motivated to accept help.

CIRCUMSTANCES

By circumstances we mean certain conditions or facts which surround or situate a human act in time and space. Since the time of Aristotle, moralists have listed seven such circumstances: who the agent is; what is done; why something is done; where; by what means; how; and when. Some circumstances make little difference to the essence of a voluntary act: e.g., whether a robbery is committed in daylight or by night, or a murder by shooting or strangulation. Other circumstances may increase or diminish voluntariness without changing the nature of the act: e.g., stealing from a rich or a poor person. Finally, there are circumstances which either change the morality of an act or add to it an additional value or disvalue: e.g., fornication becomes adultery when the partners are married to third parties.

Strictly speaking, circumstances or moral situations are not impediments to voluntariness, but together with the object and motive, they determine the morality of the act, as we shall explain in the chapter on moral determinants (specificants) and situation ethics. Aquinas gives three reasons why a moral theologian has to consider circumstances:

> First, he treats these as ordered to happiness. Whatever is ordered to an end should be proportioned to it, which, in the case of human acts, means they should be commensurate. And this requires that they fit the circumstances.
>
> Second, he considers human acts in so far as they are charged with right or wrong, better or worse. Now as we shall see, circumstances play a part in this diversity.
>
> Third, he treats human acts as well-deserving or otherwise. This is attached to them in so far as they are voluntary, which, as we shall see, is affected by knowledge or ignorance of circumstances. For these reasons a moral theologian has to take them into account.[3]

The most important circumstances are the agent himself, who the person is: an adult, a teenager, one who is single or married, a depressed person, a doctor or a priest, etc.; and what is done and why. In fact, these circumstances are so intrinsic to the act that they are more constitutive of the act itself than just situating it in time and space. For example: adultery is a sin in itself. Time and place may make little difference, though sometimes they may, e.g., when done in public. It may make a difference if the agent is depressed because of his own spouse's infidelity. Even more difficult, or even uncontrollable, is the situation of a wife whose husband demands that she use artificial birth control under the threat of breaking up the marriage and family. How free, in fact, is the wife in a situation like this? We shall return to the analysis of circumstances and their influence on the morality of human acts in our section on objective morality and situation ethics.

---

3. S.T. I–II, Q. 7, a. 2.

CONCLUDING REFLECTIONS ON FREEDOM AND RESPONSIBILITY

To the preceding analysis of voluntariness and its impediments, we may now add a few general reflections on freedom and responsibility. We may begin by referring to the Scripture and the teaching of the Church. The summary of this position is that freedom is God's greatest gift to every human person and consequently a fundamental human right. In the Bible, freedom first appears as the liberation of the chosen people from slavery: political slavery to Egypt and moral slavery to sin and idols. The New Testament points to Christ as the liberator from a double slavery: from sin which enslaves us internally, and from the law which limits our freedom externally. Thus "through his blood we gain our freedom, the forgiveness of sins," and "God sent his Son, born of a woman, born a subject of the law, to redeem the subjects of the law and to enable us to be adopted sons." Instead of an extrinsic law, the Christian lives by the law of faith and love, or "the law of the Spirit." But freedom is not license. "My brothers, you were called, as you know, to liberty, but be careful, or this liberty will provide an opening for self-indulgence" (Gal. 5: 13). Christianity is a liberating force, but Christians are free in order to serve God and each other in charity.

Some scriptural texts would seem to deny a real freedom of choice (*liberum arbitrium*) by insisting on the absolute sovereignty of God's will. The problem of reconciling the prerogatives of God's will with those of human freedom is a difficult one with serious theological ramifications, especially in regard to predestination. The truth is that the entire biblical tradition and its authentic theological interpretation consider man capable of exercising his free choice and being responsible for it, from the moment of original sin to Christ's call for conversion. This, too, is the teaching of the Church.

Human freedom is a fundamental tenet of the Catholic teaching, defined by the Council of Trent (Denz. 815), reinstated in recent papal encyclicals and by the Vatican II *Document on Religious Freedom*. The essence of this teaching is that the normal human person in the decisive stages of life can make moral decisions and be responsible for them. "The Synod ... declares that the right to religious freedom has its foundation in the very dignity of the human person, as this dignity is known through the revealed Word of God and by reason itself. This right of the human person to religious freedom is to be recognized in the constitutional law whereby society is governed. Thus it is to become a civil right. . . . It is in accordance with their dignity as persons—that is, beings endowed with reason and free will and therefore privileged to bear personal responsibility that all men should be at once impelled by nature and also bound by a moral obligation to seek the truth, especially religious truth."[4] This means that freedom and responsibility are not only facts known through reason and revelation, but also rights to be recognized and obligations to be accepted.

With this in mind, there are still a few practical questions to be examined. Having a will or a power to will, what precisely do we will? Who or what can determine our willing? How necessarily do we will anything? The question "what do we will?" is important for several reasons. One is that we always seem to will what we think is good for us, what we like. Yet in the long run, the good we will may not always be the good we ought to will, as other people, parents, society, the Church often tell us, or we ourselves eventually find out. Another question concerns the means. If we will an end, do we also will the means, e.g., when I will my health, do I also will an unpleasant diet? Moreover, if I will a legitimate end, am I also entitled to any or all means to it? This is important in some areas of activity, such as limited availability of means in medicine and economics.

THE OBJECT

The object of our volition is always a good or apparent good: the very definition of good is "what is desired." A sense of optimism pervades the entire nature when seen as essentially oriented toward good. "Willing is rational appetite, and there is no appetition except for good, because appetition is nothing other than a certain bent toward a thing that is wanted, a thing which is matching and complementary."[5] In another place Aquinas writes: "It is out of the question that any evil as such can be directly wanted, either by natural appetite, or by animal appetite, or by intelligent appetite which is will."[6] The reason why not every good is equally good and some things may, in fact, be termed evil, is the specifically human condition which entails a given ultimate goal (the necessary

---

4. Vatican Council II: *Declaration on Religious Freedom*, n. 2.
5. S.T. I–II, Q. 8, a. 1.
6. S.T. I, Q. 19, a. 9.

object of the will) and a variety of particular goods, which may or may not be in line of such ultimate fulfillment. Ignorance of a true good may be an excuse and often is. However, we have a duty to learn. But the fact is that even when we know the goodness of a thing, the will is free to choose another: a sexual gratification, for instance, in place of respect of another person or some other spiritual value.

THE MEANS

The will can be looked upon as a power which permeates all our activity and embraces both ends and means. But it can also be looked upon as a particular act of willing, in which case to will and to intend are of the ends, and to consent and to choose are of the means. Consequently, the means are as voluntary as the ends for which they are chosen. However, the will may intend an end without having to adopt the means, but it cannot adopt the means without being set on the end itself. Here two observations are in order. One is that there is a difference between a purely useful means (*bonum utile*), a means-value (*bonum honestum*) and pleasure (*bonum delectabile*). Thus, to be just and courageous is good not only as a means to social peace or the salvation of one's soul, but also in itself. The other observation along the same line is that the best ends cannot justify means which are in themselves evil. Thus, a kidney patient cannot start killing other people to obtain a transplant, no matter how desirable his own health is.

MOVING THE WILL

We take will to be a spiritual power which can freely choose among alternatives (freedom of specification) and between doing and not doing (freedom of exercise). In both areas, we perceive a passage from something not being the case to something becoming the case: from not willing to willing a thing and from not doing to doing something. In the scholastic language, this is described as the transition from potency to act or the actuation of the will. Since such actuation cannot take place without an actuating agent, the question arises as to who or what actualizes the will and how necessarily the will is actualized in regard to both its choices (specification) and its decisions (exercise). In regard to specification, the will is moved or actuated by the intellect, which presents it with an attractive object. In the order of exercise, the will is self-actuating:

autonomous not only in its own act, but also the prime mover of all other human activities. Such a power is God's gift to human persons. The question still remains how necessarily the will is moved either by the intellect or by God: a question which is important not only psychologically and morally, but also philosophically and theologically.

The intellect is the actuating agent in the order of specification. But the intellect is not alone, although all other information must pass through it. There are additional "informants" such as other people, mass media, and, of course, our own feelings and emotions. Ideally, they should all be checked by the reason before being presented to the will, but sometimes they escape such control because "the reason commands the emotional powers of desire and contention, not by exercising a despotic dominion, as a slave is dictated to, but with a kingly and civil dominion, as a free man is ruled, who holds within himself the power of resistance. So also the sensitive appetite, both of desire and contention, has its own force which is not just will-power; indeed it is able to conflict with it. Accordingly there is no reason why the will should not be influenced by it" (or by any other agent that is not under our despotic power).[7] This brings us to consider the influence not only of the reason and emotions, but also of the external world in all its variety from spiritual beings like angels and devils, through the mass media, to climate and horoscopes.

The important theological position in this regard is that while none of these factors should be dismissed as non-existent, their influence, nevertheless, is not absolute, but subject to the individual reason which alone transmits its object to the will. One must be particularly careful and suspicious of attributing choices to the influence of either angels (inspiration) or devils (possessions). Except for the impediments which we discussed above, none of these factors moves the will necessarily either in the area of specification or in the area of exercise which is the will's autonomous area.

Only God moves the will, not only in the act of specification through the instrumentality of his creation and his revealed word, but also in the act of exercise. How God moves the will in its own act of exercise without violating its freedom is a mystery which transcends human understanding. To know it would imply that we know how God acts. We can only say that "God moves it in such a way that it is not predetermined to one

---

7. S.T. I–II, Q. 9, a. 2.

object; its motion remains contingent and not necessary, except for the things on which it is set by the burden of its nature."[8]

---

8. S.T. I–II, Q. 10, a. 1.

Part III
Moral Good and Evil

6

The Nature of the Distinction

OF ALL DISTINCTIONS IN HUMAN ACTS, THE DISTINCTION BETWEEN good and evil is the most important. It is also the most debatable: not in the sense that it is affirmed by some and denied by others—this would contradict our moral experience and practice—but rather in regard to the nature and foundation of such a distinction. It seems obvious to us as Christians that obedience to God is good and disobedience evil. But how do we decide that one particular act is good or in obedience to God and another is not? To love one's neighbor as oneself is the fundamental precept of the gospel. Yet people draw different conclusions from it: the pacifists condemn every kind of violence and resistance; others believe that love can be served by justice also and include in their understanding things like capital punishment and the theory of "just war." The distinction is experienced not only on the high level of common sense and the natural law, but also in particular conduct, as when we say that the same physical act of sexual intercourse is good in marriage and bad outside it. What is the nature of this distinction; what is its foundation? How reliable and unchangeable is it? Why is "telling the truth" good and "telling a lie" bad? Was it always so; will it always be so? And there are other acts, like abortion, birth control, homosexuality, euthanasia, to mention only a few, previously considered evil, then gradually tolerated and finally some even "legalized." It is in this context that we must place our study of moral good and evil. In the *Summa Theologiae*, I–II, Aquinas devotes four questions to this issue in the following order:

Question 18 introduces the problem and discusses the nature of the distinction in general. The first four articles are a summary of tradition on the subject. Articles 5–11 are Aquinas' own development and contribution.

Question 19 is an application of this distinction between good and evil to the internal acts of the will. This is an important question, not only as a further development of the previous discussion, but also of the additional light it casts on the meaning of the moral object and the nature of conscience and other moral norms.

Question 20 applies the findings to external acts, raising also some new issues, notably the question of primacy between the internal and external act (*finis operantis versus finis operis*), the morality of the effect and double effect.

Question 21 concludes the treatise with a view on the social and spiritual dimensions of good and evil acts: a kind of projection of morality into human existence and salvation history. According to their goodness or badness, human acts are also right or wrong, praiseworthy or blameworthy in the eyes of human society, meritorious or demeritorious before God.

Considering the importance of the subject and Aquinas' lengthy treatment of some other topics (e.g., emotions, dispositions), this is rather a brief study. It would be wrong, however, to conclude that all we have to know in this regard, or that all Aquinas has to say on this subject, is contained in these four questions. In studying the morality of human acts, we must keep in mind other important characteristics of theological study: the unity of theology; the treatise on God and creation; the mystery of salvation and man's ultimate goal; Christology and the sacraments. But within the great theological schema of *exitus-reditus*, the brief treatise on the moral determination of human acts holds a special place and makes a very substantial contribution to moral thought.

BASIC TERMINOLOGY

In our discussion, we shall be using a number of terms traditional to moral theology and still current. Here is a preliminary acquaintance with some of these terms and their meaning:

Essence of morality. By essence of morality we mean that which constitutes the goodness or badness of a human act. Essence is what makes a being the kind of being it is, as different from accidental characteristics. Thus the essence of man is to be a "rational animal"; size, age, color, etc., are accidents. Our question will be, what constitutes the essence of morality, or better, moral goodness or badness?

Moral determinants or *moral specificants*. By moral determinants or specificants, we mean those elements or realities which constitute the essence of morality or give the human act its moral species, as, e.g., soul and body constitute a human being. In the case of a human act, these elements are: *object, motive,* and *circumstance*.

Norm of morality. By norm of morality, we mean a measure or standard by which object, motive, and circumstance (or the human act as a whole) are judged good or bad. Such norms are: the *eternal law* or God's wisdom (supreme norm); human reason or the *natural law* (proximate objective norm); *conscience* (or proximate subjective norm). There are, of course, other norms, positive law, customs, etc. Norm of morality must not be confused with either the essence of morality or moral specificants. These constitute an act to be of a particular kind, and the norm tells us whether the kind is good or bad.

Foundation of morality. By foundation of morality, we mean the source of moral order or moral world which is human nature or God, its creator. The term *sources of morality* has another meaning: it often applies to the Scripture, tradition, and the teaching of the Church. Aquinas also uses the term *principles of morality*, which he divides into internal, as the virtues, and the external, law and grace. It should be mentioned in this regard that the use of this terminology is not always consistent: what some authors call moral specificants, others may call the sources or principles of morality. In particular texts, however, the terms and their meanings should easily be identifiable.

PROBLEM AND ITS CONTEXT

We can now return to the problem. The question is twofold: 1) what is the nature of the distinction between good and evil in morality; 2) what is its foundation or what precisely constitutes the distinction? Is the distinction only accidental, like blackness and whiteness in human beings, or essential, like the difference between a living and dead body? If there is a difference, what is its foundation? The problem may be illustrated by the example of "lying." First, there is a difference between "telling a lie" and "telling the truth," although people may disagree about the nature of this distinction. Second, we can perceive several elements constituting a lie:

1) the physical element, e.g., the sound of the speech, the composition of words; 2) the moral element which itself is threefold: a) material, or the act of "uttering a falsehood" (telling a lie); b) formal, or the agent's intention in uttering a falsehood; c) the situation or circumstance in which this is done.

In analyzing the act of lying along these lines, we can make a number of statements, each of which may be challenged. First, we can say that the physical element makes no difference, as both lie and truth may "sound" the same. Second, we can deny that there is an essential difference between telling a lie and telling the truth; that in every lie there is some truth and that if there is a difference it is only extrinsic, e.g., that one hurts people and the other helps. Third, we can accept the difference and start arguing about its foundation. In this regard we have three elements to consider: the material element or the act of lying (uttering a falsehood); the formal element or the intention of the agent; and finally, the circumstances. If all these elements are harmonious and judged good, the act is good. The problem arises when the elements conflict; when the act of lying is said to be bad and the intention of the agent good (e.g., lying to protect the life of the innocent). The same conflict may arise between the circumstances and the other two elements. Here is the kernel of the issue. If the primacy is given to the material element, the act done, we lose something of the nature of morality, which is a free human response to value. If the primacy is given to the agent's intention and situation, we risk moral subjectivism and relativism. This is the dilemma of contemporary moral theology, and it is not a new one. A brief historical glance at the problem is in order at this point.

THE SCHOLASTIC TRADITION

The prevailing traditional position on the nature of moral good and evil has been that there is an intrinsic and specific distinction between them. Societies have lived and operated on the basis of this distinction. Yet, as already indicated, the distinction was not always taken for granted. In modern times, it has been denied by subjectivistic and positivistic ethical systems, not as a distinction but as an intrinsic and specific distinction. When an intrinsic distinction between good and evil is denied, then if there is still to be a distinction, it must depend on some extrinsic denominator, such as the will of God, the law, custom, utility, pleasure, etc. Everything that fosters love or helps to win a war is good, so some say; or as Lenin said, "Everything that contributes to create a new society on the ruins of the old is morally good."

The distinction between moral good and evil has been obscured by certain theological positions as well. Some early reformers, approaching the problem in view of human sinfulness and need for justification, held that all human acts are sin (evil) before justification and that if man is not condemned, it is because God does not impute such acts unto damnation. The Catholic theologians opposed this view, which was explicitly rejected by the Council of Trent.

A more optimistic view holds that all human acts are essentially good and only accidentally evil. This view originates from an excessive comparison of moral and physical evil and the fear that to assert an essential or substantial evil would lead to the acceptance of the Manichean dualism of good and evil. Following the metaphysical principle that being and good are the same in reality (*ens et bonum convertuntur*), everything to the extent that it "is" is also good. Evil is only a privation: absence of a due quality, like blindness of an otherwise healthy human being. Consequently, every human act, to the extent that it is a reality, is good: it is the person, timing, place, or something of that kind that is wrong.

The analogy with physical good and evil is psychologically helpful, but it also has its limitations. The Bible itself was quick to develop a sharp distinction between physical and moral evil; a distinction which culminates in the New Testament calling blessed those who suffer.

The gospel, of course, is not a moral treatise, but an invitation to conversion in faith and love. However, such conversion must bear practical fruits in "good works," as a witness to one's faith and love. Not every human act is an act of love, as the writings of the apostles already made clear. There is, nevertheless, in this beginning as well as in the early patristic writings, a more direct, simple and convincing recognition of evil without great philosophical study of it.

The scholastics about St. Thomas' time were confronted with a more complex problem due to the philosophical reawakening. The problem was how to define moral good and evil in order to discuss them. The definition of good was easier, since it implies the notion of being and perfection. The definition of moral evil was more complex. If it is to be defined—and it must be if it is to be discussed—it must be defined as something, i.e., some existence or being. But metaphysically speaking, as the scholastics maintained, everything to the extent that it exists is a being and good, ultimately caused by God who is the author of all existence. Since human acts are existing realities, the conclusion was that all human acts are fundamentally good and only accidentally evil. Thus, St. Bonaventure writes: "If we follow the common opinion that all action is from God and thus good by nature, it cannot be admitted nor can one reasonably uphold that malice is essential to human actions, because it is rather a defect in regard to some accidental circumstances of that action."[1] The trouble is that for such "accidental malice" people may go to hell. The problem was often semantic. In other places, St. Bonaventure uses the term "essential," saying that adultery is essentially wrong and love of God essentially good.

One of the most influential books of this time was Peter Lombard's *Book of Sentences*. In Lombard's conception a human act, as all created realities, is a composed being (only God is *actus purus*). The elements composing a human act are of two kinds: physical (such as walking, talking, sexual intercourse), and moral. Physical goodness comes from the physical perfection of the act, like a "perfect murder" or an articulate speech. Moral goodness springs from two additional sources: one is what Lombard calls *materia debita* or the "right object," e.g., the legitimate wife in sexual intercourse; the other source is the circumstances: time, place, subjective motives, means, etc. The conclusion was that the goodness of a human act depends on all these elements, physical and moral, objective and circumstantial. An important moral principle was drawn from this, often quoted by Aquinas himself, which says: *bonum ex integra causa, malum ex quocumque defectu* ("goodness requires complete integrity, each single defect causes evil"). But this is an ideal, hardly a common occurrence. What the conclusion does not explain is what happens if one element is evil and another good. In a sense it does: it maintains that the act is evil. But how evil? Are there any priorities, e.g., that of the agent or of the act and its circumstances? This became a divisive issue.

By the time Aquinas took up the issue, two distinct currents emerged in its regard. One current, represented by Peter Abelard and his followers, stressed the primacy of the agent (*finis operantis*); the other one came from St. Bernard and Peter Lombard, and it accented the primacy of the act done (*finis operis*). Before addressing himself to this issue, Aquinas summarizes the tradition in these terms:

---

1. *Commentarius in IV Libros Sententiarum*, L. 2, D. 41, a. 1, q. 2, Opera Omnia, 4.

Accordingly in a human act we can observe a fourfold worth. The first is generic, namely its real quality as an action, for, as already remarked, to the extent that it has active reality to that extent it has good. The second is specific, and this is taken from its being directed to proper objective. The third is according to its circumstances, which are as it were its properties. The fourth is according to its end, in other words by its bearing on the ultimate cause of goodness.[2]

This fourfold structure of the morality of human acts implies physical perfection, reasonableness of its performance, right environment, and a good intention in the line of man's ultimate goal. Thus, sexual intercourse is morally good if, a) it observes physiological and psychological conditions; b) takes place in marriage; c) respects mutual decencies and feelings; d) intends love, procreation, and ultimately one's fulfillment in God by serving him.

Aquinas was in basic agreement with this schema, but he also felt the problem raised by the agent-act controversy. Since this controversy is still current in the contemporary criticism of the "traditional morality" and "moral absolutes" as protecting the act and neglecting the agent, it will be useful to summarize the so-called "traditional" or textbook schema of moral specification, before returning to Aquinas for his explanation and its significance for contemporary theology.

CLASSICAL SCHEMA OF MORAL SPECIFICATION

The term "classical" may sound presumptuous for a position which is being criticized as inadequate to meet the moral complexities of human situations. However, the schema is more than just a memory of those who studied moral theology thirty years ago and the generations before them. We believe that it still has its intrinsic value, and the problem lies not with the schema, but with our understanding of the terms (elements), namely object, motive, and circumstances.

According to this schema, the human act is a reality, a moral reality different from purely physical beings. It is a creation whose creator is the human agent acting with knowledge and will, or the human person in the image of God. Experience testifies that some acts are good and some are bad. Where does this distinction come from?

---

2. S.T. I–II, Q. 18, a. 4.

It comes from three elements which constitute a human act. These are the *object*, the *motive*, and the *circumstances*.

What is *moral object*? In scholastic terminology, object is the specific and fundamental aspect under which something is perceived, understood, desired, or studied and analyzed. Thus, "being human" is the specific and most fundamental aspect, the first reality we see in human beings, and should be "the object" of our concern and respect; color, size, age, etc., are secondary. In morals, the object is what is the most specific and fundamental in an act; it is the act itself or what it does or achieves by its very nature: a built-in reality also called "the end of the act" (*finis operis*). Thus the object of prayer is to pray; the object of stealing is to steal; the object of lying is uttering a lie, etc.; because this is what these acts achieve. What is a motive? It is the subjective intention superimposed on an act. This has been called "the end of the agent" (*finis operantis*). The fact is that the human person has the power to interfere with the object of an act adding to it its own personal motivations. Thus, one can steal or lie to help a friend in need or danger. It is in the external acts only that the object of an act may differ from its motive. The distinction between the moral significance of *finis operis* and *finis operantis* must be momentarily postponed. What are the *circumstances*? Circumstances are the external environment or conditions of time, place, condition of the agent, means, and manners by which an act is done. They are considered to be of two kinds: the *aggravating* and/or *extenuating* circumstances, and *morality changing* (*speciem mutantes*) circumstances. To steal from a poor or a rich person is an aggravating or extenuating circumstance in the sense that it is bad to steal, and worse to steal from the poor. The morality changing circumstances affect an act in its objective value, changing it, or adding to it a new additional moral quality. Thus, to use a common example, extramarital sex is wrong (fornication); the fact that the partners are young and inexperienced people in the heat of passion may diminish the gravity of the sin. But if the partners are married to third parties, the circumstances change fornication into adultery, a specifically different act.

With this in mind, the traditional moral theology produced the following practical principles:

1. In order to be good, a human act must be good from all three specificants, i.e., from object, motive, and circumstances, or one must do the right thing at the right time for the right purpose.

2. The primary specification of an act comes from its object. The purpose of this principle is to safeguard the objective morality against relativism.

3. Motive and circumstances contribute to the moral goodness and badness of an act in the following way:

   a) an objectively good act may become better through good motive and circumstances;

   b) an objectively good act may become bad because of the motive and circumstances;

   c) an objectively indifferent act receives its morality from the motive and circumstances; and

   d) an objectively evil act can never become good from motive and circumstances.

It is with this last principle that the problem begins. It claims that "a lie is always a lie" no matter what motive or circumstances. The critics of the traditional moral theology find it difficult to accept such an absolute in this, as in some other areas of human conduct.

The classical schema of moral specification gradually developed into what the critics now consider an excessive moral absolutism and legalism: a system of universal absolutes, allowing no exception and paying no attention to personal situation, motive, and to the historical and sociological changes. In practice, there has always been a pastoral concern for the "sinners," but the rules were never questioned. The moral absolutes found their support in a number of other factors, notably in the normative interpretation of the Scripture; the dogmatic theology and infallibility of the Church's magisterium in matters of faith and morals; the unchangeability of the natural law, as well as in the patriarchal structure of the family and society.

The contemporary reaction to the moral absolutes of the past springs not only from a possibly deeper concern for the individual, but also from new doubts cast on the supportive factors. Thus the critical hermeneutics present the Scripture as culturally conditioned, an invitation to love rather than an unchangeable norm of behavior; the evolutionary theories and the plurality of cultures and religions challenge the dogmatic assumptions of creation, monogenism, original sin, and the infallibility of the Church, while the scientific revolution forces theology to extend its traditional friendly dialogue with philosophy to a more challenging dialogue with modern science. Other contributing factors to these doubts are the breakdown of family structure due to social mobility and economic pressure and biomedical control of human life, function, and procreation, challenging the unchangeability of the natural law. Instead of conformity to nature, the contemporary morality is viewed more in terms of controlling it and human conduct in terms of change and relationship. Even Vatican II's *Pastoral Constitution on the Church in the Modern World* takes notice of this change when it states: "We witness the birth of a new humanism, one in which man is defined primarily in terms of his responsibility toward his brethren and toward history."[3]

THE NATURE OF MORAL EVIL

Let us now examine what we believe to be the position of Aquinas on both the nature and foundation of moral goodness and badness in human activity. In I–II, Q. 8, a. 5 he first asks whether the distinction is in kind or specific. The objections which introduce the subject were the current scholastic questions. The first objection compares moral good and evil with good and evil in things. Since good and evil make no specific difference in things, they make no specific differences in acts: "a good man and a bad man are of the same kind." The second objection takes up the familiar argument that "evil is a lack (*privatio*), and therefore, a sort of non-being. However, according to Aristotle, a non-being cannot be a differential factor, and since this is what constitutes a species, it would seem that an act is not set in a species by the fact that it is evil. Consequently good and evil do not specifically divide human acts." The third objection states that specifically different effects result from specifically different acts. "Yet the same specific effect can follow from a good and a bad action alike: as, for example, when a baby is born from adultery and from married intercourse." There is, therefore, no essential difference. Finally, sometimes acts are good or bad on account of their circumstances. Since circumstances are accidental and make no essential difference, it follows that human acts are not of different species because they are good or bad.

In his answer, Aquinas affirms the specific difference between good and evil in human acts and proceeds to explain the reasons. This explanation is of utmost importance not only for this particular argument, but also for Aquinas' concept of objective morality in general and the

---

3. Vatican Council II, *The Church Today*, n. 54.

nature of moral evil. In his explanation, Aquinas takes for granted the scholastic position (summarized in the previous article 4) that all four elements (physical, specific object, circumstances, and the end) are the moral constituents of a human act, and that only an essential condition, never an incidental, constitutes a species. Consequently, to account for a specific difference between good and evil in human acts, there must be some essential difference in one or all of the moral specificants. Aquinas argues that there is such a difference, derived not from the physical nature of an act, but from its relationship to reason. Human acts are specifically different according as they are "reasonable" or "un-reasonable." In other words, good is according to reason, evil is contrary to reason. It should be noted in this regard that "reason" here stands not for a rationalistic morality, but for human intelligence, or even for the human person as a whole. A comparison with the physical nature of things will illustrate this point.

In the physical order, good and bad make no specific difference. This is quite obvious: a good man and a bad man are specifically the same human beings. The reason for this is that the norm for being specifically human is not our reason but the nature or the Creator of nature. We are human by reference to the human form as determined by nature.

In the moral order the situation is different. Human acts are natural, not by reference to physical nature (or even its Creator), but by reference to the human person from whom they proceed. Human person is the creator of human acts and consequently their norm. For this reason it is only in the moral order that good and evil make a specific difference: the difference is to be according to or against reason. "As the species of physical things are constituted from forms existing in the world of nature, so the species of moral acts are constituted from forms as conceived by reason."[4] So as in the physical order, "to be according to nature" and "to be contrary to nature" makes a specific difference, in the moral order, "to be according to reason" and "to be against reason" makes a specific difference. "Clearly then when we observe a difference between good and evil in objectives we are seeing them in relation to the reason, an essential reference by which they are judged to be reasonable or unreasonable. Acts indeed are termed 'human' or 'moral' in so far as they issue from reason. Consequently it is evident that good and evil are specific differentiations

---

4. S.T. I-II, Q. 18, a. 10.

which set up diverse kinds of moral acts."[5] Human intelligence, according to Aquinas, has a double moral function: one is to specify what is according to reason, *secundum rectam rationem esse*; the other function is to put this "theoretical" knowledge into practice, which is done through the will (*appetitus rationalis*), under the command of practical reason. This command, as we saw in our discussion of freedom, is not despotical but political, which means that the will does not of necessity follow it. We shall see later on that reason is the immediate, not the ultimate norm of moral goodness or badness, which means that in order to be an authentic norm, it must itself be objectively right: *recta ratio*. Fooling oneself never helped anybody. But with this warning, the reason has the first word, which must be respected and obeyed. It is in disobedience to it on the practical level, through the lack of honesty and courage, that the guilt (sin) occurs. It will be the role of virtues, the good dispositions of the mind, to make the reason a competent commander and the will well disposed to follow it against internal and external obstacles.

The answers to the objections, which introduced the subject, contain a few additional clarifications. One concerns the physical nature of the act. As stated above, good and evil make no specific difference in nature or the physical reality of the act. Yet the physical reality itself may be according to or against reason, in which case it becomes morally significant and specifically different. "Intercourse in marriage and in adultery when considered in relation to the norm of the reasonable are specifically different acts with specifically different effects; one deserves praise and blessing, the other blame and penalty. Consider them in relation to the physical powers of reproduction, and of course they are not then specifically different, and they have the same sort of effect."[6] The same goes for circumstances if they represent a condition opposed to reasonable behavior.

A second clarification concerns the nature of moral evil. This, as we observed in the case of the scholastics, has been described as a defect or privation, for fear of the Manichean dualism. Aquinas' analysis leads to a more "positive" conception of moral evil. "Evil is not just a blank, but a deprivation affecting a determinate power. An act is called a bad kind of act, not because it has no objective, but because that objective cannot be squared with reasonable living; thus to take what belongs to another. In

---

5. S.T. I–II, Q. 18, a. 5.
6. S.T. I–II, Q. 18, a. 5 ad 3.

so far as the objective is something real and positive it may determine the kind of bad act that is performed."[7] To use another example, this means that in the moral order, adultery is not just a defect (*privatio*) of a basically good sexual act, but it is basically a bad act, because it is against reasonable living: *habet objectum non conveniens rationi*. Evil is "to be against reason," as good is "to be according to reason." Such a positive conception of evil does not lead to the Manichean dualism. We are talking about human acts, not about the human person, who is never entirely depraved. In this sense and in the words of St. Augustine, we can love the person and hate his vices: *cum dilectione hominum et odio vitiorum*.

THE MEANING OF OBJECTIVE MORALITY

Related to our present discussion are two contemporary and somewhat controversial issues: the meaning of objective morality and situation ethics. The first issue concerns the relationship between the object and intention, or what is called the end of the act (*finis operis*) and the end of the agent (*finis operantis*). In practical terms, this becomes a question as to whether morality stands for obedience to "moral absolutes" or obedience to conscience: a free response to values as seen personally. Contemporary criticism of the traditional morality has been the latter's apparent legalism and objectivism at the expense of personal freedom and psychological and sociological conditions. The question arises not only when the object of the act conflicts with the intention of the agent, e.g., lying to protect the life of an innocent friend, but also when they morally coincide as in the case of a legitimate intercourse in marriage whose end is both love and procreation, yet one may be preferred to the other. This question must be distinguished from what is called the "double effect." The conflict in the double effect is not between object and intention, but rather between two objects: the life of the mother or the life of the fetus.

What precisely is a moral object? The general impression we get from most (though by no means all) of the moral manuals of the recent past and their contemporary critics is that the moral object is a reality (physical) entirely outside voluntariness; something "in itself," an external deed to be praised or blamed for what it is. This is not Aquinas' concept of the moral object.

7. S.T. I–II, Q. 18, a. 5 ad 2.

In scholastic terminology, the object is that which, in an act, first and foremost stands out in relation to a cognitive or appetitive faculty. Thus, the object of lying is to "utter falsehood" because this is what the mind first perceives in the act of lying; who, when, how, why, etc., are circumstances. From this perspective, the primacy belongs to the object; to say otherwise would be like saying that color or age are more important than being human in a person. The problem, however, lies in the fact that people may have different perceptions of the object itself. This is particularly the case in the external acts, in which what one person sees as the first and foremost reality may not be seen as such by others or by an "objective" moral standard.

Aquinas takes up the issue by asking two questions: a) is the act morally specified by the end intended? and b) is the moral kind which comes from the end contained as under a genus in that which comes from the objective, or is the reverse true?[8] This is the same as asking: does the end of the agent (intention or *finis operantis*) specify the morality of the (external) act, and if so, which specification, from the end of the agent or from the end of the act, is more fundamental and primary to moral specification? If the emphasis and primacy is on the end of the act done (*finis operis*), we are depersonalizing morality; the moral agent who is a human person in the image of God becomes secondary. If the emphasis and primacy is on the end of the agent (*finis operantis*), we risk subjectivism and relativism in morals.

Responding to such a dilemma, Aquinas takes two unequivocal positions. One is that morally speaking, there is no such thing as a purely external, "in-itself" human act. In the moral order, all human acts must proceed from the intrinsic principle of knowledge and will: "we started by saying that certain acts are 'human' in as much as they are voluntary." Nevertheless, "we find a double activity here, namely the will's own internal activity and its externalized activity, and each of these has its objective." In other words, in every external act we find two realities: one is what the will wills; the other one is what is willed. The internal act of the will is entirely the will's own business; the external (imperated) act happens to have in addition its own specific status from the kind of act it is: "the end intended is the objective for the will's internal act, while the objective for the external act is what is engaged with." A subtle distinction is here

---

8. S.T. I–II, Q. 18, aa. 6–7.

The Nature of the Distinction 87

at play, as the external act appears under a double objective: the objective intended by the will (*finis operantis*) and the objective of the act (*finis operis*) or the moral status that the act has in the eyes of other people.

Having recognized this distinction, Aquinas takes a second position, which boldly states that what formally and primarily specifies even the external act is not its own objective, but the objective intended by the will: "Now the part played by the will shapes the performance of the external deed, for the will applies members like instruments to the execution of an action: indeed our outward acts possess no moral significance save in so far as they are voluntary. Hence the specific character of human acts is assessed as to its form by the end intended and as to its matter by the objective of the external deed. That is why Aristotle observes that he who steals in order to commit adultery is directly more adulterer than thief."[9] It is interesting that in this entire treatise, *De Actibus Humanis*, Aquinas never explicitly uses the distinction between *finis operis* and *finis operantis*, because, as he writes in the *Commentary on the Books of Sentences*, the end of the act is always reduced to the end of the agent: *finis operis semper reducitur in finem operantis*.[10] Thus, in the context of the contemporary theological dilemma between the morality of personal responsibility and the morality of law, Aquinas is on the side of the person. This position will be reaffirmed as we proceed with our analysis, especially on the subject of conscience.

A different problem we are confronted with in this regard is that such understanding of objective morality may lead to moral subjectivism and relativism, which are contrary to Catholic moral tradition. We shall address ourselves to this issue in our concluding remarks of this section. As an introduction to it, we would like to pursue the present analysis by pointing out another distinction which easily escapes attention. This is the distinction between the intention or the end of the agent and the motive of the agent. The traditional schema of moral specificants is simpler in this regard. Since the object of the act is the act in itself, or act done, it is easy to distinguish it from whatever motives a person may have. A lie is always a lie, no matter what motivated it. But when the object of the act is identified with the agent's perception and intention of it (*finis operantis*), the distinction is less obvious. Yet there is a distinction, as our familiar

---

9. S.T. I–II, Q. 18, a. 7.
10. Thomas Aquinas, *Scriptum super Libros Sententiarum*, L. 2, D. 1, q. 2, a. 1.

example of lying may show. In the act of lying, we may distinguish the traditional objective element or "the act done" (uttering falsehood); the formal objective element or what the agent perceives and intends in the act, e.g., that "uttering falsehood" to save an innocent life is not really "uttering falsehood" (a lie), but "saving a life." According to our analysis, it is this formal objective element that gives the act its primary specification. But in addition to this specification, or basic understanding of the nature of the act, the agent may have some ulterior, subjective motives, e.g., to "save an innocent life by uttering falsehood" in order to save his own life, to preserve companionship, to obstruct the enemy, to receive an award, etc. These are secondary, subjective motives, good or bad as the agent may perceive them, but different from his original perception of the act of saving as good in itself. It is one thing to perceive that "uttering falsehood to save an innocent life" is not a lie but saving a life, and another to think that such is the case, but to do it for other motives we may choose, e.g., a monetary reward. The first may be an erroneous conscience; the second is an arbitrary intent. The danger of relativism is not that people may be wrong in their perception of values, but in thinking that they can arbitrarily decide what is right. Consequently, our motives are not the first and formal moral specificants, but our intentions following the perceptions of intelligence are. A final reason why the moral primacy belongs to the intention rather than to the external objective is the will's universality. It is again one of those scholastic assumptions which makes sense in practice: the more universal an agent is, the more extensive is its power. The proper object of the will is the universal good or the ultimate end. "The will, which has our final end as its proper objective, is the universal motive-power for all our psychological powers, whereas their proper objectives are the objectives of particular acts."[11] Since all external acts have only their own particular objectives, they fall under the universal objective of the will, as the tactical dispositions of this or that military unit fall under the general goal of winning the victory.

But this now opens a new vista on the entire process of moral specification and the meaning of objective morality, bringing more and more into the picture the role of the ultimate goal. This may be stated in the following propositions: 1) An external act is morally insignificant unless embraced by the will's intention. (An involuntary lie is not a lie: "there is

11. S.T. I–II, Q. 18, a. 7.

more of an opposition to the moral virtue of truth where someone utters truth intending falsity, than where one utters falsity intending truth.")[12]
2) The right and burden falls on the will which must a) be good in its own act, i.e., have the right intention in the line of an authentic ultimate goal, and b) correctly evaluate the proportionality of the external act to such an end. In other words, as free and responsible human agents, we must have an authentic vision of our human goal, examine the value of particular acts in relation to it, and have honesty and courage to pursue them when found worthy.

MORALLY INDIFFERENT ACTS

Before our concluding remarks on objective morality and as a corollary to moral specification, a word must be said about morally indifferent acts. Are there any human acts which are neither good nor bad? Is there a value-free zone of human activity? In answering this question, Aquinas makes a distinction between the theoretical and practical levels of human activity.[13]

Human acts may be considered abstractly: e.g., we can talk and write about stealing, adultery, singing, talking, playing the piano, etc., without reference to a particular agent. It is quite obvious that on this level some acts are morally neutral and others are not. Playing the piano, taking showers, going for a walk, have no specific for-or-against relationship to reason, as stealing and adultery do. Consequently, and speaking abstractly, some human acts are morally neutral. On the practical level, however, the situation is different if we are talking about the human acts done with knowledge and will. Since all human acts are *in particularibus*, this difference is important.

Given the scale of goodness and badness in human conduct, the fact that adultery will, in general, be considered worse than just talking about it, some moralists believe that there is room for indifferent acts even in a particular case. Aquinas holds a different position. He maintains that every individual act is morally determined, if not from its object, then from motive and circumstances. One plays the piano for relaxation, practice, and many other reasons, and to play when others try to study will also make a difference. If there is no motive, or if the playing is just a matter of habit, then the act is not properly human but only an act of man.

12. S.T. II-II, Q. 110, a. 1 ad 1.
13. S.T. II-II, Q. 110, aa. 8–9.

The issue of indifferent acts has a special moral significance when applied to various professional activities. Skill and competence are morally neutral in themselves, but whether the individual scientists, doctors, sportsmen, business people, artists, etc., can claim such neutrality in personal and particular exercise of their profession is a different matter. A particular human act implies awareness of some purpose and circumstances which make the act good or bad.

In conclusion, therefore, we admit that abstractly speaking, there are morally neutral acts and that even in a particular case, some acts are better or worse and neutral by inadvertence or the force of habit. But we feel it necessary to affirm that there are no morally indifferent individual human acts, if by human act we mean what is done with knowledge and will, and what is more, there should not be any. It is our human privilege and duty to give a "moral touch," a personal meaning, to all our activities according to the words of St. Paul: "Whether you eat or drink, or anything else, do all for the glory of God."

CONCLUDING REMARKS

The preceding analysis of the "moral object" suggests a conclusion in favor of a personalistic morality: a morality based on the primacy of the end of the agent, which is also a favorite current in contemporary moral thinking. Our references to Aquinas show that it is not necessarily a novelty in the Christian moral tradition.

Since the proximate norm which measures the morality of a human act is the agent himself (the person), or the concrete human person (conscience), we must now ask two additional questions: 1) Can we still have an objective moral order and a moral science (moral theology) of such an order? and 2) how does the individual person relate to it?

The first question is not a specifically moral problem; it is an epistemological problem, a problem of knowledge in general. Our position is based on two assumptions: that there is an active mind (subject) and a real world (object) of both physical and moral realities. Positivism and skepticism of modern philosophy introduced doubts in regard to both, the power of the mind and the reality of the world. This is an epistemological crisis of which moral science has been singled out as a special target, as logical positivism and the emotive theories of ethics testify. Confronted with the real moral issues of the contemporary society, the current is losing its original academic popularity. So far as we are concerned, we take for granted, although not without sound arguments, the reality of both an active mind and a real moral order.

It is from individual moral realities, the particular human acts as situationally experienced, that through conceptualization we arrive at universal concepts. From the particular acts of justice we arrive at the concept of justice; from instances of adultery and lying we arrive at the notion of adultery and lying. Such conceptualization enables us to recognize a particular act when it occurs, to communicate our experience, and to construct a moral science and system of moral values. In line of our understanding of objective morality, however, and more than in the case of natural sciences, we must be careful in applying these general concepts back to particular human acts, because of the nature and contingency of moral realities and the individuality of human activity. Moral science is not mathematics. But with this precaution, we claim the possibility of an objective moral order and a meaningful science of it.

The second question is a specifically moral problem because it takes us back to our issue of the primacy of the subjective versus objective morality. We answer this question by affirming two facts: one is that primacy belongs to the person (*finis operantis*); the other one is that the person we are talking about is a human individual. This means that we have to remind ourselves of what we already know about the human person in particular, namely, that he is always acting for an end and at least implicitly for an ultimate end; that formally, although not materially, we all concur in one ultimate end (happiness); that from our Christian perspective such an ultimate end consists in the vision of God; and finally, that man's natural condition is to live in society, in the Christian context, a fellowship under God. Our human existence is always a coexistence. Consequently, if we really want to be ourselves and give primacy to ourselves, it must be to ourselves as we really are, a community under God. Moral life is deeply personal only when it is deeply interpersonal.

Translated into moral application, this means several things: a) that being social we need to communicate our values and learn from one another; b) that our moral dialogue must be real, and consequently, we must seek objectivity; c) that beginning with the primacy of the agent, it becomes a moral call of everyone in virtue of being human and social to objectify oneself in a true fellowship. Morality becomes a discipline of giving away something of oneself in favor of what one perceives to be a higher good for all.

One last question remains about the objective moral order itself. While we see the need and possibility for a dialogue of values, we still have to ask whether these values are something real, or just a social convention and convenience subject to arbitrary change.

Our answer must be that moral values are not a matter of convention and convenience, but something real, and that at least some fundamental values remain constant. They are constant on two grounds: human nature and the unity of the human goal.

When we introduce human nature and goal as a point of reference for the reality and constancy of moral values we are, in fact, introducing the concept of the natural law, which has traditionally served this purpose. But the natural law tradition, too, has been a subject of considerable reexamination in contemporary theological thinking. Two specific objections are frequently raised against the traditional natural law argument: one is its physicism or biologism, especially in regard to human sexuality; the other one is its codification, or the attempt to declare as universally binding precepts and prohibitions which may, in fact, be historically conditioned and changeable.

Human nature is a complex concept. It coincides with our understanding of what it means to be human. This may not be easy to define, as the contemporary medical and legal debates about the beginning or the end of human life illustrate. It is, nevertheless, safe to assume that at any given time, all human beings manifest some basic common qualities and reactions, which are not conventional agreements but real and naturally known facts. Some of these facts are physical and biological, like the instinct of self-preservation; others are specifically human and moral, like the search for truth and happiness and living in society. The natural fact-perception leads to the natural value-perception so that from the natural instinct of self-preservation, we derive the natural rights to life, food, shelter, and from the search for happiness, the rights to, and respect for, freedom, work, marriage and family, etc. It is true that some of these conclusions are not as constant as the basic facts of self-preservation and living in society, but as long as they relate to them, they are not a matter of arbitrariness and convenience. Moreover, it is precisely through such specific derivation that the basic facts themselves are explicated in practice. To do good and avoid evil is self-evident, but it does not take us far enough. Human contingency and changeability may not permit a definite codification of the natural law. The conclusions derived from it are alterable, but this does not diminish their (even provisional) reality and significance for moral dialogue.

We shall have a few additional observations on this subject in the next section on Situation Ethics. From what we have said, we may conclude that the cause of relativism is not our mutual trust as free agents but rather our indifference, in the first place, to what we can reasonably know, and ultimately, to our common goal and human fellowship. If such indifference comes from human weakness and ignorance, it may be excused; if it is voluntary and selfish, it is a sin. The danger of relativism is not in respecting personal conscience and perception of values. If this is a risk, we must take it to safeguard the dignity of the person. God took this risk when he created man free and responsible. Morality is an opening of oneself to God and others: a process of formation by perfecting one's knowledge and will.

7

Situation Morality

RELATED TO OUR ANALYSIS OF MORAL GOOD AND EVIL, AND AN important issue in itself, are the circumstances better known in the contemporary context as "situation ethics." We shall first outline the traditional understanding of the role of circumstances as moral specificants and then evaluate contemporary situation ethics.

CIRCUMSTANCES: THE TRADITIONAL VIEW

The traditional moral specification was not a black or white issue. The world of human activity is a contingent world, in which no individual act could ever fully be measured by the abstract types. Aquinas is persistent in saying that *actus humani sunt in particularibus*; "human acts are particular": they have their "nature," but each one with its own flesh and bones. This, indeed, is a good way to describe circumstances. The classic mnemonic list since the time of Cicero and going back to Aristotle contained seven circumstances: who, what, why, by what aids, where, how and when. As we mentioned in an earlier section, some circumstances are more fundamental than others, e.g., who the agent is, what and why something is done. Human conduct reflects a person's talent and temperament, sex, age and health, and religious and social conditions. The circumstances of "why" and "what is done" are intimately related to the moral object itself. However, as we said earlier, there is still a distinction between "why" as an additional motive or motives and "the end of the agent" as the primary moral specificant. Similarly, there is a distinction between "what" as "the end of the act," and "what" may circumstantially be done by an act, such as killing an innocent bystander in a legitimate act of self-defense.

Other circumstances are morally significant if and when they are perceived as morally good and bad. Thus, for the circumstance of time and place, it is not enough that something is done on a Sunday in church; it must be perceived as morally good or bad to be done in that way. When so perceived, to commit murder in the church is not only a crime, but also a sacrilege. The circumstance "with what aids" plays its own important role in the area of moral cooperation and in choosing the means, which may or may not be appropriate even for a good end.

While the distinction between the object, motive, and circumstances is obvious and useful, in practice there is no separation. Every act, specifically every external act, is always situational, with its own flesh and bones. Even an internal act is situational by the fact that it is always the act of a particular person. Consequently, in evaluating the morality of a human act, the circumstances must always be taken into consideration. In order to do this, the traditional morality offers a number of distinctions and subsequent principles concerning the role of circumstances.

The main distinction is between two kinds of circumstances: those "changing the morality" and those "modifying the morality" of an objectively good or bad act. The first kind of circumstances simply adds a new value or disvalue to the objective morality of an act. The reason is that in themselves, these circumstances contain their own conformity or deformity with the rational nature of the human person. Thus, the circumstance of the religious vow of chastity adds a new specific value to the practice of chastity. On the other hand, adultery is not just modified fornication, but a new species of such a sexual act because of its additional deformity of injustice and infidelity to the legitimate spouses.

The second kind of circumstances are those modifying morality without changing the specific nature coming from the object. They only aggravate or diminish the objective value or disvalue of an act. Thus, a state of depression because of a pending divorce may diminish but not change the evil of adultery, as stealing from a poor person aggravates the act of stealing without changing its nature. With this distinction in mind, the traditional moral theology offered a set of principles determining the role of circumstances among the other moral specificants. The principle concerning the circumstances changing morality is simple: these circumstances are in fact just another moral object in their own right. The principles concerning the circumstances modifying morality are the same as those stated in regard to motive. An objectively good act may become better from circumstances: such was the widow's mite in the gospel. A good act may become less good, like praying when one should attend his duties, or even simply bad on the account of circumstances, e.g., returning a stolen gun to a convicted murderer. A morally indifferent act becomes good or bad from circumstances, like singing for a charitable cause, or driving in a state of drunkenness. The evil of a bad act may be diminished through circumstances, such as an occult compensation in the case of an obvious injustice. But a bad act may also become worse because of circumstances, as in the case of extravagant living in a poor and depressed area. The concluding principle of this series maintains that an objectively bad act can never become good on account of circumstances. It is this last principle that has become controversial, bringing us to the issue of situation ethics.

SITUATION ETHICS

The question of moral circumstances has become a specific moral issue in contemporary ethical debate under the name of "situation ethics," or what is sometimes also called the "new morality." A familiar book on the subject is Joseph Fletcher's *Situation Ethics* (Philadelphia: Westminster, 1966). Karl Rahner is the best known Catholic theologian who often passes for an advocate of situation morality. The idea inspired a number of minor works and a considerable number of articles in the sixties and in the aftermath of the second Vatican Council.

The Church's first official reference to the "new morality" goes back to Pius XII, who in several of his addresses in 1952 and 1953 describes it as "existential ethics ... ethical individualism ... ethical actualism," etc.

On February 2, 1956, the old Holy Office condemned as dangerous to faith and morals what it called the "new morality" which, according to this condemnation, seeks to detach itself from the principles of objective ethics. The document rejects the new morality on the grounds that it holds that the ultimate decision of conscience does not come from the application of an objective, universal norm to a particular case, but that such decision is and ought to be made through a direct light in each particular situation. Furthermore, the document states, the new morality dismisses the validity of the natural law, since according to it, "being human" is historically conditioned and changeable. Finally, it rules out the role of authority and leads to moral relativism.

A proximate reason for such official reaction against the "new morality" at that time was the feeling that the theologians were making too great a concession to modern philosophy, especially to Marxism, and to the social changes after World War II in general. It was, in fact, the war with all its implications, prison camps, and resistance movements, that brought the Catholics and non-Catholics, priests and laymen, intellectuals and workers, closely together, abating the old dogmatic and other separating differences of the past.

The roots of the new morality go deeper than such immediate war and postwar experience. Indeed, the tension between the subjective and the objective is at the very heart of moral history. Situation ethics is a reaction against an excessive objectivism in morals, as existentialism is a reaction against the excessive rationalism in philosophy. Both are coupled in life by the emergence of the modern mass society and what is seen as the technological control of the individual. A special momentum was given to existentialist thought by the discovery of a semi-forgotten nineteenth-century Danish writer, Søren Kierkegaard. His reaction against German idealism, accompanied by his personal loneliness, with a deep religious feeling yet in conflict with his established Lutheran Church, made him an attractive symbol of existentialism. For him, ethics was life: an either / or issue, not in abstract principles but in concrete decisions. Subjective tensions, anxieties, and social conflicts became familiar existentialist themes, supported by arguments that the human subject has been lost in the complexity, competition, automation, and oppression of modern society.

There are other factors which, from a moral perspective, bring the issue closer to home. One of the basic claims of the situationalists (if we may be allowed to use that name) is that the traditional treatment and role of circumstances is unsatisfactory in modern times. The world we live in is not just another situation. It is another world with a new man in it: a man who is more mature and less free. The examples are many: a Catholic businessman working in a materialistic (whether capitalist or communist) economic system; a Catholic doctor in a state hospital practicing abortion; a judge presiding in a divorce case; soldiers and spies in modern war, etc. These, it is argued, are situations in which even the most conscientious Christian finds it impossible to obey absolute norms. Technology has changed the ways of life; e.g., the availability of contraceptives puts sex and marriage into a different perspective, as mass media changes traditional education and lifestyles. The old virtues of patience, forgiveness, and obedience to government seem to be modern vices, prolonging unjust oppression, which revolution and disobedience might change.

We may add two additional observations. One is that while the analysis of modern society and human experience in it may be valid, we must not rule out moral weakness and laxity as people seek excuses for what they want to do and to escape the responsibility which life imposes. Another observation is from religion itself: the revival of "charismatic theology." Although the charismatic movement may be a result of modern existentialism, it is also a contributing factor to it. The fact is that the Bible, as well as the Christian history, abound in examples of great individuals who took exception to rules and establishments of their time.

MORAL ESSENCE AND EXISTENCE

Situation ethics, as we said earlier, is closely related to and reflects existentialist philosophy. This philosophy, which gives primacy to existence over essence, has its own view of the human person and condition, and even its own language in describing them. Man is not just a being; he is also a becoming; he is free, but his freedom is coexistential with the freedom of others and limited by them. Every human existence is a particular existence: every person is unique. In existentialist language, facticity means factual existence in time and space; unicity stands for the uniqueness of the person. Consequently, no abstract, universal norms can apply to the individual. Human conduct cannot be conceptualized.

As every human being is factual and unique, so every human being is subject to change in a changing world. Facticity, unicity and changeability are not invitations to laxity and irresponsibility. At least Christian existentialism claims that in every particular situation, there is only one authentic answer to God's call. There may not be universal norms, but there is still one true response to God's calling us to do the right thing in a particular situation. The agent must listen to this call and respond to it. There is an ethical invitation in every situation and an ethical response to commitment to it. How we know the right response is not clear. Since we do not know what the true response is, the only response we can give is to "commit" ourselves. Morality becomes not a matter of knowledge but a fact of commitment.

Situation moralists offer what they call situation moments as the factors which make the individual situation factual and unique. Among these are: geophysical factors, such as climate, seasons, day, night, etc.; psychosomatic factors, like sex, age, health, temperament; cultural factors, like education, intelligence, profession; social factors, like family, race, class, residential area; historical factors of one's past life, e.g., prisoners of war, former marriage, divorce; moral factors, such as moral sensitivity and emotional responses, and religious factors, like the fact of redemption, faith experience in the local church, liturgical life, etc.

The traditional morality should have no quarrel with the circumstantial role of these factors. The difference begins with the emphasis and the exclusiveness of their role, i.e., when these factors become the only moral determinants. Moral existence (situation) need not be in conflict with moral essence. The existentialist slogan "existence precedes essence" is wrong not in what it says, but in what it does not say. It is from existence, the concrete experience of moral good and evil, that we arrive at their essence. But there is no reason why we could not, or should not, apply our cumulative experience back to new existences, even with all due respect for their own particularities. The weakest point of situation ethics is not its emphasis on existence but its denial of essence: the denial of the possibility of conceptualization, which is only a short step from a denial of human fellowship.

Situation morality, as we said earlier, is not necessarily an anti-normative morality. But in this regard there is a difference between Christian and non-Christian or atheistic existentialists.

Christian existentialists believe in God and feel a personal responsibility to him. Consequently, our actions are not indifferent, but either good or bad according to the authenticity of our response. Christian existentialists differ from those holding the traditional objective morality in their refusal to admit the possibility of conceptualization of the individual moral experiences into a moral context which could be socially shared. The absence of such sharing makes every moral decision a personal guess in hope and prayer that it will be the right one. This explains the great existentialist themes of anxiety, loneliness, life as a struggle, conversion, commitment, etc.

As a philosophical and religious reaction, existentialism marks a return to a more real philosophy: to the mysterious, the religious and the ultimate in life, which modern rationalism, pragmatism, and positivism disengaged from human consideration. But such a reaction can also be overdone.

Atheistic existentialists have their own additional disadvantage: they have no God speaking to them and no norm to follow. Their morality has no support and no purpose: the human person is left in the dark and life becomes absurd.

CONCLUDING OBSERVATIONS

Our concluding comments will be limited to the Christian situation morality, or a believing existentialism. A discussion of atheistic existentialism, important as it is for a general knowledge of contemporary moral problems, would require a substantial analysis of the development of modern philosophy. Even the Christian or believing existentialist must not be treated as a single class, since there are many individual differences. Nevertheless, the following general observations may help us to grasp and evaluate some common aspects and consequences of situation morality.

The main difference between the traditional treatment of moral circumstances and that of contemporary situation ethics is the emphasis on their importance. In the traditional moral schema, the circumstances are one of three moral determinants, and not the most fundamental one. They are related and ordinarily subject to the objective value of the act as perceived by the agent. Situation morality considers the circumstances or the situation as the only norm-making factor of every human act.

Now as we already indicated, this must not be interpreted as indifferentism or relativism in the ordinary sense of the word. Christian situation morality claims that every person must give a personal response to God's command; the command is there and the response must be authentic. It may not be applicable to another person or another situation of the same person. But every person in every situation has an "objective" (authentic) norm given by God, who must be obeyed.

In this context, the gap between an authentic objective morality, such as that of Aquinas, and situation morality becomes rather illusive, which is evidenced by the fact that Aquinas himself is often taken for an existentialist. The real issue, therefore, is not whether an agent must make his own personal decision, because ultimately this is what he must do; it is rather a question whether such a decision is or can be in isolation from and in disregard of the human fellowship in all its historical, psychological, and religious reality. Rejecting such fellowship of minds and hearts, it is difficult to see how in practice one can escape subjectivism and relativism, unless we accept personal revelations as the ordinary way of knowing God's command. For this reason, Protestantism, legally and hierarchically less structured, became a more fertile ground for situation morality. Catholic moral theology takes the visible Church as the normal channel of God's communication and guidance. It does not exclude the possibility of exceptional personal revelations nor the working of God's grace in every individual person. But it warns us that in our human situations it is not only God who speaks but very often also our own weakness and sinfulness as well as the devil through his temptations. St. John tells us in his first letter, "Do not trust every spirit, but put the spirits to a test to see if they belong to God."

Among the consequences of situation morality in the contemporary Christian and, more specifically, Catholic experience, has been a certain confusion of values. The traditional morality speaks of a hierarchy of values and consequently, also of degrees of malice. For instance, within the Catholic context of faith, virginity and celibacy are higher values than marriage and family, and priesthood takes precedence over the lay state. Similarly, justice is a higher virtue than temperance; adultery is graver than fornication, and murder is worse than theft. Situation morality does not accept such a differentiation, since all difference comes exclusively from who the individual person is and what his situation is. Now no one denies that for a particular person it may be better to be married than celibate, a layman rather than a priest. But objectively speaking, i.e., given God as our ultimate goal and the division of gifts in the witness of the kingdom, there is still a difference between dying for one's faith and only singing for it in a church choir.

The traditional moral theology, notably that of St. Thomas, took for granted that all human acts are *in particularibus* and that there is always a limitation to the application of universal norms to particular cases. Two specific virtues, wit or the flair for the exceptional, the Greek *gnomen* in the area of prudence and equity in the area of justice, remind us of such contingency of the norms, as both deal with exceptional situations in which a judgment must be made or a thing done besides and above the ordinary moral rules. We may call it exemption, but a better word is transcendence. Situation morality takes a different direction: it speaks not about application and exemption or transcendence, but of adaptation. This suggests a change in universal norms and their subjection to the particular situation, bringing back the issue of changeability and unchangeability of natural law. To complement what we have already said on this subject in our previous chapter, we can only indicate Aquinas' line of thinking in regard to the meaning of natural law and the difference which emerges between Aquinas and situation morality.

Aquinas takes into consideration that in order to be effective, the natural law must go beyond the universal principle of doing good and avoiding evil and voice some concrete precepts, e.g., prohibiting the killing of the innocent. But he is also cognizant of the fact that such precepts are often historically and culturally conditioned and, thus, changeable. In *Summa Theologiae*, I–II, notably in question 94 on natural law, Aquinas refrains from codifying the natural law and accepts a certain changeability of human nature. What is unchangeable, in his view, is the basic human aspiration for good and happiness. Since human happiness comprises physical, animal, and rational good, he thinks that self-preservation in being, self-perpetuation in one's offspring, and rational development by living in society and knowing truths about God, are the immediate and universal human tendencies and therefore of natural law. The forms or precepts of these tendencies may change from culture to culture and the more remote they are from the original perception, the more uncertain they become. Moreover, the reason may be clouded by passions and the will weakened by bad habits.

A second characteristic to be mentioned is Aquinas' conception of natural law as an "ordinance of reason" which shares in the Eternal law. Consequently, the unchangeability of natural law is not primarily grounded in the unchangeability of biological laws of nature, but rather in the unchangeability of the Eternal law, which the intellectual creature shares. This may appear to open the way to situation morality, but a difference gradually emerges as the human experience and revelation are brought in as the normal channels of such a sharing. The physical and psychological reality is a part of our human make-up and cannot be reasonably dismissed as irrelevant. One does not love another by torturing him. Still, moral good and evil are differentiated, as we said, not by reference to the physical nature as such, but by reference to reason or the human person as the image of God. God is the ultimate goal of the human person. Consequently, it is the unchangeability of God which gives the moral continuity to human actions and norms. The norms are unchangeable, in so far as they participate in the unchangeability of God. It is for our faith and reason, coupled with historical and sociological experience, to discover which particular mores belong only to a particular time and culture and which may indeed be valid for all times and people.

The Second Vatican Council, whose personalistic traits are reflected in all its documents, puts an unequivocal emphasis on the communal and social dimension of the human individual as inseparable from his personality. "Profound and rapid changes make it particularly urgent that no one, ignoring the trends of event or drugged by laziness, content himself with a merely individualistic morality."[1] Stating that "every man has the duty and therefore the right to seek the truth in matters religious, in order that he may with prudence form for himself right and true judgments of conscience," the Council also states that "truth ... is to be sought after in a manner proper to the dignity of the human person and his social nature."[2]

This also puts the question of individual adaptation into a different perspective. To the extent that situation morality rests on personal dignity and responsibility, limiting the absoluteness of moral norms by the consideration of the individual person, Aquinas would have no quarrel with it. It is when the individual person rejects the consideration of moral norms on the grounds of his separateness that situation ethics deviates from authentic morality. As such, it is unacceptable intellectually because it offers no proof that moral experiences cannot be conceptualized and profitably shared as a moral science; it is unacceptable socially for the reason that it becomes unworkable; it is unacceptable theologically because as Christians it is our duty to listen to God through the channels of reason and revelation and as free persons to dominate situations and not be dominated by them.

---

1. Vatican Council II, *The Church Today*, no. 30.
2. Ibidem.

8

Conscience

OUR ANALYSIS OF MORAL GOOD AND EVIL MAY APPROPRIATELY BE summed up by a discussion of conscience: the core of moral decision. Today, perhaps more than in the past, there is a new awareness of and emphasis on conscience as a fundamental human right. In social and international relations, this is partially due to a renewed struggle for individual and political freedom and still widespread violation of it. Sensitive to both, the United Nations' *Universal Declaration of Human Rights* declares in Article 1: "All human beings are born free and equal in dignity and rights. They are endowed with reason and conscience and should act toward one another in a spirit of brotherhood." In the Christian and Catholic context, a new impetus has been given by Vatican Council II, emphasizing the essential link between spiritual growth and a free and responsible conscience.

It is often said that every true morality is a conscience morality. This, we believe, is the conclusion of our own explanation of the meaning of objective morality as one which gives primacy to the agent and his intention. Nevertheless, the subject of conscience is still a complex one, not only in the practical sphere of possible conflicts, but also in regard to its mysterious origin. There are, therefore, many approaches to conscience, and we shall survey some of them.

Since conscience is a norm of moral actions, it is appropriate to begin the subject with an outline of moral norms in general. The phenomenon of moral norms arises from the fact that the moral specificants (object, motive, circumstances) have to be themselves evaluated by some kind of reference or standard, that something or somebody has to say that to love is good and to hate is bad or that stealing from the poor is worse than stealing from the rich.

The traditional moral theology listed three such norms: *eternal law* or the divine wisdom as the supreme objective norm; *human reason* or natural law as the proximate objective norm; and *conscience* as the proximate subjective norm. There are, of course, other moral norms which we experience, such as the will of God manifested in the Scripture, the laws of the Church, the will of parents and superiors, positive laws and customs, which are all intermediaries between eternal/natural law and subjective conscience. Accepting, as we do, that God is the ultimate goal of every human person and that we all share a common human nature and live in fellowship, it is obvious that the higher and more common the wisdom, the higher and more universal is the norm. Thus, divine wisdom or eternal law has a primacy over human wisdom or natural law, and both in an objective order over individual conscience. Yet in practice, it is our conscience to which we first appeal and act upon. This recalls the familiar problem of subjective versus objective in morality.

The most common notion of conscience is that of a judgment made by a person concerning the morality of his actions. As such, it is a universal human experience. Conscience is not the same as consciousness. Consciousness is a broader notion, which stands for an awareness of oneself and things around oneself. Thus we talk of a person as being conscious or being unconscious, e.g., in a coma. Consciousness is direct, immediate, intuitive, and thus different from discursive knowledge and conclusions. It is a psychological reality which precedes and underlies all other sensitive and intellectual perception. Conscience is consciousness applied to what is to be done: a moral dimension of consciousness. But this is only an initial understanding of conscience. Contrary to what is sometimes said of conscience as being a "power" or a "moral sense," Aquinas considers conscience as primarily an act of the practical reason; a concrete application of one's moral knowledge (*cum-scientia*). Consequently, conscience as an act is the result not only of a direct intuition, but also of acquired knowledge and experience. For this reason, Aquinas becomes more concerned with prudence as the virtue of conscience than conscience itself. Subsequent moral theology maintained the concept of act-oriented conscience without the same emphasis on prudence, ending gradually in a legalistic and casuistic conception of conscience. Contemporary moral theology reacts against this conception, and Vatican II reflects this reaction when it calls conscience "the most secret core and sanctuary of man" and "the voice of God."

With these introductory observations, we propose to survey the more significant approaches to conscience both sacred and secular, beginning with the biblical concept.

BIBLICAL AND EARLY CHRISTIAN CONCEPT OF CONSCIENCE

There are two ways to search for the meaning of conscience in the Bible: a search for the word and a search for the spirit or fact of conscience. The word, which in Greek is *syneidesis*, is practically nonexistent in the Old Testament, except for a few occurrences in the Wisdom literature. In the New Testament, the word is primarily found in the epistles, notably in St. Paul, who uses it some twenty times. If the word is not used, except in the New Testament, the fact of conscience runs through the entire Scripture. The words commonly used in the Old Testament are "heart," "knowledge," "wisdom," but more important is the assumption that man is free, that he can listen to God, and respond to his love, as well as harden his heart. There is no definition of conscience in the Bible, but its presence is manifested in a person's relationship to God, to his tribe, family, aliens, and in the New Testament, to the Christian community and to the world: conscience is the human person in dialogue with God and others. The biblical conscience is neither a threat nor a personality cult, but a person's internal forum, accessible only to him and to God who "scrutinizes the reins and hearts of man."

There are several significant characteristics of conscience in the Bible, and especially in St. Paul, who, as we said, also uses the Greek word *syneidesis*. Here are some of these characteristics:

Conscience is the core of the human person and the center of all authentic morality: "Let your hearts be broken, not your garments torn" (Joel 2:12). It is an internal reality, not an external observance: "The real Jew is one who is inwardly a Jew, and the real circumcision is in the heart—something not of the letter, but of the spirit. A Jew like that may not be praised by man, but he will be praised by God" (Rom. 2:28–29).

Conscience is a universal reality: "[Pagans] can point to the substance of the Law engraved on their hearts—they can call a witness, that is, their own conscience" (Rom. 2:14–15). Conscience is binding, autonomous, but not absolute. "We all have knowledge; yes, that is so, but knowledge gives self-importance; it is love that makes the building grow" (1 Cor. 8:1). It is God related: "God is greater than our conscience and he knows everything" (1 Jn. 3: 19–21) and community related: "We who are strong have a duty to put up with the qualms of the weak without thinking of ourselves" (Rom. 15:1). St. Paul also gives a typology of conscience, speaking of "clear conscience," "weak conscience," and "branded conscience," but the most important conclusion to be drawn from the biblical concept of conscience, and explicitly emphasized by St. Paul, is that conscience must never obliterate love.

The early Christian and patristic concept of conscience is Bible inspired and lacks the later scholastic elaboration of it. The reality of conscience is manifested in its omnipresence as judge and counselor, joy and remorse, a call and the voice of God. Two characteristics are evident, especially in St. Augustine, significant for later development. One is the identification of conscience with the person as a whole and as related to God and Christ. The other one is a double role of conscience, in the sense that conscience is not only a person as a whole, but also his ability to make concrete moral judgment; in other words, conscience is also an act.

Although the biblical conception of conscience continues into the medieval period, occasional departures from such a conception set in, giving it a more juridical direction. Two examples may be quoted: one is the so-called "libri penitentiales," confessional manuals between the seventh and tenth century; the other one is St. Bernard's argument against Abelard, in which he subordinates subjective conscience to the objective norms to the point that, in his view, even an invincibly erroneous conscience is a sinful conscience. St. Thomas will disagree with this position.

SECULAR CONCEPTS OF CONSCIENCE

The Bible is not the only source from which Christian theology draws its information about conscience. There is also secular information stemming from primitive culture, classical definitions, and contemporary psychology. Since conscience is a universal human phenomenon, there are similarities between the biblical and later theological and the primitive and later psychological conceptions of conscience. But there are also differences. A common trait of the early biblical and primitive cultural conception of conscience is the absence of a definition. Conscience is simply an experience: good people are rewarded, bad people are punished. The French sociologist, Emil Durkheim, suggests a parallel between such primitive experience of conscience and the early stages of a child's conception of good and evil.

Anthropologists speak of some other characteristics of primitive conscience. One is its externality, meaning that the goodness and badness of human activity is primarily measured by the external standard of success and failure. Health and long life are signs of moral goodness; sickness and disaster are signs of evil. An appeal to magic to decide good and evil is a common practice in primitive morality.

Another characteristic of primitive conscience is its collectivity, in the sense that the individual finds identity in a group (family, tribe) rather than in oneself, very much like peer group identification.

The Greeks and subsequently the Romans developed a more precise concept of conscience, giving it the name of *syneidesis* in Greek and *conscientia* in Latin. Its primary role was the knowledge of oneself, often associated with the inner presence of a deity. Thus Seneca wrote: "A sacred spirit dwells within us, an observer and guardian of our good and bad deeds."

From a general historical perspective, we may detect two contrary approaches to conscience: one we may call a hostile or fear conscience; the other is a cult of conscience. Fear conscience watches and condemns: "No witness so fearful, no accuser so terrible as that which dwells in the soul of every man" (Polybius).

Cult conscience absolutizes the individual freedom, regardless of other persons and values. The ancient stoics and some extreme modern "conscientious objectors" fall into this category. In 1521, Luther made his famous appeal to conscience at Worms: an example of a kind of conscience—absolutism, which grew from the subjectivism and anthropocentrism of the Renaissance. St. Paul seems to allude to such ethos conscience in his first letter to the Corinthians. Some Christians of Corinth, under the influence of stoic philosophy, claimed for themselves a deeper knowledge of good and evil and decided to eat the meat of pagan sacrifices. Their argument was reasonable: such sacrifices make no sense anyway, since there are no pagan gods and all things are from God. But their action scandalized some "weaker brethren," and this worried St. Paul. Judging by the words he uses, "having knowledge ... being right ... being free," it seems that such was their concept of conscience. St. Paul grants them their freedom, but only to a certain extent, warning them of the possible scandal to the weak brethren. It is not their conscience but the worship of their conscience that St. Paul condemns, calling himself a slave for the sake of others.

In the history of moral philosophy, Kant is often credited for having a more balanced role of conscience, as not only an accuser but an excuser as well. He spoke of conscience as a faculty of judgment, which evaluates a particular action in view of a universal principle, and holds before man his duty for acquittal or condemnation.

Contemporary secular approaches to conscience are heavily psychological and behavioristic, with particular interest in child development. Sigmund Freud exercised a considerable influence here, although by no means universal. In his psychic apparatus of *id* (instinctive drives), *ego* (a self-adjustment of *id*) and *super-ego* (adjustment to authority and culture), conscience pertains to the level of *super-ego*. Since the *super-ego* is authoritatively and culturally imposed upon the *ego* and *id*, conscience becomes an enemy, oppressive and in conflict with a person's natural drives.

Another negative characteristic of some sectors of modern psychology in regard to conscience is its amorality: a tendency to reject the spiritual and moral depth of conscience. Although there is a great deal of talk about guilt and guilt feelings, the guilt is more a psychological condition than a moral reality: a sickness to be treated, not a sin to be confessed. The responsibility for guilt is often transferred to other factors: authority, society, culture, or the biological and psychological conditions in childhood.

A somewhat different position is held by some contemporary existentialists, who view guilt not just as a psychological state, but as an ontological and cosmic reality: a dichotomy between what is and what could and ought to be in the world. Human beings participate in this cosmic dichotomy, searching for a fulfillment which they can never find. Anxiety and guilt become a natural condition, with conscience interminably torn by ethical dilemmas. Once again, the response to this situation varies: the atheistic existentialists usually reject conscience as a valid moral norm: the Christian existentialists accept its mysterious role as the voice of God and mediator between sin and grace.

THEOLOGICAL CONCEPT OF CONSCIENCE

The first systematic treatment of conscience in the Christian tradition appears with the Scholastics. It was prompted by the familiar issue of objective versus subjective morality, which the dispute between St. Bernard and Peter Abelard brought to the surface. Abelard was a subjectivist. St. Bernard, on the other hand, defended objective morality, to the point of writing to his monks that conscience must always be on the side of objective truth and that even what we would call an invincibly erroneous conscience was a sinful conscience. St. Thomas rejects this argument, as we shall shortly point out. There were other differences among the Scholastics, for instance, the intellectual position of Aquinas versus a more affective and voluntaristic stand of St. Bonaventure. But they shared a common ground as well. One was the distinction they made between conscience (*syneidesis*) as an act and *synderesis* (or *synteresis*) as an inner disposition to make moral judgments. Although some of his contemporaries considered *synderesis* a power of the soul, Aquinas thinks of it as a disposition. In his view, conscience is an act of this disposition, as developed and enriched by experience and enlightened by grace. Aquinas' view is grounded in his psychology of the human person, notably in his understanding of the nature and operation of the powers of the soul: the intellect and will. This is discussed in the First Part of the *Summa*, in the treatise on man, especially in Question 79, on the intellectual powers of the soul. A parallel text may be found in *De Veritate*, Questions 16 and 17.

According to this psychological analysis, the human intellect is a two-dimensional power open to a double perfection. First, there is an intuitive knowledge (similar, although less perfect, than in the angels): the intuitive understanding of the first principles of knowledge which Aquinas calls *intellectus* or *habitus primorum principiorum*. Different from such intuitive understanding, although built on it, is the discursive knowledge of inquiry and conclusions, which is more proper to man. Since the human person is not only a thinking subject but also an active agent, Aquinas argues that, analogous to the speculative understanding of the first principles of knowledge, there is also an intuitive understanding of the first principles of action, a *habitus primorum principiorum agibilium*, e.g., that good is to be done and evil avoided. He calls this disposition *synderesis*: a habitual light which pertains to the very nature of the soul.

Conscience could be and sometimes has been synonymous with *synderesis*: a disposition or habitual conscience. Aquinas believes, nevertheless, that it is more appropriate to consider conscience an act of *synderesis*: the working of this disposition in particular situations, telling the agent what is to be done here and now. The result of such an "act" concept of conscience is that in concrete human life, conscience becomes an application not only of *synderesis* (the initial intuition of good and evil), but also of the acquired knowledge and experience built upon it and ingrained in the virtue of prudence. Such application of conscience is made in three ways:

> First, in that we acknowledge that we have done something. . . . In this case, conscience is said to witness. Knowledge is applied in a second way when through our conscience we judge that something ought to be done or ought not to be done. In this case conscience is said to incite or bind. A third application is when by conscience we judge something already done to have been done well or ill. In this case we speak of conscience excusing or accusing or tormenting. It is obvious that all these things follow actual application of knowledge to what we do. Hence strictly speaking conscience is the name of an act.[1]

This gives a balanced view of conscience as neither a threat nor cult, but as an impartial, inner witness and judge, excuser as well as accuser, as warranted in each particular situation.

In the treatise on the morality of human acts in general (*Summa Theologiae*, I-II, QQ. 18-21), Aquinas devotes two articles to conscience specifically: articles 5 and 6 of question 19, which deals with the morality of the internal acts of the will. It is natural that conscience be discussed in this context since morality, as we already established, consists primarily of the internal act of the will: the end or intention of the agent. According to Aquinas the goodness or badness of the will depends on the object of the willing (intention) alone. Such object is presented to the will by reason. Consequently, the goodness or badness of an act depends on its rational specification, which is the role of conscience. Our dictum, therefore, that human acts are good or bad as they are according to or against reason, may be reworded by saying that they are good or bad as they are according to or against one's conscience. Once such a subjective or conscience morality is granted as a starting point, Aquinas proceeds to

1. S.T. I, Q. 79, a. 13.

examine other norms, notably eternal law and the divine will. Since God is the ultimate goal of the human person, eternal law takes precedence over the individual conscience, because "the light of reason within us can show us what is fair and guide us in so far as it reflects the light of God's countenance."[2] While this is obvious in principle, it is not without tension in practice, if conscience is the first interpreter of the eternal law in a particular instance. The problem for the Scholastics was, as it is for us today, the invincibly erroneous conscience. If conscience is the voice of God to be obeyed, what happens if it is invincibly wrong? It is the invincibly erroneous conscience which, in fact, tests our honesty about conscience. As this is the core of the meaning of true morality, it is proper at this point to have a deeper look into the theological interpretations of conscience. We propose to do this with reference to three specific sources: Aquinas, legalistic, and the contemporary theological concept, as synthesized in the documents of the Second Vatican Council.

AQUINAS' CONCEPT OF CONSCIENCE

Conscience would seem to play a minor role in Aquinas' moral theology, at least in comparison with the later moral manuals which sometimes devote one-third of their total work to conscience and moral systems. Aquinas is more concerned with prudence and, ultimately, with the human person as a moral agent. It is reason, as we already explained, which specifies the moral value and presents it to the will for action. Moral goodness and integrity of the will depend upon the response to reason: "The goodness of an act of will properly depends on the objective. This is presented to the will by the mind, for the object proportioned to will is a good, as intelligently perceived, not a good as sensed or fancied— this last corresponds to our power of emotion. The will can reach out to universal good apprehended by the mind, whereas sense-desire stretches no further than to particular goods apprehended by the powers of sense. Accordingly, an act of will depends on the mind in the same way that it depends on the objective."[3] If the word conscience is rare, its meaning, which is that of rational activity, permeates Aquinas' entire morality. As we know, such reasoning in morality must always come down to a particular decision, which is what conscience is: an application of knowledge

---

2. S.T. I–II, Q. 19, a. 4.
3. S.T. I–II, Q. 19, a. 3.

to a determinate deed. In this role, conscience is the proximate, subjective norm of morality: the first to tell us what is or is not to be done, the first to be obeyed. Conscience is the first but not the ultimate norm of morality. It is subject to eternal law and objective truth. This subjection rests on two, by now familiar, facts: God as our ultimate goal and human fellowship as our natural condition. "In a directly causal series an effect depends more on the first cause than on a secondary cause, since the secondary does not act save in virtue of the first. That the human reason is the rule for acts of human will so that it measures their goodness comes because it derives from Eternal Law, which is the divine reason."[4] Man cannot deny God or human fellowship without denying himself. To do so knowingly and willingly is irresponsible. The question is: what if it happens that he does so unknowingly and unwillingly, that his conscience is invincibly erroneous? "Does a mistaken conscience bind?" In answering this question, Aquinas remains faithful to the primacy of the end of the agent in morality and lays grounds for an authentically free and responsible conscience as expounded in the *Pastoral Constitution on the Church in the Modern World* and the *Declaration on Religious Freedom* of the Second Vatican Council.

"Is a mistaken conscience binding?" This is the title of article 5, question 19 of the *Prima Secundae*, already referred to. Aquinas sets the stage in the first objection: "It would seem that an act of will out of step with a mistaken conscience is not bad. For as we have said, the reason is the measure for human willing as deriving from Eternal Law. But reason when mistaken does not derive from the Eternal Law. So then an act of will is not bad if in that case it is out of step." Not so, will be the conclusion. To arrive at this conclusion, Aquinas summarizes some theological opinions of his time and then reacts to them. He writes in the same article: "On this matter some theologians have distinguished between three classes of act, some good of their kind, some neutral, some bad. They go on to teach that if reason or conscience command that something should be done that is good in itself then no mistake arises there, and likewise, if it forbids something to be done that is bad in itself: for the same cause good is prescribed and bad prohibited." This is clear and simple: such conscience reflects the objective truth and remains a legitimate and good moral norm. But according to these same theologians, the situation is

---

4. S.T. I–II, Q. 19, a. 4.

different "if reason or conscience tells a man that he is under precept to do what is in itself bad or not to do what is in itself good, then it is mistaken." Conscience is also mistaken when it tells a man "that what is neutral in itself, for instance to pluck a stalk, is enjoined or ruled out." In both instances, we have a mistaken conscience, but the theologians proceed in an inconsistent way: "They conclude that reason or conscience obliges on neutral matters, so that an act of will against it is bad and a sin. But that when the reason or conscience is mistaken in commanding what is bad in itself, or in forbidding what is good in itself and necessary for salvation, then it is not binding; and in that case an act of will that goes against it is not bad." Aquinas rejects this inconsistency: "To maintain this is unreasonable" (*irrationabiliter dicitur*). Morality may deal with contingencies, but it must still remain consistent. If conscience is good and obliging in judging mistakenly a neutral act as good or bad, why not if it judges mistakenly a bad act as good? "Not only may what is neutral take on the character of good or bad, but good can take on the character of evil, and evil the character of good, and all this because of the way an object is apprehended by the mind." To make his point, Aquinas gives two striking examples:

> Take an example; to avoid fornicating is good, yet the will is not set on this course save in so far as it is recommended by reason as good. If a mistaken reason presents it as bad, then the will pursues it as wearing the aspect of evil. The act of will, then, will be bad, since it is willing evil, not indeed what is evil in itself, but what is evil by another factor, namely the reason casting it in that part. Take a similar example: to believe in Christ is good in itself and necessary for salvation; all the same this does not win the will unless it be recommended by reason. If the reason presents it as bad, then the will reaches to it in that light, not that it really is bad in itself, but because it appears so because of a condition that happens to be attached by the reason apprehending it.

The examples reinforce Aquinas' position on the primacy of the agent over the act done and state his unequivocal stand for freedom of conscience. They are a direct rejection of any forced conversion. Although without explicit reference, the *Declaration on Religious Freedom* echoes Aquinas' argument when it states that "it is by personal assent that men are to adhere to the truth" and that "it is one of the major tenets of Catholic doctrine that man's response to God in faith must be free. Therefore no one is to be forced to embrace the Christian faith against his own will."[5]

Such an affirmation of the freedom of conscience is, nevertheless, far from a cult of conscience. Conscience is not only free; it must also be responsible. This responsibility is not extrinsically imposed, but intrinsically a part of human nature. It springs from the fact that the ultimate goal of human activity is God; that we are by nature social, and are liable to err. "The Eternal Law cannot err, but human reason can."

Man is other-directed and ultimately God-directed for his fulfillment. Our understanding of conscience is therefore inseparable from our understanding of God as man's ultimate goal and society as his existential condition. The possibility of being wrong subjectively in regard to God and other people must be kept in mind. Consequently, conscience may be wrong in regard to Eternal Law and objective human truth. In the case of conflict, Aquinas suggests two basic principles: *a person must never act against conscience; a mistaken conscience does not excuse unless the mistake is involuntary.* To determine involuntariness or invincibility of such ignorance, Aquinas brings back his psychological analysis of human responsibility and its impediments. Freedom of conscience is inseparable from its responsibility, because a human person is inseparable from human fellowship under God. As the *Declaration on Religious Freedom* says again: "Truth ... is to be sought after in a manner proper to the dignity of the human person and his social nature."[6]

Once again, morality is placed in the human person's self-objectification. It is not by claiming its right but by rejecting responsibility that conscience fails, separating itself from its roots in the wisdom of God and the love of others. The true setting for an authentic understanding of conscience as moral norm is a harmony between freedom and responsibility. The human person is free, and his conscience must be obeyed and respected. But we must never become egocentric, because our condition as creatures and social beings forbids it. A person, as free moral agent, must continually enlarge his vision of himself in his relation to God and to others, following the advice of St. Paul: "My brothers, remember that you have been called to live in freedom—but not a freedom that gives free rein to the flesh. Out of love, place yourselves at one another's service. The

---

5. Vatican Council II, *Declaration on Religious Freedom*, nn. 3, 9.
6. Ibid., n. 3.

whole law has found its fulfillment in this one saying: you shall love your neighbor as yourselves" (Gal. 5:13–14). From a Christian and theological perspective, conscience is never a purely "private matter."

Our analysis of Aquinas' concept of conscience may be best summarized in the following statements from the *Declaration on Religious Freedom*:

> [T]he highest norm of human life is the divine law—eternal, objective and universal—whereby God orders, directs and governs the entire universe and all the ways of human community, by plan conceived in wisdom and love. Man has been made to participate in this law, with the result that, under the gentle disposition of the divine Providence, he can come to perceive ever increasingly the unchanging truth. Hence every man has the duty, and therefore the right, to seek the truth in matters religious, in order that he may with prudence form for himself right and true judgment of conscience, with the use of all suitable means.[7]

In an earlier passage we read:

> It is in accordance with their dignity as persons—that is, beings endowed with reason and free will and therefore privileged to bear personal responsibility—that all men should be at once impelled by nature and also bound by a moral obligation to seek truth, especially religious truth. They are also bound to adhere to the truth, once it is known, and to order their whole lives in accord with the demands of the truth.[8]

MODERN LEGALISTIC CONCEPT OF CONSCIENCE

We employ the term legalistic to the period between scholastic and contemporary moral theology, aware that while it helps as a title, it does not do justice to the period itself. Not all theologians of this period were legalistic moralists. The fact is, nevertheless, that the period saw the emergence of the moral manuals with a casuistic, "act-oriented" conscience. As it often happens in history, modern theology reflected the spirit of its time, with positive sciences replacing metaphysics and voluntaristic conceptions of law and authority taking hold in morals. The Reformation and a general secularization of society provoked in the Church a disciplinary

7. Ibidem.
8. Ibid., n. 4.

response, with particular concern for ecclesiastical jurisdiction, seminary formation of priests, and private confessions of the faithful, all directed to safeguard the objective truth and traditional moral values. In the process, the biblical concept of conscience as a dialogue with God, and even the scholastic *syneidesis*, yielded to an "act-oriented" conscience, as the moral primacy of the agent shifted to that of the act done. The Cartesian philosophy of clear and distinct ideas had its counterpart in the search for clarity and certainty in moral decisions. This led to the formation of the so-called moral systems of conscience, ranging from rigorism (tutiorism), which demanded an absolute certainty in a fundamentalist observance of the law, to laxism, which was practically indifferent to it. Between these two extremes, both rejected by the Church as a valid form of conscience, the moralists advanced and defended various degrees of probability, some more on the side of the law, others on the side of conscience. St. Alphonsus is credited with introducing "aequiprobabilism," which in the case of conflict and doubt gives an equal right to the freedom of an upright conscience as to the law. This was a return to a more compassionate concern for the human agent, against the Jansenistic pessimism about his freedom.

Such historical circumstances explain why the treatise on conscience held a central place in the moral manuals which multiplied in modern times and became familiar textbooks in theological schools and seminaries well into the twentieth century. The contemporary criticism of these manuals is not entirely justified. Such criticism may be correct, to the extent that the manuals lost the spiritual and moral interiority of the human person in their often casuistic defense of objective norms; but their pastoral concern and clarity of their explanation may still be an inspiration and service. Their classification of conscience, which we propose to summarize, is an example in point.

CLASSIFICATION OF CONSCIENCE

The common conception of conscience is as an act or dictate of practical reason about a deed done or to be done here and now. It is a proximate, subjective norm of morality, presupposing conformity with objective truth and the eternal law. As such, conscience has a triple relationship: to the act it commands; to the eternal law which it reflects; and to the person or agent whose conscience it is.

1. In regard to the *act,* conscience is: *antecedent* (preceding the act), and *consequent* (judging an act done). Antecedent conscience may be: commanding; prohibiting; consulting; or permitting. The force of obligation differs between a conscience which is commanding or prohibiting and one which is only consulting or permitting. Consequent conscience is approving or disapproving an act done with the results of joy or remorse, respectively.

2. In regard to the *eternal law,* conscience is: *true* or *right,* when it is conformed to the eternal law and objective morality; *false* or *erroneous,* when it is contrary to it. A false or erroneous conscience may be such, either invincibly or vincibly. Special forms of false conscience are: *scrupulous* conscience, which fears sin from all sides; *perplex,* which is confused and indecisive; *lax,* which has little or no concern about right or wrong; *callous,* which is a habitual laxity; and *hypocritical,* which is scrupulous in minor or external observances and lax in important things.

3. In regard to the *agent,* conscience is: *certain,* when there are no reservations about something being true or false; *probable,* when more weight is put on one course of action than another; and *dubious,* when clear evidence for one side or the other is missing.

A doubt may be "theoretical" (*dubium juris*), about the existence or validity of a law and "practical" (*dubium facti*), about the applicability of a law in a concrete situation. Thus, a person may doubt whether there is still a law of fast and abstinence during Lent, and whether such a law applies to an expectant mother.

A doubt may also be *positive* or *negative.* A positive doubt is with arguments for or against an action, e.g., a doubt about conjugal intercourse when the husband insists on birth control. A negative doubt is when there are no clear arguments either for or against an action, e.g., when a person does not remember whether he made the right restitution and debates whether to make it again or not. Moreover, a subjectively certain conscience is not necessarily a true conscience. Certainty is a psychological state, truthfulness an objective reality. A person may be invincibly certain that what he does is right, yet objectively he may be wrong.

PRACTICAL GUIDELINES CONCERNING CONSCIENCE

With this classification of conscience in mind, the following practical principles determine which conscience and when is a legitimate norm of action:

1. Only true and certain conscience is, per se, a legitimate norm of action. Such conscience must be obeyed whenever it commands or prohibits something to be done. There is no strict obligation when conscience is only consulting or permitting.

2. Invincibly erroneous conscience is, per accidens, a legitimate norm of action. It must be obeyed when commanding or prohibiting. To act otherwise would amount to acting against one's conscience and, therefore, to sin.

3. Vincibly erroneous conscience is not a rule of action. One must not act either against or according to a vincibly erroneous conscience, but seek information.

4. Only certain conscience is a legitimate norm of action. Such certainty is perfect if there are no reservations about law or its application; imperfect if there are doubts about law or its application.

5. One should not act with a practical positive doubt. Such action would amount to moral indifference and exposure to sin.

6. In an action which is pressing, doubtful law does not bind, common opinion should be followed, and, if the doubt persists, the presumption in favor of the person prevails.

7. Other forms of false conscience are not legitimate norms of action, but rather a matter of moral and psychological counseling. Scrupulosity is a frequent phenomenon in religious experience and could be very painful and frustrating for both the penitent and the confessor. A good psychological and moral understanding of the situation on the side of the confessor and a humble and confident obedience on the side of the penitent may be the best beginning of treatment. A perplexed conscience may be confronted with real alternatives, e.g., a wife feeling obliged to tell her husband about their daughter's dating and protecting her for fear of the father's irascibility. A perplexed person should be

advised about freedom to choose between the alternatives; one should also know that no one is obliged to do the impossible. Of course, callous and hypocritical consciences are more a moral blindness than a mental illness; they are not a legitimate norm of action, but a sinful state of the person.

In applying these principles, attention must be paid to the state of the agent and his needs, as well as to the gravity of the matter involved. The framework is intended for pastoral help and leaves ample room for prudential judgment.

CONTEMPORARY THEOLOGY AND THE SECOND VATICAN COUNCIL

Contemporary moral theology reacts against the manualist act-oriented conception of conscience, as it does against legalistic morality in general. Such reaction developed gradually through the revival of biblical studies and in response to new, personalistic philosophical currents, such as existentialism. While there is an underlying agreement on conscience as a function of the total human person, growing in moral awareness of oneself and others, there are significant differences as well, as some theologians adhere to a moral affective interpretation of conscience, and others, the neo-Thomists, continue to emphasize the intellectual element.

As in all other areas of theology, the Second Vatican Council reflects and synthesizes their developments, not as a systematic treatment, but as a pastoral concern. Nevertheless, the historians of the Council speak of the painful development of the statements on conscience in the *Pastoral Constitution on the Church in the Modern World*, when the document was still known as Schema 13.[9] The section on conscience is included in the chapter on the *Dignity of the Human Person*, nos. 14–17, rightly suggesting that the understanding of conscience is inseparable from a broader understanding of the human person in the natural condition and supernatural vocation. The statements on conscience are developed from the ontological and theological make-up of human beings, emphasizing the following elements:

The *unity and sanctity* of the human person, composed of material body and spiritual soul. Man "regards his body as good and honorable, since God has created it and will raise it up on the last day."

---

9. See Moeller, *L'Élaboration du Schema XIII*.

The reality of sin: "Nevertheless, wounded by sin, man experiences rebellious stirrings in his body. But the very dignity of man postulates that man glorify God in his body and forbid it to serve the evil inclination of his heart."

Openness to a supernatural fulfillment: "Man is not wrong when he regards himself as superior to bodily concerns, and as more than a speck of nature or a nameless constituent of the city of man. For by his interior qualities he outstrips the whole sum of mere things."

Personal relation with God: "He finds reinforcement in this profound insight whenever he enters into his own heart. God who probes the heart, awaits him there. Thus, when man recognizes in himself a spiritual and immortal soul, he is not being mocked by a deceptive fantasy springing from mere physical or social influence. On the contrary, he is getting to the depth of the very truth of the matter."

From this ontological and theological understanding of the human person follows his intellectual and moral dignity:

> Man . . . by his intellect surpasses the material universe, for he shares in the light of the divine mind. His creativity is manifested in two areas: art or technology and conduct or morals. He makes progress in practical sciences, technology and liberal arts. "In our times he has won superlative victories, especially in his probing of the material world and in subjecting it to himself.

But:

> [H]e has always searched for more penetrating truths and finds them. For his intelligence is not confined to observable data alone. It can, with genuine certitude, attain to reality itself as knowable, though in consequence of sin, that certitude is partly obscured and weakened.

For this reason, man can and needs to grow in knowledge of truth and practice of virtue: "The intellectual nature of the human person is perfected by wisdom and needs to be. For wisdom gently attracts the mind of man to a quest and a love for what is true and good. Steeped in wisdom, man passes through visible realities to those which are unseen." Human wisdom is further perfected by the grace of God, because it is "through the gift of the Holy Spirit that man comes by faith to the contemplation and appreciation of the divine plan." These statements affirm that man is endowed with reason and will, to be perfected by intellectual and moral virtues and enriched by the gift of the Holy Spirit.

This is the natural and supernatural anthropology into which the document introduces the notion of conscience as a person's highest value, and one shared by all human beings in virtue of being human. The document makes the following points:

1. Conscience is the first norm of action. "In the depth of his conscience, man detects a law which he does not impose upon himself, but which holds him to obedience. Always summoning him to love good and avoid evil, the voice of conscience can, when necessary, speak to his heart more specifically: do this, shun that. For man has in his heart a law written by God. To obey it is the very dignity of man; according to it he will be judged."

2. Conscience is the voice of God. "Conscience is the most secret core and sanctuary of a man. There he is alone with God, whose voice echoes in his depths. In a wonderful manner conscience reveals that law which is fulfilled by love of God and neighbor."

3. Conscience is a universal reality and value. "In fidelity to conscience, Christians are joined with the rest of men in search of truth, and for the genuine solution to the numerous problems which arise in the life of individuals and social relationships."

4. Conscience is not absolute. "Conscience frequently errs from invincible ignorance without losing its dignity. The same cannot be said of a man who cares but little for truth and goodness . . . or conscience which grows practically sightless as a result of habitual sin."

5. Conscience is free and responsible. "Only in freedom can man direct himself toward goodness. Our contemporaries make much of this freedom and pursue it eagerly; and rightly so, to be sure. Often, however, they foster it perversely as a license for doing whatever pleases them, even if it is evil."

CONCLUDING REMARKS

Some commentators argue that the Council's teaching on conscience presents a substantial departure from the traditional, legalistic treatment of it. In particular, they believe that against the primacy of the law and an act-oriented conscience, the Council gives the primacy to a person-oriented conscience; an expression of human heart rather than an act of the practical reason, and binding not because of an objective order but because of the love of God. Such comments reflect the familiar tension between the subjective and objective, or the end of the agent versus the end of the act morality, which we discussed earlier and hopefully put into proper perspective. Something similar is called for in this present context. Two specific issues will serve the purpose: one is freedom versus obedience, and the other one habitual versus actual conscience.

The Council affirms the freedom of conscience as "an exceptional sign of the divine image within man," and as a moral prerequisite since "God has willed that man be left 'in the hand of his own counsel' so that he can seek the Creator spontaneously and come freely to utter and blissful perfection through loyalty to him. Hence man's dignity demands that he act according to a knowing and free choice. Such a choice is personally motivated and promoted from within. It does not result from blind internal impulse nor from mere external pressure." It is significant, however, that the Council speaks of conscience not only as a law in itself, but also as an obedience to the law and an obligation to a correct conscience: "[T]he more that a correct conscience holds sway, the more persons and groups turn aside from blind choice and strive to be guided by objective norms of morality." Once again, the true issue of morality comes through as one shifting the moral concern from fear and limitation of individual freedom to the personal responsibility of self-objectification.

In the human condition, freedom of conscience is not only a gift to be enjoyed, but a talent to be developed, as man is called to achieve his full dignity by freeing himself from the captivity to passion, reaching through intelligent and responsible choice of moral values his ultimate goal in God. This, too, needs God's continuous support. "Since man's freedom has been damaged by sin only by the help of God's grace can he bring such relationship with God into full flower. Before the judgment seat of God, each man render an account of his own life, whether he has done good or evil."

Before proceeding with a few additional reflections along this line, a word must be said about the distinction between an actual and habitual conscience. This distinction seems to be an attempt to reconcile the traditional "act-oriented conscience" with the renewed emphasis on the "person-oriented conscience." Aquinas speaks of conscience as an act of reason, determining the rightness or wrongness of a particular action. It is an act of prudence, founded on *synderesis*, the intuitive perception of good and evil, but enriched by acquired practical knowledge and experience, and enlightened by God's grace. As long as sufficient care is taken to use all these resources, in other words, as long as sufficient effort is made in the formation of conscience, Aquinas has no hesitation in giving primacy to the actual conscience in a given situation, even when such conscience happens to be invincibly erroneous.

The contemporary view of conscience, including some of the Vatican II statements, seems to prefer the concept of a habitual conscience, i.e., a continuous quality of the human person, "the core and sanctuary of man" and "the voice of God," a virtue rather than an act. Aquinas would have no serious quarrel with such a conception of conscience, and call a person "conscientious" even when we do not see him actually in action, as we can call him prudent because we know his qualities. But there must still be a transition from a habitual conscience to a concrete act of conscience and an evaluation of it. It is on the level of actual affirmation of conscience that moral problems and conflicts arise. This brings us back to the question of the freedom and responsibility of conscience. Conflicts of conscience arise from the fact that man is both individual (free) and social (responsible). Conscience must, therefore, be examined in its basic relationships, which are one versus many (individual versus the community), and the individual versus authority, especially, perhaps, the authority of the Church.

The first thing we have to say in this regard is that conscience grows and reveals itself in human fellowship. Such fellowship acts on the individual conscience in two significant ways: by forming a person's habitual and by challenging his actual conscience. Man is a social being, and no matter how much we emphasize his autonomy and freedom, he is always influenced by his group and environment and feels comfortable when in agreement with them. Nevertheless, moral theology firmly holds that such influence is not deterministic, as some behavioristic psychologists more readily assume. If such were the case, it would be hard to explain how a person could react against his own environment and change. The point we want to make is that habitual conscience is never in a pure personal state, but is rather a combination of one's individuality and social input, and that for moral purposes, it is important to distinguish the personal from the social elements.

As we said earlier, there is still need for an actual conscience to deal with a particular situation. Since particular situations are variable and contingent, actual conscience must show flexibility and independence. Consequently, the true meaning of conscience as a norm of action is realized in the actual conscience as one which applies the common standard to its action or modifies it according to its judgment.

AUTHORITY AND THE FORMATION OF CONSCIENCE

There are different forms of conflicts of conscience, some internal and others external. One of particular importance is the conflict with authority. Authority is a kind of crystallized fellowship: a community standard expressed in parents, educators, bishops, governments, and other persons embodying social or group morality. On the one hand, such an authority is more likely to influence the formation of habitual conscience. On the other hand, it is the actual conscience which conflicts with authority in practice. The reasons for such conflicts are mostly practical, such as an authority too demanding or morally unconvincing, or an individual convinced in his own righteousness. Today, this conflict is even more acute, because of the uncertainty of social moral standards on the one hand and the danger of collectivization of human minds by mass media on the other.

In this regard, of particular interest to us is the authority of the Church. Besides practical reasons which apply to conflicts in general, theologians also speak of historical reasons in regard to the contemporary crisis of conscience and authority in the Church. Individualization and secularization of society has something to do with this. The first Christians seem to have been more community oriented, not only by faith, but also by force of circumstances, such as their small numbers in a pagan world. This made interdependence and community support more indispensable and authority more necessary. Conflicts are always less likely in smaller and coherent groups with clear purpose and a common adversary. Whatever the real situation might have been in the early Church, things became different as the administrative structure grew more complex and the letter of the law replaced the spirit of community. There are, of course, other reasons for contemporary tension: often there are wrong interpretations of authority and its extent, opinions are put forward as dogmas, and heretics are seen on all sides.

Our analysis of conscience clearly suggests a need for its formation, and this concerns both those in formation and those responsible for it. Although there are no blueprints for forming a conscience, a few assumptions based on our understanding of conscience and morality may yield a few suggestions.

One assumption is that nobody is really born with a conscience, more precisely an actual conscience. A person grows in it, and growth takes time. The intuition of first principles is not enough: one must become competent to discern good and evil in a concrete situation. This means that an individual person, before being responsible to his conscience, is responsible for his conscience.

A second assumption regards authority, which is meant to help the growth of conscience. The contemporary interpretation of authority as "service" is not without a message in this regard. The most important thing for society and authority is to provide an authentic and convincing value system.

The authority of the Church should still be viewed somewhat differently from other forms of authority, because of its divine origin and a faith commitment of Christians. But the basic methodology still holds.

With the assumption that a conscience grows, that society is here to help the growth, and that Christian conscience involves God and his authority, and thus prayers and sacraments, the rest becomes a pedagogical and pastoral method. To describe this method means to explain the entire moral theology and its application, notably: the respect and primacy of the human person; development of freedom and responsibility; proper motivation in view of an ultimate human fulfillment as we know it from revelation; intellectual and moral virtues; and a just society.

9

Social and Spiritual Dimension of Human Activity

THE PRINCIPLES EXPLAINED IN THE PRECEDING CHAPTERS ON MORAL good and evil apply to both internal and external acts. The essence of these principles is that there is a specific difference between moral good and evil in human activity determined by moral object, motive, and circumstances; that the reason or conscience is the proximate, subjective norm of goodness or badness of an act; and that conscience itself is measured by an objective moral order and ultimately by the eternal law of God, because of a person's social nature and the transcendental reality of the ultimate goal.

In the course of our analysis, we pointed out, nevertheless, certain distinctions in human activity. One such distinction was between internal and external acts. There are several reasons why the distinction and the moral nature of external acts are of particular significance. We may summarize these reasons by recalling some of our previous statements.

We stated, first, that all external acts also must be internal or imperated by the will, since all human acts must proceed from the intrinsic principles of knowledge and will. We pointed out, nevertheless, that it is a characteristic of external acts to have a built-in reality or object, which may or may not coincide with the intention of the agent. Thus, sexual intercourse with a built-in objective of procreation may also be intended as an expression of love or satisfaction of passion. Similarly, stealing has a meaning of its own, although intentions may vary from one thief to another.

This raised the question of priorities: does the moral goodness or badness of an act consist primarily in the act done (*finis operis*) or in the intention of the agent (*finis operantis*)? We discussed this as one of the most important issues in morality and pointed out a double danger: that of legalism and a conformist morality, which could be destructive of personal response to values, and that of subjectivism, which may destroy objective morality.

Our own conclusion was that the moral order is different from the physical order, and that moral good and evil consists primarily in the agent's free and internal response to values, as seen by reason or conscience. This is what makes a person in the image of God. But in giving such primacy to the end of the agent, we did not deny the need for and existence of an objective moral order and our possibility of knowing and duty of conforming to it. We call this moral objectification which, respecting our subjectivity, reminds us of our socio-theological condition of human fellowship under God as the ultimate end of each and all. Morality is placed where it belongs: the human mind and heart within the framework of an objective order under divine wisdom. In conforming to this order, we need not only our own personal openness and willingness (self-formation), but also external help through education, the help of God's grace, and, though to a lesser extent, positive law and commands. With this in mind, we turn now to some specific aspects of external acts.

THE NATURE OF EXTERNAL ACTS

As the word suggests, an external act or action is a deed that is visible and tangible in time and space or physically experienced. Such a deed is always imperated by the will, which is the condition of all human activity. But the external acts are elicited by other faculties or organs and bodily members such as hands, tongue, feet, eyes, sexual organs, and emotional functions, which are the instruments of the will to effect its intention in extrinsic reality. Consequently, there are two characteristics and subsequently, two relationships in all external acts.

The characteristics are: a) an external act is always a projection or externalization of a person's internal intent: a social and physical manifestation of an internal commitment; b) every external act or deed adds to the internal act a physical effect, or what is called its own (material) reality. Although the intent to kill is a morally complete act, there is nevertheless still a difference between wanting a person dead and actually killing him. The fact is that such externalization makes a tangible impact which is by itself good or bad. Thus, religious practices, almsgiving, visiting the sick, etc., stand in the eyes of other people for something good, even when they are done hypocritically. Similarly, stealing and lying stand for something bad, even when internally justified or at least excused.

There is a twofold relationship in external acts: one is to the will which commands the act, or to the intention of the agent. The other is to the act's external status, as good or bad, acceptable or unacceptable, and helpful or harmful effects which accompany it.

This raises two questions: the first is by now a familiar one: what is morally more important, the intention of the will or the external deed; the "why" or the "what" of an act?; the second is whether the externalization or the deed in any way modifies the internal morality of the act. It is a question of the freedom and flexibility the agent has in regard to a deed which enjoys an established moral and social status; e.g., how free is a person in his intention in regard to an act which, like lying, is considered to be bad. Notwithstanding the primacy of the end of the agent, the fact is that it is the external act which we ordinarily experience in our relationship, and that socially, we are more affected by what people do than by what they think. In the religious context, the question of external acts is related to some other theological themes, like the efficacy of the visible and sensible signs in sacraments and the place of rubrics and ceremonies in worship. Finally, two specific questions arise from external activity: the morality of the effects and the particular issue of the double effect.

THE ACT RELATED TO THE WILL

In discussing the morality of external acts (*Summa Theologiae*, I–II, Q. 20, aa. 1–6), Aquinas maintains his basic position of the primacy of the agent, but with full recognition of a specific moral identity of external acts, and their significance for personal moral responsibility. The reasoning underlying his procedure may be summarized in the following propositions: a) moral acts are always specified by their ends; b) moral ends are specified by the reason; c) the reason enjoys its normative role in virtue of its participation in the eternal law or the divine reason. In this schema, the external act or deed is viewed as an end presented to the will by reason, presumed to interpret the eternal law of God. The morality of the external act may therefore be seen in a double perspective: what the act is in itself, as perceived by reason, and what it is in the intention of the will. Thus, to give alms is good when all due conditions are observed, and bad when it is intended to show off or to bribe. Now what the act is in itself does not depend on the will, but on the reason or understanding; but what the act is in intention depends on the will.

The ideal and normal situation occurs when the intention of the will corresponds to the reality of the act in itself and both are good; e.g., giving alms to alleviate poverty of others, which is what the act is meant to do. But this may not always be the case. The conflict may occur on two levels: on the level of apprehension when the reason thinks an act to be in itself what in fact it is not, e.g., that fornication is good and legitimate; and on the level of execution when the will performs the act for its own intention, e.g., giving alms as bribery. The first level is a case of erroneous conscience; the second is the will's responsible refusal to follow the reason, which is morally wrong. Aquinas explains this in the following statement: "You can consider a double good or evil in an outward deed, one according to the due matter and circumstances, the other according to its ordered purpose. The last indeed depends entirely on the will, but the first depends on the reason; and on this the will hinges in that it turns to an object as presented by the mind."[1] Aquinas' moral dialectic unfolds on two levels: one is the objective ethical reasoning by which we arrive at universal, objective values, e.g., that telling the truth, defending widows and orphans, is something good, and that lying is bad. This knowledge is the basis for moral science. The other level is personal morality, or the subjective response to these values. The two levels are without prejudice to each other. The moral integrity of the agent depends on his own response; but the total goodness of his action depends, in addition, on the objective value of the act. "Remember," writes Aquinas in the same article, "that one single defect is enough to make any act bad, though for it to be unreservedly good one good point is not enough, since it must be sound throughout. If then an act of the will is good on the two accounts both of appropriate objective and end, the exterior act will also be good in consequence. For the exterior act to be good it is not enough for the will to be good merely because of the end it intends; the will may be bad, either from the end intended or from the objective willed, and then the result will be a bad outward deed."

---

1. S.T. I–II, Q. 20, a. 2.

This means that a bad intention vitiates a good act, but a good intention does not justify a bad act when perceived as bad. The reason for this is that it is within the power of the mind to see the relationship (*proportionalitatem*) between the external acts in themselves and the human end (*finis vitae humanae*) for which they are chosen. In the context of human fellowship under God, the intention must always aim at an end which is in line with the ultimate end of human fulfillment. If an external act is not seen in this light, it must not be chosen. Exploitation of the weak is not a means to justice, nor wild parties to temperance. Not all such relations are equally obvious; a good reason why moral formation through virtues becomes of utmost importance.

It has been our argument that the moral order is different from the physical order and that the external physical good and evil are morally relevant only to the extent that they are within the human choice and responsibility. An earthquake is a physical evil, but we are not responsible for it. There are, however, physical evils for which we are, or could be, responsible, e.g., poverty, wars, discrimination, torture, and similar evils. It is the characteristic of external acts to have such physical effects on human welfare, whether good or bad. Another characteristic of external acts is its limitation of our human possibilities and intentions. If I can and want to help one person, I may not be able to help another. As human beings we are limited by time and space, the condition of our age and health, the means available to us, and by other physical factors. Such limitations are not a moral evil, but because we can feel them, they can hamper our intentions.

THE ACT IN ITSELF

The preceding analysis of the relationship of the external act to the internal act of the will contains, in substance, an answer to the question: how free is a person in his intention with regard to an external act which enjoys its own moral and social status? Our ability to choose actions we want to effect is an integral part of our moral autonomy and self-determination. Yet our moral autonomy unfolds within a given human reality, which cannot be ignored without affecting the society and ourselves. We must remain consistent in affirming that morality consists primarily in the agent's internal act of the will; nevertheless, the will cannot arbitrarily determine the nature of an external act. The two, in the words of Aquinas, "are not so separate that they do not affect one another; the good intention overflows into the outward act, also the good in the texture and circumstances of what is done into the intention."[2]

The principle which determines the agent's freedom and/or limitation in regard to external deeds is that of "due proportion" (*debita proportio*), or what is also described as "due matter" (*debita materia*). The meaning of this is that an external act ought to be related to what a person intends by it, such as observing a regular diet or exercise for good health. What is or is not proportionate and due matter is not always easy to determine, as many contemporary dilemmas, particularly in bioethics and social ethics, attest. Is the experimentation on fetuses proportionate to the benefit of treating birth defects? Is invasion of privacy proportionate to combating organized crime, or a hunger strike for a just political cause? The moralists agree that the act itself must be good or at least indifferent, since good ends do not justify bad means. Consequently, the agent is not authorized to choose just any acts for his intended end, but only those which are proportionate to it in the totality of his orientation to the ultimate goal. This can make an act legitimate in one situation and not in another. Sexual intercourse is a proportionate act to love in marriage; it is not proportionate to love outside marriage, as reason and experience prove. A particular question concerns the physical or ontic evil, which we cannot consider indifferent. How much physical evil can one allow or undergo to achieve moral ends? The assumption is that, in general, the human mind can see such proportionality or the lack of it, and make moral decisions within the framework of a moral decision-making process, as already explained in previous discussions on moral determination and conscience. This means that a person may be invincibly erroneous about proportionality or due matter in a particular case.

A summary of this section may be in order at this point. This must include, once again, our consistent position that morality is primarily an internal commitment of the will and that a moral act is complete in the act of the will, so that "if a man looks at a woman lustfully, he has already committed adultery with her in his heart" (Mt. 3: 27).

The externalization of such an act has, nonetheless, its own reality which affects its total goodness or badness. The externalization of the act implies a kind of numerical addition, in the sense that a person not only

---

2. S.T. I–II, Q. 20, a. 3.

wills to do something, but that he actually does it. Another effect is the extension and intensity of the act. The fact that one person carries out his intention and another does not tells us something about the moral character of that person. The externalization of an act is also a sign of the will's intensity and a way of strengthening such intensity since the physical experience of an act is associated with pleasure and pain, which are important stimuli of activity.

From another perspective, the externalization of an act of the will meant to be external, supposed to be done, is of its essence. In other words, good intentions are not enough for what is meant to be done in life. A student is not morally good by only intending to study; he must actually do the work. Sometimes such externalization may not be within one's powers, in which case it cannot be seriously intended. An intention to make a pilgrimage to Rome is not really an intention but a simple desire, if the journey and expenses are not feasible.

There are some other effects to be taken into consideration. One is that by external effort, we are in a better position to create a moral disposition, as when the willing of temperance is strengthened by actually practicing it. Finally, there is the social impact of external acts, their ontic good or evil, good or bad example, heroism or scandal. For this reason, the external acts produce certain juridical effects as well; they are declared valid or invalid and are subject to reward and punishment. In pastoral ministry, external acts must be taken into consideration and specifically dealt with in counseling and confession.

THE MORALITY OF THE EFFECTS

A further characteristic of the external acts is that they are not only related to the will and an ontic reality in themselves, but that they may also have a series of related secondary effects or consequences. Thus, a car accident is not only a physical fact, a collision, voluntary or involuntary as the case may be. Such an event may result in additional good or bad effects. The accident may delay other people getting to work, or cause a person to miss a plane; it costs the insurance agency money, which in turn may raise insurance premiums for other clients; it may result in stricter traffic laws, demand additional police patrol to enforce them, higher taxes to the public, etc.

The effects are not always predictable; often they may not be intended and sometimes they may actually be different from the initial intention. The principles determining the morality of the act, in view of its effects, are basically those of direct or indirect voluntary. The initial distinction to be made is that between the foreseen and unforeseen effects. "If foreseen it certainly adds to the moral good or bad of the action. That a person thinks of the evil consequences that can follow and nevertheless does not on this account refrain from doing it is clear evidence how much more his will is disordered."[3] If the effects are not foreseen, then a further distinction must be made between the foreseeable and the unforeseeable effects, or the events which ordinarily follow or do not follow an action. A husband may expect his wife's anger and depression in a routine family disagreement, but not ordinarily an immediate divorce suit. The degree of responsibility is judged by how vincible or invincible such lack of foresight was, and the gravity of obligation depends on the gravity of the consequences. There is a difference between testing a new, harmless beauty product and a new drug which may jeopardize a patient's life.

The following specific principles should be kept in mind in determining the morality of the effects:

1. An effect or consequence that is foreseen and intended adds either goodness or badness to the act by whatever is good or bad in the effect. Thus, a divorce which is foreseen and intended in committing adultery adds the malice of divorce to the adultery.

2. An effect foreseen but not intended adds malice if it is bad, but not goodness if it is good. The reason is that goodness must always be intended in order to be credited; evil, on the other hand, must always be avoided, even if not directly intended.

3. A foreseen bad effect, nevertheless, in order to be imputable to the agent, must be within his power to avoid (possible to prevent) and there must also be an obligation to prevent it.

This brings us to a last characteristic of the external acts, which is the possibility of double effect, good and bad, of the same action.

---

3. S.T. I–II, Q. 20, a. 5.

THE PRINCIPLE OF DOUBLE EFFECT

The principle, or rather perhaps, the phenomenon of double effect, draws considerable attention in contemporary moral theology.[4] The phenomenon of double effect is the moral experience of conflicting choices and consequences, some good and others evil, of the same action; the principle is an attempt to provide the moral guidelines under which such an action may or may not be permitted. A frequent example is the termination of pregnancy to save the life of the mother, knowing that the fetus must die. Contemporary advancement in technology, biomedicine, and nuclear energy, world population and environmental problems, social and economic conflicts and similar factors, stir additional interest in the subject. Was the atom bomb on Hiroshima justified in terms of its intention to end the war? Is the killing of innocent noncombatants permitted to disarm an aggressor, or storming a high-jacked jet with danger to the innocent passengers? Research with recombinant DNA promises great benefits such as cheaper medicine, better knowledge, cure of cancer, and increase in food production, but it may also cause world epidemics and provide new tools of militarism and possible control of the mind: is this legitimate research?

Given the complexity of human existence and moral dilemmas, the traditional morality did not forbid an action with double and conflicting effects, provided certain conditions were observed. These conditions are: 1) the act itself must be good or at least indifferent; 2) the intention of the agent must be good or the bad effect must not be intended; 3) the effects must follow independently, i.e., the bad effect must not be the means to achieve good; 4) there must be a proportionate reason for permitting the action or allowing the evil to occur.

The principle of double effect has been abundantly applied in the contemporary teaching of the Church's magisterium, especially in the areas of abortion, sterilization, and indiscriminate destruction of life, either in war or in the hospital, e.g., euthanasia. The Second Vatican Council hesitantly admits that "as long as the danger of war remains and there is no competent and sufficiently powerful authority at the international level, governments cannot be denied the right to legitimate defense once

---

4. See: Van Der Poel, "The Principle of Double Effect"; Knauer, "The Hermeneutic Function of the Principle of Double Effect"; McCormick and Ramsey, *Doing Evil to Achieve Good*.

every means of peaceful settlement has been exhausted," but it denies that any means is a legitimate means to it, condemning "any act of war aimed indiscriminately at the destruction of entire cities or of extensive areas along with their population as a crime against God and man himself."[5] While defense is legitimate, indiscriminate destruction must not be a means to it, because it is intrinsically evil.

In the same vein, the Church opposes abortion whenever it appears as a means even to a good purpose and not just a side effect. Thus, Paul VI restating the teaching of his predecessors, writes in *Humane Vitae*: "We must once again declare that the direct interruption of the generative process already begun, and above all, directly willed and procured abortion, even if for therapeutic reasons, are to be absolutely excluded as licit means of regulating birth."[6] According to the same document, nevertheless, "the Church does not at all consider illicit the use of those therapeutic means truly necessary to cure diseases of the organism, even if an impediment to procreation, which may be foreseen, should result therefrom, provided such an impediment is not, for whatever motive, directly willed."[7]

This is a clear example of the double effect principle. It forbids a directly willed evil action, such as abortion and sterilization for whatever purpose. But it permits: 1) a good or indifferent action (e.g., surgery) for therapeutic reasons, even if an impediment to procreation; 2) provided the intention is to cure; 3) impediment to procreation is not a means to it nor directly willed for whatever motive, and 4) assuming a proportionately grave reason such as the life of the mother. This is all well and good, but it may also result in somewhat awkward conclusions. Thus it has been argued that the removal of a cancerous uterus is permitted even if this implies the death of the fetus, provided the death is not intended. But to remove only the fetus in order to heal the uterus is evil because the killing of the fetus appears as the means to healing the uterus. It is difficult to grasp why losing both the uterus and fetus is permissible and losing only the fetus is not.

In the light of what appears to be inconsistent in itself and different from the way people think and act, contemporary moral literature finds two main objections to the traditional principle of double effect: one is

---

5. Vatican Council II, *The Church Today*, nos. 79–80.
6. Paul VI, *Humanae Vitae*, n. 14.
7. Ibid., n. 15.

the fragmentation of the human act by an artificial separation of the effects into direct and indirect voluntary; the other is an overemphasis on the physical condition of the act. The first objection maintains that the distinction between the direct and indirect effect is inadequate, because it is psychologically difficult to make such a separation. A transplant surgeon is not thinking in terms of *mutilation* (which he must not directly will) on the one side, and *implantation* to save life on the other side, but in terms of transplant as one act. It seems, moreover, that some actions which directly cause harm and death are, nevertheless, morally right in some circumstances, like the execution of a criminal which causes death to him and possible harm to his family and dependents. The second objection is critical of the emphasis on the physical nature of the act (*finis operis*) at the expense of the intention of the agent (*finis operantis*). The use of rhythm, for instance, cannot be judged on the basis of its physical nature: the act is good or bad according to the couple's intention and life situation. Similarly, it is argued that the excision of an organ must not be judged by the physical condition of the organ ("mutilation" if it is healthy and "life-saving" if it is sick) but by what is intended by the excision.

While the objections to the traditional (manualist) interpretation of the principle of double effect are valid, the contemporary alternative suggestions are not without their own shortcomings. It is beyond our scope to analyze in any significant detail the contemporary literature on the subject. A fairly comprehensive survey of the issue may be found in an already-quoted work, *Doing Evil to Achieve Good*, by Richard McCormick and Paul Ramsey. Although the contemporary explication of the principle of double effect is far from unanimous, there are some common trends permeating the search for its meaning in practice. Among these are the emphasis on the intentionality of the act as its primary moral specification; another is the moral unity of the action, and finally, the principle of *commensurate* reason as the key concept in the formulation of the principle of double effect. This is the view of Peter Knauer, S.J., who holds that the principle of double effect is, "in reality, the fundamental principle of all morality."[8] According to Knauer, the principle of double effect means "that to cause or permit an evil without commensurate reason is a morally bad act." The situation changes if there is a commensurate reason: "If the reason of an act is commensurate, it alone determines the *finis operis*, so

---

8. Knauer, "Hermeneutic Function."

that the act is morally good." Further on, the author states that "evil may be accepted in exchange if, in relation to the whole, the smallest possible evil is exchanged for the highest possible good. The whole is the determinative point of view for morality." The whole or total value and goodness of the act becomes the criterion for permitting it without any other casuistry. "True responsibility," observes the author, "is always a function of the best possible choice in terms of the interrelated whole." And he concludes: "In most manuals the principle of double effect is explained in such a way that it concerns only the eventual permissibility of permitting or causing a physical evil in the sense that the act is not expressly forbidden. . . . My interpretation of commensurate reason shows that someone can be so obliged in given circumstances to the causing or permitting of an evil that there is scarcely any other choice for him."

What for Knauer is the whole, for others, like Cornelius Van Der Poel is "the community-building or destroying aspect of the action," and for Van Der Marc "inter-subjectivity," or the effects the action has on the total relationship among the human subjects, with other criteria being proposed such as "proportionate reason," "promotion of human welfare," and even the utilitarian principle of the greatest good of the greatest number, which seems to be the position of Joseph Fletcher.[9]

A common denominator of these trends is a combination of a general dissatisfaction with the traditional physical understanding of the human act and a certain movement toward consequentialism as the proper response to the problem. But how to define the greatest good or determine that a particular action is community building or destroying, and what kind of community are we talking about, is not clear. The approach is reminiscent of the principle of fundamental option which, as we pointed out in discussing the subject, is an attractive and in a sense traditional conception of morality, but lacking the traditional precision of determining the morality of particular acts by their objects, motives, and circumstances. No Catholic theologian accepts the principle that the end justifies the means, but as Richard McCormick observes, "Unless one specifies a bit what counts for community-building and how we know this, then that criterion can be squeezed to yield almost any conclusion—

---

9. Fletcher, *Situation Ethics*, 95. For a survey on the morality of consequences, see: Connery, "Morality of Consequences."

for instance, the immorality of all abortions, or the morality of abortion on demand."[10]

This is a sketchy presentation of both the traditional principle of double effect and its contemporary refinements, but sufficient perhaps to attempt a few concluding reflections on the principle itself. We propose to do this by reference to Aquinas, whose treatment of the issue inspired both the traditional formulation of the principle and its contemporary criticism, as well as in the light of our own previous analysis of moral specification.

AQUINAS AND THE PRINCIPLE OF DOUBLE EFFECT

The example which Aquinas uses in this regard is self-defense. It occurs in II–II, question 64 on homicide. In article 7 of this question he asks: "Is it legitimate for a man to kill another in self-defense?" Here are the main statements contained in the answer:

> A single act may have two effects, of which one alone is intended, whilst the other is incidental to that intention. But the way a moral act is to be classified depends on what is intended, not on what goes beyond such an intention, since this is merely incidental thereto...
>
> In the light of this distinction we can see that an act of self-defense may have two effects: the saving of one's own life, and the killing of the attacker. Now such an act of self-defense is not illegitimate just because the agent intends to save his own life, because it is natural for anything to want to preserve itself in being as far as it can.
>
> An act that is properly motivated may, nevertheless, become vitiated if it is not proportionate to the end intended. And this is why somebody who uses more violence than is necessary to defend himself will be doing something wrong.

The rest of the article reinstates the legitimacy of using controlled counterviolence in self-defense, "for a man is under greater obligation to care for his own life than for another." It also reemphasizes the purity of intention: "It remains, nevertheless, that it is not legitimate for a man to actually intend to kill another in self-defense, since the taking of life is reserved to the public authority acting for the common good."

---

10. Ramsey, *Doing Evil*, 20.

Our first observation concerns the act, which, according to the traditional principle must be "good or at least indifferent." Since all human acts are singular (*in particularibus*) and no individual human act is indifferent, the clause may be misleading. The act must always be morally good or perceived as good, even if abstracted from such particular situation the act happens to be physically evil. If the act is indifferent *in abstracto*, it becomes good or bad from subjective motive and circumstances. The fact that "a single act may have two effects" is a circumstance which must be considered for the total action in its good and its bad effects. From this perspective, the double-effect action is no different from any other external action and must be specified in the same way, namely from its object, circumstances, and motive. In doing this, we must keep in mind what we said about the true meaning of moral object as that which is perceived as such by the reason (conscience) and presented to the will in that light, as well as what we said about circumstances and subjective motives in relation to the object. Moreover, our consideration must bring into the picture the legitimacy or illegitimacy of a "mistaken reason," no less than the duty of moral objectification in view of a common ultimate goal and human fellowship under God. This observation is in line with the contemporary emphasis on the unity of action and the primacy of intention (*finis operantis*), but within the traditional schema of moral specification of individual acts as the best way of avoiding loopholes and vagueness in moral decisions.

Our second observation concerns the physical act, often de-emphasized in the contemporary analysis of double effect. Aquinas seems to have a different view. "An act of self-defense is not illegitimate just because the agent intends to save his own life [but] because it is natural for anything to want to preserve itself in being." The total goodness of self-defense stems not only from a good intention, but that the good intended is naturally good in itself. For this reason, a good intention or "an act that is properly motivated, may be vitiated if it is not proportionate to the end intended." This happens if someone "uses more violence than is necessary": such an act ceases to be self-defense (which is natural) and becomes an attack (which is not natural). Is this contradictory to the primacy of the agent (*finis operantis*)? Not really; it only puts the external physical reality of the act into proper relationship to the will, as explained earlier in this chapter. The external act is not only a means to the will's intention; it may also be the end of the will's intention, in which case it becomes the source of morality. On these grounds, sexual abstinence and rhythm are proportionate to planned parenthood; abortion and sterilization are not, even if the intention and the effects are the same. The reason is supposed to see such proportionality or the lack of it, although not every reason does. The human mind, in virtue of its participation in the eternal law, determines what is, and what is not, proportionate to a goal in a given situation and presents it to the will in that light. Such determination becomes binding for the will, even if the reason is invincibly mistaken, as we explained in the section on conscience. The traditional principle of good motive must be understood as a motive according to reason.

The principle that the effects must be independent or that the bad effect must not be the means to achieve good calls for a similar explanation. It may be difficult to prove that the effects are independent or even mentally separable. The bad effect is an unfortunate circumstance of a single act intended to be good. Strictly speaking, in an authentic double-effect action, the bad effect cannot be a means to a good effect, because it is "incidental" to it: an undesirable aspect of an otherwise good action. Consequently, an attack which exceeds the limits of self-defense ceases to be proportionate and becomes bad, not only as a means but as the total action. It is the circumstance *quibus auxiliis* which must be proportionate to the good intended. In this light, we can accept the possibility not only of physical evil (such as pain), but even of moral evil (such as a lie) as an unfortunate *quibus auxiliis* of a good action. Nevertheless, because of the gravity of such circumstance, the entire action must be seriously weighed.

That one must not do evil to achieve good is a standing rule of Christian morality, affirmed by St. Paul in his letter to the Romans (3:8). In the case of double effect, however, we are dealing not with two actions as means to each other, but two effects of the same action. Consequently, one must never kill in order to preserve life—this would be doing evil to achieve good—but one may preserve life even if this implies another death. The point to be made is how the action is conceived, not only as intended, but as naturally proportionate to the intention. In practice, of course, it is not always easy to make such a point. Moral dilemmas are always an agonizing experience.

A word, finally, about the proportionate reason itself. The theologians who propose the principle of proportionate or commensurate reason as the key concept for the entire issue of double effect have a point, considering the role of an ultimate goal in human life and Christian morality. The problem, as we mentioned earlier, is the content of such an ultimate end, "what it is when realized," and the way a particular act is specified as commensurate to it. Because of this problem, we believe that the role of the proximate ends, i.e., the traditional object, motive, and circumstances, must not be dismissed. Commensuration, writes Aquinas, is attained by its comparison to a rule. "The human will is subject to a two-fold rule: one is proximate and on its own level, i.e., human reason; the other is the first rule beyond man's own level, i.e., the eternal law which is the mind of God."[11] In this context, an act of fornication lacks its due commensuration, not only in regard to the external law (or some cumulative human goodness), but in regard to the reason which sees such an act as contrary to what it considers to be a good, normal sexual relationship. In other words, the act is objectively bad. We must repeat what we said earlier, namely that morality must be both total and specific, as we cannot love God (whom we must love above all) without loving our neighbor in a concrete, everyday situation. Consequently, in the case of a double-effect action, proportionality (or commensuration) is not only an important criterion, but it must itself be considered on two levels: one is between the effects (in the sense that to save cows is not a commensurate reason for killing people); the other is between the (physical) action as a whole and what it intends to achieve, not only as the intention of the agent, however primary, but also by itself. This is the ground for public opposition to the nuclear arms race, even if the purpose is self-defense. We must add that every such action itself, like all of our moral life, must be commensurate to the *finis vitae humanae*.

RIGHT AND WRONG—SIN AND GUILT

Aquinas concludes the treatise on moral specification of human acts with a brief reference to what he calls "the consequences of human acts by reason of being good or bad."[12] The consequences are that human acts by reason of their goodness or badness are also right or wrong, praiseworthy or blameworthy, well-deserving or ill-deserving before men and God. Human society and moral science are familiar with these ethical concepts, but their priorities, order, and sometimes their meaning are not always in harmony. Are human acts good because they are right, or right because

11. S.T. I–II, Q. 71, a. 6.
12. S.T. I–II, Q. 21.

they are good? Are praise and blame, reward and punishment only extrinsic denominations, or are they intrinsic qualities of human acts? What constitutes sin and guilt? These are some of the questions touched upon in this context by Aquinas; we say "touched upon," because some of these moral realities, e.g., sin, call for an in-depth theological consideration of their own, and Aquinas treats them as separate treatises.

The first point to be made is that these consequences of human acts are grounded in the moral nature of the human person in its twofold aspect: individual freedom with responsibility and social nature or human fellowship under God. With this in mind, Aquinas thinks that good and evil are the most fundamental moral notions because of their ontological identity with being itself. Good and being are convertible, so that every being in so far as it is, is also good. Evil is a privation of a good due to a being in virtue of what it is. So the will is also good in virtue of its natural bent toward good in general as its proper function; a defect in this function becomes evil. But the true goodness or badness of the will derives not from its general inclination, but from its acting for a specific end by moving itself (and other faculties) toward it or deviating from it, and this is what makes the will's action right or wrong. Right or wrong are the good and bad in acting for an end: a narrowing down of the ontological goodness and badness to the goodness and badness in action. It should be noted that right, in this context, is not a substantive, the *ius* of justice, it is an adjective, meaning rightful (*rectus*) or straight, as different from crooked. Consequently, the issue between a morality based on good versus a morality based on right does not arise at this point. It is clear, nevertheless, and morally significant that in Aquinas' line of thinking, the right as *ius* (what is due to another), like all other social and political rights and duties, must be rooted in what is morally good in itself.

From this perspective, right is an agreement with the proper end or the nature of things, and wrong a deviation from it. This may happen in natural (non-rational) movement, in which case we speak of a defect or failure; when it happens in the operation of the will, it is not just a failure, but a sin (*peccatum*) or a culpable failure, because of the will's rational and thus responsible activity for an end. In other words: anything may go wrong, but when the will goes wrong it is not only wrong, it is a responsible wrong, which is called sin. Going right or wrong depends on certain rules. The rules for the will are human reason and eternal law. "Whenever, therefore, a human act goes out to an end according to the order of reason and of the Eternal Law, then it is right but when it goes awry then it is termed a sin. Now it is clear from our premises that any human act is bad in so far as it departs from the order of reason and of the Eternal Law; and that it is good when it keeps to this. It follows that according as it is good or bad so also it is rightful or sinful."[13]

By reason of being good and bad, right or wrong, human acts are also praiseworthy and blameworthy. Praise and blame are intrinsic to the goodness or badness of human acts, but not their cause, "for to be praised or blamed is nothing else than to be charged with responsibility for a good or bad deed. This arises when it lies within the power of the doer, namely it is under his control. Such is the case with all voluntary acts, since, as we have already observed, a person is master of his activity through the will. We are left with the conclusion that only in voluntary activity does good and bad constitute the reason for praise or blame; and in them evil, failure, and culpable fault are identical."[14] The technical term in this regard is that such acts are "imputable" to the agent (*actus humani imputantur*). The emphasis here is not only on the mastership of one's activity (voluntariness), but also on the rightness or wrongness of the action in view of an authentic human goal. For this reason, an artist who willingly breaks the rules because of his own proximate end is a good (original) artist, but a bad person if he breaks the rules of his ultimate goal. How free an artist, a technician, or scientist is in breaking such rules for professional ends is an issue already considered in the section on indifferent acts.

The manuals of moral theology follow St. Augustine in defining sin as that which is said, done, or desired against the eternal law (*dictum, factum vel concupitum contra legem aeternam*), or Aquinas, who considers sin to be an act against right reason, or simply an act contrary to human nature. As a help in pastoral and confessional ministry, a further specification is added, which says that for every grave sin there must be clear knowledge or awareness, free consent, and grave matter.

In the Christian moral tradition, however, sin is not only a moral (voluntary) fault, but also a religious phenomenon; a reality in experience and a mystery to understanding, in the words of Psalm 19: "But who can detect his own failings? Wash out my hidden faults." In the Bible especially, sin is not so much contrary to virtues as it is to faith: a turning away

---

13. S.T. I–II, Q. 21, a. 1.
14. S.T. I–II, Q. 21, a. 2.

Social and Spiritual Dimension of Human Activity 145

from God, believing in one's own righteousness. This is why the fundamental sin is pride. On the basis of Scripture, especially the teaching of St. Paul, Christian theology speaks of original and personal sin. Original sin is a collective alienation of the human race from God, depriving each and all human persons of the supernatural gift of eternal life, and wounding, but not destroying, man's natural capacities for righteousness. The original righteousness and the title to eternal life have been restored by Jesus Christ, the firstborn of a new creation. In view of this, every personal sin is now a refusal of this new offer of grace. It has its roots in the weakness left over from original sin, but with grace at our disposal, it has no excuse.

By reason of their goodness or badness, human acts also have the quality of merit or demerit, reward or punishment. This, too, is an intrinsic quality, in the sense that they are meritorious or demeritorious whether or not they are actually recognized as such. The formal recognition or retribution, nevertheless, comes from another person, the community, and God. Such retribution is a matter of justice, which is the virtue of human relations. The basis for it is the fact of human fellowship, the *naturaliter sociale*, as the existential condition of human living. Since human persons are by nature social, whatever a member of a community does affects the entire community. This is true even for those acts which seem to help or harm only the agent or just another person, because the condition of each part affects the condition of the whole, like hurting a person by hurting his hand. The communal dimension of human activity is fundamental to morality. Because human acts are voluntary, i.e., a free personal contribution or detriment to the common good, they call for reward or punishment by the community. How the community exercises its rights and duties in this regard is a matter of social and political systems, laws, and above all, justice.

Finally, human acts have the quality of merit or demerit before God. The question of supernatural merit cannot be developed at this point. It suffices to say that it is a standing theological position, the teaching of the Church, and a rational postulate that human acts are rewarded or punished by God according to their goodness or badness in this world. In the words of St. Paul: "For all the truth about us will be brought out in the law court of Christ, and each of us will get what he deserves for the things he did in the body, good or bad" (2 Cor. 5:10). The entire Scripture is an invitation to conversion and perfection. The reasons Aquinas gives in his concluding article are entirely in the line of his community-based morality and the place of the ultimate goal as a common good in it. Since God is our ultimate end, it is fitting that all our acts be judged by him. "Consequently, he who does an evil deed, which cannot be fitted into this service, fails to give God the honor due to him as our last end."[15] Moreover, in every community "it is the ruler above all who takes care of the common good and it is his office to requite the good and evil done in the community. God is the governor and ruler of the whole universe . . . and especially of the world of intelligent creatures. Therefore it is clear that human actions will meet their reward and deserts from him; otherwise it would follow that he exercised no care over them."[16]

There are two significant aspects of this theological insight. One is that no human act goes unnoticed; if it is not seen, rewarded, or punished by a human community in this world, it will be rewarded or punished by God, who sees in secret. Moreover, no political community can claim the entire person and consequently, it may not judge every individual act by its own standard. "A human being is not subordinate to the political community entirely in his whole self and with all he possesses, and therefore it is not required that each of his acts should be well or ill deserving within the political order. But all that a man is, all that he can do, and all that he has is within God's order; and therefore every good or bad act deserves well or otherwise from God in correspondence with its character."[17]

Another aspect of the same insight is the vision of a universal human fellowship under God: a universal kingdom of all creation in which human persons freely and responsibly participate in their own individual way, according to their talents, contributing to and receiving from the same common good that is God himself. As all creation, so we, too, are moved as instruments by God, "yet in such a way as not to rule out our own self-motion through free choices. . . . It is by our own acts that we have merit or demerit before God," and although God in himself can gain nothing nor suffer any loss through our actions, "yet, inasmuch as it is in us to do so, we can offer our service to God or withhold it by maintaining or not the order of things instituted by God."[18]

---

15. S.T. I–II, Q. 21, a. 4.
16. Ibidem.
17. S.T. I–II, Q. 21, a. 3.
18. S.T. I–II, Q. 21, a. 4, ad 1 & ad 2.

We find in these theological reflections an affirmation of our human worth, not only within our human social structures, but also within God's own government of the entire universe. By the same token, our concern and moral responsibility transcend subjective narrowness and call for moral objectification of our conception of values in view of a common good, which finds its harmony of minds and hearts in the one true good that is God himself, our ultimate goal.

Part IV
Emotions

10

Nature and Morality of Emotions in General

IN THE FOREWORD TO *SUMMA THEOLOGIAE* I-II, QUESTION 6, introducing the treatise on human acts, Aquinas writes that he will discuss first the acts which are specifically human, and then the acts which are "common to humans and animals," namely, "the passions of the soul." Following this distinction we, too, devoted our preceding study to a kind of "pure" morality, namely, to the acts as they are specifically human through knowledge and will. By introducing emotions, we are not really changing the subject. There is no such thing as "pure" morality; there is only human morality, and emotions are an integral part of it. "If man were only a disembodied intellect his aim would be achieved by a comprehensive thought system. But since he is an entity endowed with a body as well as mind he has to react to the dichotomy of his existence not only in thinking but also in the process of living, in his feelings and actions."[1]

The schema of moral specification of human acts, although correct in principle and indispensable for moral knowledge and dialogue, is, nevertheless, insufficient to describe indiscriminately an individual person's moral response. Neither a particular human act nor individual person can ever be entirely covered by books and theories without a continuous contact with the material substrate, the principle of individuation. It is desirable, nevertheless, that our books and theories come as close as possible to the real and particular human situation, to the flesh and bones of the human person, if the moral science and framework which we need are to have a practical significance, and the practical experience a scientific relevance. The study of emotions, and more precisely, their integration

1. Fromm, *Man for Himself*, 55.

into morality, is a step in this direction. It is, in fact, from our experiences of loving and hating, desiring and spurning, hoping and despairing, our feelings of joy and sadness, that we climb the ladder of moral perception, deliberation, judgment, and decision. The climb is not without tension, and sometimes it may not even reach the heights of an ideal rationality. By the ideal rationality we do not mean "pure" rationality, but rather a situation in which reason is neither the slave of emotions nor their tyrannical oppressor. It will be our main argument that a true human morality calls for a harmonious unity of rationality and affectivity, as distinct but not separated powers of the same human person.

These introductory remarks suggest that the moral issue of emotions is primarily one of balance between too much and too little feeling. Contemporary moral theology is struggling for such a balance for two specific reasons: one is an inherited suspicion of emotional expression common to most religious attitudes, including the Catholic; the other is a kind of social revolt against the rationalistic morality of the past and present by giving a carte blanche to any emotional feeling and gratification. In Rollo May's observation, the most prevalent unanalyzed assumption about emotions in our society is that "Emotions . . . are forces which put you into motion, and so to be 'emoted' in whatever you happen to feel at the moment."[2]

Aquinas wrote a treatise on emotions, which is still praised for its insistence on the psychosomatic unity of the human person and mental events, and appreciated for its many and perceptive psychotherapeutic insights. Of course, psychology, depth psychology, psychiatry, and psychotherapy are new sciences. They brought changes and advances in the vocabulary, as well as knowledge of psychosomatic phenomena unknown to Aquinas. But the basic fact of emotional experience has not changed; today as always, people are hungry and sexual, exuberant and depressed, they fear and hope, seek pleasure, and avoid pain. It is this basic experience which, from a moral perspective, is our primary concern, suggesting that whatever new factual knowledge of emotions becomes available, there will always be room for a moral and theological contribution to it.

---

2. May, *Love and Will*, 90.

THE NATURE OF EMOTIONS

As in the case of all human acts, there are two aspects of emotions; psychological and moral. This means that to evaluate emotions morally, we must first know them psychologically in their causes and effects. Such knowledge, however, is an enormous task, which modern psychology has made its own with little consensus. "The psychology of affective processes is the most confused chapter in all psychology. Here it is that the greatest differences appear from one psychologist to another. They are in agreement neither on the facts nor on the words."[3] Aquinas was a pioneer on the subject for his own time, gathering as much information on man's emotional life as possible from both the classical pagan and Christian sources. His lengthy treatise (*Summa Theologiae*, I–II, QQ. 22–48) is predominately psychological, with only 3 questions out of 26 dealing with specifically moral aspects of emotions: question 24 on the morality of emotions in general and questions 34 and 39 on the morality of joy and sadness in particular. Yet the purpose of Aquinas' research was not psychological, but moral and theological. Besides being a fact of life and perhaps because of it, emotions are the concern of two cardinal virtues, courage and temperance, with a broad ramification of adjunct virtues like patience, perseverance, continence, gentleness, modesty, as well as their contrary vices of impatience, obstinacy, wrath, lust, and similar dispositions, all in some way dealing with emotions.

A dialogue between moral theology and psychology on the subject of emotions must begin by recognizing certain distinctions between their respective roles. Professionals in the subject emphasize that the role of the theologian must not be confused with that of clinical analyst. From a moral point of view, emotions are not a psychological problem, but a natural phenomenon. This is not to deny the unfortunate and frequent "mental disorder" requiring treatment. But such disorders are a different issue, known in theology as moral impediments, as was pointed out in our discussion of *Conditions of Responsibility*. An important aspect of such a treatment is the discernment between what and how much is a somatic or psychic malfunction and what and how much is mental or indeed moral disorder. Keeping in mind the reality of psychosomatic diseases, we must accept, nevertheless, that there is an emotional life, which cannot be called disorder or disease and which enjoys a specific place in

---

3. Claparede, "Feelings and Emotions," 157.

moral consideration. The basic moral position, therefore, must be that emotions are not hazards, although they could be, but an essential and indispensable force in a person's moral activity; they are not disturbances, although they could be, but an integral part of one's personality, grounded in the substantial union of soul and body. "It is better, writes Aquinas, "that a man should not merely have the right intention, but also perform the good action; it is better that he be bent on good, not merely with his will, but also with his sensory orexis . . . the presence of emotions in sensory orexis is a sign of the will's intensity, and hence an index of greater moral worth."[4]

The distinctive role of psychology and theology must not suggest their separation. "The belief that spiritual and mental disorders are independent of each other saves a great deal of trouble to the specialists in the treatment of both, and a misapplication of the venerable distinction between the 'natural' and the 'supernatural' supplies a ready rationalization to justify the convenience. But the belief is as untenable in the light of the traditional theological principle that 'grace perfects nature' as it has been shown to be unsound and disastrous therapeutically. But neither are the risks wholly illusory, so long at least as the respective roles of theologian and psychologist, or pastor and psychotherapist, are not clearly distinguished and coordinated," so writes Victor White in his *God and the Unconscious*.[5] C. G. Jung writes in the Foreword to the same book: "Long years of experience have again and again taught me that a therapy along biological lines does not suffice, but requires a spiritual completion."[6]

What do we mean by "emotions?" The answer, as already indicated, is not as simple as it may sound. The term is differently described and explained by different psychologists. The only common agreement seems to be that emotions or emotional states signify a complex reaction involving bodily changes and excitement, which may interfere with the mind's rational function and a person's moral conduct. Beyond this description, we find a controversial field with psychologists complementing, correcting, and sometimes demolishing each other's theories.

Although the term emotion is now commonly in use, Aquinas and most of the classical philosophers used the term "passion," which is closer

4. S.T. I–II, Q. 24, a. 3.
5. White, *God and the Unconscious*, 83–84.
6. Ibid., 13–14.

to its Greek original *pathe* and *paschein*, Aristotle's tenth category, meaning susceptibility of interference and change. Today the word "passion" is often reserved for more violent emotional reaction, as when we talk about sexual passion. Consequently, the term emotion seems to express more accurately what Aquinas is talking about under the word passion. Other terms have been used, such as affections, feelings, sentiments, disturbances, or inclinations, but these are even less satisfactory, being either too broad or too narrow to express adequately the phenomenon of emotions. It is characteristic, nevertheless, that they all point to a common psychological reality, which is a sensory experience of attraction or repulsion of different intensity and with bodily transmutation. It is with this common phenomenon, the fact, namely, that we do experience sensory reactions which can support as well as impair our normal moral conduct, that as moralists we are primarily concerned. Emotions, as is commonly known, may be a useful stimulus as well as a hindrance to objective moral decisions, strengthening our commitment and clouding our judgment.

Since it is a common assumption that somatic changes accompany emotional experience, some psychologists, reflecting the positivistic and mechanistic mentality of modern science, look for emotional causes and effects in the organic functions of the body. But this can be overdone, at the expense of both the psychological and moral role and usefulness of emotions. Of all theories of emotions, the behavioristic and instinctive interpretations of emotional experience exemplify most explicitly this extreme. These theories favor an entirely somatic and/or instinctive nature of emotions. The James–Lange theory is an example of the somatic and Freud's psychology of the instinctive interpretation of emotions.

Emotions in the James–Lange theory are the result of what happens in an organism, so that there is no emotional manifestation without a physiological event. "My thesis is . . . that the bodily changes follow directly the perception of the existing fact, and that our feeling of the same changes as they occur is the emotion."[7] According to James, there would be no emotions if the vascular and visceral modifications were suppressed. "Without the bodily states following on the perception, the latter would be purely cognitive in form, pale, colorless, destitute of emotional warmth. We might then see the bear, and judge it best to run, receive the

---

7. James, "What is an Emotion," 19.

insult and deem it right to strike, but we could not actually feel afraid or angry."[8]

The reduction of emotions to organic sensation was criticized by other psychologists who, like W. B. Cannon, found it experimentally inconvincible. Emotions, according to this argument, are not subject to laboratory tests as other physiological effects are, which means that they cannot be entirely identified with them. As a substitute, Cannon offered his "thalamic theory," suggesting that the incoming sensory impulses receive additional emotional quality in their transit through the thalamus and become an experience *sui generis*. Cannon's theory was not immune to further criticism and other suggestions, most of them, however, still primarily organ-function oriented.

A person whose influence on modern psychology cannot be ignored is Sigmund Freud. He, too, attempted to explain passions in terms of the mechanistic-naturalistic thinking of his time. Freud considered emotions to be instincts. "He assumed that those passions which were not the obvious expression of the instinct of self-preservation and of sexual instinct (or as he formulated it later of Eros and Death instinct) were, nevertheless, only more indirect and complicated manifestations of these instinctual-biological drives."[9] Disagreeing with Freud, Erich Fromm writes: "[B]rilliant as his [Freud's] assumptions were they are not convincing in their denial of the fact that a large part of man's passionate strivings cannot be explained by the force of his instincts. Even if man's hunger and thirst and his sexual strivings are completely satisfied 'he' is not satisfied."[10]

Opposite to behavioristic and instinctive theories are the intellectualist interpretations of emotions. These theories consider emotions as an affective expansion of intellectual activity. "We suggest that an emotion or an affect can be considered as the felt tendency toward an object judged suitable, or away from an object judged unsuitable, reinforced by specific bodily changes according to the type of emotions."[11] Magda B. Arnold and J. A. Gasson, the writers of "Feelings and Emotions as Dynamic Factors in Personality Integration" (in *The Nature of Emotion*), specify that "the individual must perceive and judge the object in relation to himself (as

8. Ibidem.
9. Fromm, *Man for Himself*, 54.
10. Ibidem.
11. Arnold and Gasson, "Feelings and Emotions as Dynamic Factors in Personality Integration," 203.

suitable or unsuitable, good or bad for himself) before an emotion can arise" and that while "in the animal, such judgment will be an estimate based upon sense knowledge and sense memory; in the human being, the present estimate always includes rational elements which have entered into the situation in the past and are recalled in the present."[12] This conception differentiates emotions not only from reflexes (*actus hominis*), but also from feelings and moods, although this latter distinction is more difficult to delineate. "There are some feelings, for instance, which are called emotions when they become intense, and there are some emotions which are called moods when they last for a considerable length of time."[13] Feelings and moods are indicators of an inner state of the agent; emotions are movements to action aiming at a suitable object.

The intellectualist theory of emotions is close to Aquinas' own conception of emotions as "the passions of the soul." He emphasizes, nevertheless, that the effect on the body is not a mere expansion of intelligence, but what materially and properly constitutes the nature of emotions. The soul is the subject of emotions as the "form of the body," and there are no emotions without the body. The basis for this position is the substantial union of soul and body, a fundamental tenet of Aristotle's and Aquinas' psychology. They both maintain that it is the soul which is the subject of emotions; not as an intellectual substance in itself, but as the form of a physical body. To make his point, Aquinas narrows down the meaning of passion from a general sense of any change or interference, even good, such as the change in the mind by learning a new truth, to the more specific sense of change when a quality is either gained or lost, as when a sick animal is healed or a healthy one becomes sick. It is this last kind of change which is most properly called passion. "Now *passio*, in each of these three senses, may be found in the soul. For first, the remark *thinking and understanding* are in some sense passions applies to that kind of passion which involves reception pure and simple. Those kinds of passion in which some quality is lost, however, always involve some bodily change; passion strictly so called cannot therefore be experienced by the soul except in the sense that the whole person, the matter-soul composite, undergoes it. But here too we must distinguish: the bodily changes may be for the better or for worse; and it is in the latter case that the term pas-

12. Ibid., 203–4.
13. Ibid., 210.

sion is used more properly. Thus sorrow is more naturally called a passion than is joy."[14]

Aristotle's psychology, which Aquinas follows, is in contrast to Plato's dualism, appearing in some Christian conceptions of a "soul in exile," only dwelling in the body as in a boat or even a prison. If the body is the soul's prison, emotions are its jailers, and one could hardly say anything good about them. Characteristically, the term itself was rarely used without its degrading adjective: "inordinate" passions. The substantial union conception of the human person liberates emotions not only from their mechanistic and instinctive behaviorism, but also from other negative attitudes, giving them a human dignity as *passiones animae*. Man is body and soul; hungry, sexual, and inquisitive, because "the soul is the ultimate principle by which we conduct every one of life's activities; the soul is the ultimate motive factor behind nutrition, sensation and movement from place to place, and the same holds true of the act of understanding" (*anima enim est primum quo nutrimur et sentimus et movemur secundum locum, et similiter quo primo intelligimus*).[15]

According to Aquinas' rational psychology, the soul is the principle of life and operations. The operations of the soul are distinct, but not isolated. The soul operates through its powers or faculties. Some of these are organic, like the vegetative and sensory functions, and some are inorganic, like reasoning and willing. On both levels, there is also a vertical distinction between the apprehension or cognitive powers and appetition or orectic powers, or between the intellect and will and sensory perception and sensory appetite. In the sensory appetite itself, Aquinas distinguishes between the concupiscible or affective and the irascible or spirited powers; a distinction between a normal attraction to a good and repulsion from evil, and an attraction and repulsion involving difficulty and strain because the good is hard to achieve or evil hard to escape.

Within this psychological schema, the location of emotional experience becomes more precise. Since emotions are sensory reactions to good or evil with some bodily transmutation, it is obvious that neither the intellect nor the will are their immediate locus. On the sensory level itself, the emotions take place more properly in the appetitive (orectic) powers than in the cognitive, because good and evil affect our desire more than

14. S.T. I–II, Q. 22, a. 1.
15. S.T. I, Q. 76, a. 1.

our knowledge. It is when a person feels attracted to a good or repulsed from an evil that emotions arise. We must add, nevertheless, that because of the substantial union of soul and body in one human person, there is a continuous interaction between the intellectual (or spiritual) and the emotional in man: the bodily experience affecting the mind to the point that it may impede a rational judgment, and spiritual joy and sorrow overflowing into the bodily feelings of pleasure and pain.

CLASSIFICATION OF EMOTIONS

The purpose of the classification of emotions is to have a better perception of emotional diversity and thus, perhaps, be in a better position to evaluate and treat emotional reactions in particular situations. Human acts are particular and have to be evaluated on this level. It makes a difference whether the emotional experience in a person's activity is one of a smooth, affective response or a matter of continuous tension, anger, and frustration. A classification of emotion will help to determine as much as possible the particular kind of emotional reaction, which is important if the reaction is such that it calls for a psychological and moral attention and treatment. The remedies for anger may not apply to fear and despair.

On the surface, the classification of emotions appears rather simple, since the way a person is affected by a sensory object seems rather limited; the object is either good or bad, present or absent, easy or difficult to obtain or to avoid. Aquinas' list of eleven emotions fits into this schema. Most authors remark that it is not a perfect classification, but nobody has produced a better one. The problem of classification lies not only in diversity and subjectivity of emotional experience, but also in diffusiveness and even deceptiveness of emotional reactions; what appears to be daring may in fact be a hidden fear or an anger disguised as despair.

The first important distinction which Aquinas makes in this regard is between emotions and dispositions. Emotions are movements of the sensory appetite; dispositions are more continuous character traits of a person. The distinction is difficult to grasp and comes to full light only with the notion of moral dispositions which we call virtues; the good quality of mind which makes a person good and his action good as well. Virtues dispose a person to act promptly and joyfully yet freely, according to the prudential judgment of the situation. This cannot be said for emotions, which could be good or bad, sudden and unpredictable. Although emotions are not dispositions, a person may still be disposed to different emotional reactions.

The distinction between emotions and dispositions is followed by a second distinction between the affective or concupiscible and spirited or irascible emotions. The basis for this distinction is the smoothness of the first and hardship of the second kind, between a simple sentiment and a tension in emotional experience. Affective emotions relate to objects which are reachable and simply pleasurable or painful. The irascible emotions exert effort; we hope, fear and are angry or aggressive, not because it is pleasant or painful to do so, but because it is necessary in obtaining a pleasure or avoiding a pain.

Affective emotions are our normal responses to good and evil as such, like *love* of good (*amor*) and *hatred* of evil (*odium*). If the good and evil are absent, something we do not yet possess, love passes into *desire* (*desiderium*) and hatred into *aversion* (*fuga*). When good and evil are present, then love and desire terminate in *joy* (*delectatio*), and hatred and aversion in *sadness* (*tristitia*). The spirited or irascible emotions are the tense reactions to situations in which good or evil are difficult to obtain or to avoid. The classification of these emotions depends on how possible or impossible such good or evil are. If the good in view is difficult yet possible, we have *hope* (*spes*); if it is impossible, we have *despair* (*desperatio*). If the evil is absent and threatening yet possible to resist, we have *audacity* (*audacia*); if it is impossible to escape, it becomes *fear* (*timor*). When such evil falls upon us as something present, the reaction is *anger* (*ira*). Thus, this schema contains six emotions in the affective and five in the spirited powers of the soul. All are also in pairs of contraries, like love-hatred, hope-despair, except anger which has no contrary, since good, which was hard to hope for and to obtain, is not hard any more once it is possessed. Explaining this classification, Aquinas writes: "The affective emotions display a greater diversity than do the spirited, for they comprise both elements of movement (as in desire) and elements of repose (as in joy and sadness); whereas the spirited emotions display no elements of repose, only those of movements. For the object of spirited orexis is something difficult of attainment: and a thing is no longer difficult of attainment once one has come to rest in its possession or endurance."[16]

---

16. S.T. I–II, Q. 25, a. 1.

Because sense-good and sense-evil, present or absent, possible or impossible, are what provoke emotional reactions in us, Aquinas offers the following order of their occurrence: "First comes love and hatred; second desire and aversion; third hope and despair; fourth fear and audacity; fifth anger; sixth and last, joy and sadness, which come after all emotions."[17] In this order, joy and sadness, hope and fear are the four principal emotions: "Joy and sadness . . . because in them all the others have their end and fulfillment . . . fear and hope are called principal not in the sense that . . . all the others find fulfillment in them, but in the sense that they are the last stage of orectic movement towards some objective: for where the objective is some good, orectic movement begins with love, passes into desire and ends in hope; where it is some evil, it begins with hatred, passes into aversion and ends in fear."[18]

Because good has a greater power of influence than evil (we hate evil because it deprives us of some good and we would have no evil to hate if we did not have a good to love), love comes out as the first and most fundamental emotion permeating and developing through both affective and spirited reactions to two terminal emotions of joy and sadness. Joy and sadness are the principal emotions in the order of intention; in the order of occurrence the first emotion is love. Most contemporary psychologists agree on this point.

MORALITY OF EMOTIONS

The morality of emotions may be considered under a double aspect. One is the way emotions occur in particular, subjective instances of human activity in relationship to reason, as when a person acts in anger or from fear. This aspect can properly be treated only on the subjective level, within our understanding of the moral determination of human activity and the role of moral virtues. The other aspect is a general evaluation of sensibility to reason and will, or simply the value of emotional input as a unique factor in morality. It is this second aspect of the morality of emotions which we have in mind in our present consideration.

Emotions, as we already know, can be a support as well as an obstacle to rational moral decisions. A person who is not only rationally but also emotionally committed to a cause is more determined to achieve it

---

17. S.T. I–II, Q. 25, a. 3.
18. S.T. I–II, Q. 25, a. 4.

But emotions can also interfere with free decisions to the point of moral irresponsibility. In our chapter on "Conditions of Responsibility," we outlined how such emotional interference with moral responsibility may be evaluated. Our present analysis intends to elaborate on those principles in a more general and positive direction, considering emotions not just as moral impediments, but as an integral part of human personality and thus an integral part of the moral decision itself. Such an approach to emotions has not always been explicit enough in moral treatises, often suspicious of emotions as merely psychological disturbances. But in spite of such instances of negative attitudes to emotions, the prevailing theological position has been one of rational balance between extremes. The extremes may be described in terms of suppression of emotions on the one hand and submission to them on the other. Two classical examples of these extremes are the stoics who viewed emotions as disturbances to which rational man must never yield, and the hedonists who claimed that pleasure and pain are the ultimate principles of good and evil. Neither one of these extremes is ever fully concretized in individual life, for the simple reason that the human person is naturally unfit for such extremes. But by temper, education, and social mentality we may gravitate to one or the other, not without some practical moral effects. If our understanding of emotions tends to lead to their suppression, then things related to the body must appear bad. The result is that many truly human needs, psychological as well as sociological, may be unreasonably rejected by ourselves and denied to others. Suspicion of the erotic in marriage and social indifference to material needs of people, on the supposition that only the soul matters, may be examples of this. If, on the other hand, our understanding of emotions rests on the theory of submission, then the body and material interests become normative and every physical gratification and social exploitation is justified.

Aquinas, of course, is in favor of a balanced moderation and makes his own theological contribution to it. As we mentioned earlier, in the lengthy treatise on emotions in the *Summa*, I–II, QQ. 22–48, only three questions are devoted to the moral aspect of emotions: question 24 is an overview of moral goodness and badness of emotions in general, and questions 34 and 39 discuss the goodness and badness of joy and sadness, respectively, as the terminal emotions in their respective areas of attraction to good and repulsion from evil.

In an earlier discussion (*Summa Theologiae* I–II, Q. 17, a. 7) on the extent of rational control over the sensory and organic functions, or acts which may or may not fall under such control, Aquinas maintains that sensory appetite, unlike purely biological and vegetative functions, falls under the will or at least is amenable to rational guidance and thus morally significant. This cannot be said for mere physical reactions and bodily reflexes which, in general, evade such control. These reflexes serve the essential interest of physical self-preservation and procreation. They are instinctive, like hunger and thirst, although some higher reflexes like sexual arousal may have a more direct origin in emotional stimulation. Opposite to such bodily reflexes are the voluntary motor reactions, the commanded movements (*usus passivus*) of the bodily members and organs. Thus, in a situation of fear, a person may stop talking or fleeing, but will not stop shaking. Emotional responses are somewhere between the voluntary and purely bodily reactions, because they have a greater share in the life of reason, although they are still sense related. It is on these grounds that neither an extreme intellectualist nor purely behavioristic and instinctive theory of emotions can be accepted without destroying the specific psychological and moral role of emotions. It is still true that our emotional responses depend not only on our psychological ability and rational control, but also on our physiological disposition, such as sex, age, and health. Women, for instance, are more quickly moved to tears than men. While the psychological side, which results from the perception of sensory good or evil, falls under the reason as a more universal power, the physiological or somatic does not, being, as it is, a disposition of the body. However, even in regard to the sensory side, the control (power) of the reason is limited: it is "diplomatic" rather than "despotic," as Aristotle would say. This means that we can never control our emotions the way we control our hands and legs. But we can control them better than our heartbeat or breathing.

There is, one may say, a moral classification of emotions. We may look at the morality of emotions in two ways: intrinsically, or as they are in themselves, and extrinsically, or as they are subject to the control of reason and will. "Now intrinsically of course the emotions are simply movements of the non-rational orexis; one cannot therefore ascribe to them moral good or evil, which we have shown to involve the reason."[19]

19. S.T. I–II, Q. 24, a. 1.

In other words, emotions in themselves are not human acts, but rather the acts of man. They become human acts to the extent they are subject to reason and will. In this case they become voluntary either by being deliberately aroused and sustained or "at least by not being guided and checked as they could be."[20] This means that not to moderate and channel emotional reactions when this can be done is morally as responsible as to voluntarily enhance them.

Although emotions are in themselves, or intrinsically, morally neutral, they do not remain so in particular instances. To be frightened or angry may in itself be morally neutral, but not when we know what fear and anger can do to us or to others and when we can have some control over them. Failure to exercise such a control is itself morally bad. In this context, we must add another qualification to moral neutrality of emotions, the fact namely, that in particular instances, emotions themselves may not be so indifferent but good or bad before becoming such by a voluntary intention. Thus, anger may not be appropriate to express and support an act of forgiveness, even if this is what we intend.

As there are two ways of looking at emotions, there are two ways also of looking at their relationship to reason and will: antecedently and consequently. Antecedently, emotions may cloud the rational judgment on which the moral value of an act depends. In this regard, an act which is purely or even primarily emotional loses some of its moral value so that, e.g., an "act of charity is more praiseworthy when done from deliberate choice than simply from feeling or pity."[21] In consequent emotions there are two possibilities: "First, it may take the form of a kind of overflow: the higher part of the soul is so strongly bent upon some object that the lower part follows it. In this case, the presence of the emotion in the sensory orexis is a sign of the will's intensity, and hence an index of greater moral worth. Second, it may be the outcome of choice: i.e., a man may make a deliberate decision to be affected by an emotion so that he will act more promptly, thanks to the stimulus of the sensory orexis. In this case, too, emotion adds to the action's worth."[22]

When emotions are subject to reason, they fall under the same consideration as the external acts. "We must here apply to passions what we

20. Ibidem.
21. S.T. I-II, Q. 24, a. 3 ad 3.
22. Ibidem.

have already found to be the case with actions: that they are to be classified from two different points of view. First, they may be classified merely as natural phenomena; from this point of view, moral considerations are irrelevant. But second, the passions and emotions may be classified from the moral point of view, in so far as they are part of the life of free and rational choice. In this way, a particular kind of emotion may be good or evil by its very nature, because its object is one that is in tune with right reason, or at odds with it: for instance, modesty, the fear of unchastity, or envy, chagrin over another person's good fortune. Such emotions share in the morality of the particular kind of external action to which they correspond.[23] The meaning of this is that emotions, like other external acts, may have a moral significance of their own as perceived by reason and presented to the will either as an end to be intended in itself or a means to another end. They may also have a morality as intended by the will. Consequently, we are dealing here with two levels of moral goodness or badness of emotions; first, the intention of the will must be good, and second, the supporting emotions must be proportionate to the intention, and ultimately to a true human goal. In simple terms, one cannot support an authentic friendship by envy or choose anger as a means to forgiveness.

Looked at as supportive of intentions, the emotions are morally determined by the morality of intention, provided they are proportionate to it; looked at as the end of the will, they determine the goodness or badness of the will. Thus, sadness over a friend's misfortune is a good emotion, making the will accepting it good; jealousy over another person's fortune is bad and makes the will bad. The use of terms such as "choosing" or "commanding" emotions could be misleading. Emotions are not like a dress one puts on or takes off at will. They enjoy a certain spontaneity, as one cannot cry or laugh on command. But once they arise, the mind can take an attitude toward them and gradually integrate them into its proper activity and intention. When the will so chooses or consents to a particular emotion as a value in itself, the goodness of the will depends on the goodness or badness of the emotion in that situation. If emotion is only a means, then its value depends on the will's end, provided, as we said, that it is proportionate to it. If the emotion so chosen is good in itself, it adds additional goodness to the act, becoming "an index of a greater worth," as an act of charity becomes better when it is also the impulse of pity. If the

---

23. S.T. I–II, Q. 24, a. 4.

end or intention are bad, then whatever other feelings we choose or experience in support of that intention are also bad. The question whether we can employ any emotion for a good intention brings us back to the issue of "due matter" and "proportionality," which we discussed in regard to the external act. In principle, the will can intend envy and anger for a good purpose, for instance, to bring about a social reform or to protect a friendship, but whether such emotions are in themselves proportionate to these ends is a different question, and most people would feel that they are not. The will may imprint (imperate) its own moral value on emotions as long as they are (or perceived to be) proportionate to the will's intention, which itself must be good.

In a more general sense, the emotions add to the will a significant moral dimension given the substantial union of the human person; "because the nature is composed of soul and body and intellectual and sensitive nature, it pertains to the good of man that he submits himself entirely to the virtue, namely his intellect as well as his body" (*quia natura hominis composita est ex anima et corpore et ex natura intellectiva et sensitiva, ad bonum hominis pertinet quod secundum se totum virtuti subdatur scilicet et secundum partem intellectivam et secundum corpus*).[24]

Within the substantial union of soul and body, the role of emotions is to support the agent in his commitment to good as perceived by reason and pursued by the will. Consequently, their suppression is unreasonable and harmful, as long as the reason itself is not suppressed by them. But this, too, calls for reflection. Can one really be "rationally emotional"? How bad is it to be "overcome" by emotions? People get angry and say things they would not say otherwise. They may apologize for that, but should they also apologize for not being "only rationally" angry? In this regard, Aquinas offers an insight which is significant both psychologically and pastorally. The fact is that in an emotional state, the power of reason diminishes and sometimes gives way. This is particularly true in strong emotions of pleasure, such as sexual pleasure, but the same may happen in other emotions, like anger and pain. Aquinas' observation is that temporary "withdrawal" of reason is not necessarily sinful. "The reason itself demands that the exercise of reason be sometime discontinued."[25] Since we are not pure spirits, it would be unreasonable to expect rationality in

---

24. Fromm, *Man for Himself*, 55.
25. S.T. I–II, Q. 34, a. 1.

every single instance of our behavior. Sometimes we "blow up." Of course, such moral "digression" must itself be justified within the framework of the human person and his ultimate goal; if not directly a means to it, at least indirectly, helping the person to know his character better, relieve tension and mature morally. Thus it makes a difference to lose one's temper and to "blow up" for a good reason or for no reason at all; and, similarly, to be overwhelmed by sexual passion in marriage, on the one hand, or in fornication and adultery on the other.

A final note concerns the significance of emotions for morality as a whole and more specifically, for moral continuity and stability. In one of our previous discussions, we pointed out that the unchangeability of physical nature is not necessarily the main argument for moral unchangeability. Yet, the physical order becomes morally significant when brought into the moral context, and the stability of its laws cannot be entirely dismissed. Emotions may have a say in this regard. Are the basic emotional reactions always the same? Are people always going to love some things and hate others, or get angry for the same reasons? These questions may be both a challenge to, and a support of, objective morality.

11

Love, Pleasure, and Pain

THE FOREGOING SURVEY OF THE NATURE AND MORALITY OF EMOTIONS is only an introduction to the nature and morality of emotions in particular. But the nature and morality of particular emotions is a vast area of psychiatry and religious counseling, which hardly can be undertaken within the study of general principles. This is the work of personal competence and luck in guiding oneself or others in particular situations. It is possible, nevertheless, even in regard to particular emotions, to highlight some general causes, effects, and perhaps remedies, which can promote better understanding of an individual case. A general knowledge of what makes people angry and what angry people usually do may help to deal with a particular instance of anger. However, like all human acts, emotions are singular (*in particularibus*) and must be treated on that level.

Our concluding observations must, therefore, be limited to a brief examination of some general causes and effects, not of all, but of those particular emotions which are psychologically and morally more fundamental to human life. These are considered to be love, pleasure, and pain. Since we follow Aquinas' thought on this subject, we wish to add that our survey cannot be a valid substitute for the original reading (*Summa Theologiae*, I–II, QQ. 26–48) and that his own "therapeutic" insights into these, as well as other, emotions may still make a valuable contribution to modern psychology and morality.

LOVE

Aquinas and Freud are in agreement that love is the first and underlying emotion. But while Freud confines love to the sex-instinct which he calls libido, Aquinas' *amor* is an all-pervasive phenomenon of nature found in everything that manifests a tendency toward something else. "Love is wanting things that accord with the nature of the one who wants."[1] It is a movement: an emotion on the sensory level, and an act of the will on the intellectual level. The sensory and intellectual appetites (*orexes*) are active in putting themselves into motion, so that to love is an immanent activity. But the prime mover on both levels is external: the object of attraction which is the *causa finalis* of love. The appetite first experiences the attractiveness of an object, and then it gives rise to a movement (desire) towards it. There is, as Aquinas remarks, "a certain circularity" in the orectic or appetitive process: First the object works on the orexis, imprinting itself there, as one may say; then the orexis moves towards the object, with the purpose of actually possessing it; so the process ends where it began. The first effect produced in the orexis by the object is love, which is simply a feeling of the object's attractiveness; this feeling gives rise to an orectic movement towards the object, viz., desire; and finally this comes to rest in joy.[2]

If love wants things that accord with the nature of the one who wants, there will be as many kinds of love as there are kinds of natural bents. Rollo May writes that there are four kinds of love in Western tradition. "One is *sex*, or what we call lust, libido. The second is *eros*, the drive of love to procreate or create—the urge, as the Greeks put it, toward higher forms of being and relationship. A third is *philia*, or friendship, brotherly love. The fourth is *agape* or *caritas* as the Latin called it, the love which is devoted to the welfare of the other, the prototype of which is the love of God for man. Every human experience of authentic love is a blending, in varying proportions, of these four."[3] Aquinas has a different approach and suggests three basic categories. The first he calls "natural love," which is an instinctive bent to what is fitting to things or in accord with their nature "not through their own knowledge but through that possessed by the Author of their nature." His example is the law of gravitation: a heavy body's bent to its natural place of rest. The second kind of love is found

1. S.T. I-II, Q. 26, a. 1.
2. S.T. I-II, Q. 26, a. 2.
3. May, *Love and Will*, 37–38. This book and Erich Fromm's *The Art of Loving*, may be profitably read on the nature of love from a contemporary, psychological, and sociological viewpoint. Both authors are critical of the modern, commodity-concept of love and its negative effects.

in the sensory orexis which follows sense perception. This is common to all animals, which instinctively perceive and love what is fitting with their nature. Humans share in this sensory love with one difference, namely, that it can and ought to be guided by reason as the more universal faculty of perception. Finally, there is love which follows intellectual knowledge as such: the love of the will, which is specifically a human act. "Natural love is not confined to the vegetative powers of the soul, it is found in all the faculties of the soul, in all parts of the body, and indeed, in all created things; as Dionysius says, all things tend to love what is beautiful and good: for everything has a built-in sense of affinity with whatever accords with its nature."[4]

Such an initial conception of love contains a profound psychological and moral insight. It affirms love as a cosmic reality, a natural movement towards what is fitting, a network of relationships, unfolding from instinctive and unconscious attraction (*amor*) to a conscious and voluntary choice of whom and how we love (*dilectio*). From this perspective, the gospel law of love is not only the first law of morality; it is also a cosmic reality which gradually grows into a specifically human and Christian love through conscious and spiritual purification of attractive objects and our attachment to them.

This brings us to some particular aspects of love as a human emotion. Human love, too, is first of all a reality, a bent, in the sense that we, too, are naturally attracted to what is fitting with our nature. We are dependent on, "vulnerable" to other things and persons. But while love, as an attraction, is an immanent and instinctive movement, the concrete object of love in our case is more optional, subject to discernment, not only on a purely intellectual level, but on the sensory level as well. We are not determined to sensory good in the same measure the animals are; we do not need to love the first thing which comes our way. As Rollo May remarks in the book quoted earlier: "The human being does not stop with the naive delight, but he paints a picture, or he writes a poem, which he hopes will communicate something of his experience to his fellowmen."[5]

Another aspect of specifically human love is the distinction which arises from the difference between attractive things and attractive persons. The things, including animals, are loved possessively, by what

---

4. S.T. I–II, Q. 26, a. 1 and S.T. I–II, Q. 26, a. 1 ad 3.
5. May, *Love and Will*, 267.

Aquinas calls a "love-of-desire" (*amor concupiscientiae*). Other persons must not be loved possessively, but by a "love of friendship" (*amor amicitiae*). The idea coincides with the longstanding ethical principle explicitly formulated in Kant's well-known maxim that "no man must be the means for the ends of another man." History abounds with egalitarian aspirations, from the golden rule to socialism; it abounds equally with various forms of their violation from ancient slavery to modern totalitarianisms.

The movement of love, writes Aquinas, has a twofold object: "The good thing which is wanted for someone, whether oneself or another person; and the one for whom it is wanted. The former is the object of love-of-desire; the latter is the object of love-of-friendship. Within this division there is a certain order of precedence. The object of love-of-friendship is loved for its own sake, and in the primary sense of 'love'; the object of love-of-desire is loved for the sake of something other than itself, and not in the primary sense of 'love.'"[6] Love-of-friendship is not the same as friendship or friendliness, nor love-of-desire the same as desire (concupiscence). Love-of-friendship and love-of-desire are rather the emotional dimensions of both friendship and concupiscence, although in the latter case, the difference is less perceptible, a question perhaps of whether we only like a thing or whether we actually want it. Friendship, on the other hand, is a virtue adjunct to justice: a good quality meaning agreeableness to people in general and above the strict requirements of justice, as when we say that some people are friendly and others are not. Since emotions have a specific, sensory object, the love-of-friendship, or friendship as we ordinarily understand it, is a more particular and limited phenomenon, involving intimacy and interaction of only two or a few persons. We can be friendly to strangers, but not really friends.

The point we want to make is that there is a difference between an emotional involvement with things and an emotional involvement with another person or persons. Things which fit with our nature, like food, a comfortable home, or a pet, may legitimately and naturally be loved by love-of-desire, although discernment must still be made about what and how much truly fits our nature and deserves such love. Although the emotion of love is psychologically and morally significant in all its variety, as in the love of a home, sport, or a pet (people become emotionally attached to different objects), the attachment to other human beings calls

---

6. S.T. I–II, Q. 26. a. 4.

for special consideration. Since human beings are of the same nature and our human fellowship is the existential condition of our life and growth, we cannot treat other people possessively, as we do homes or pets. Yet other people are "fitting with our nature," and some more than others. Experience testifies that a possessive love of other persons is not only morally wrong, but psychologically destructive of authentic friendship. Such a relationship usually never lasts. Yet it must be noted that even a love-of-friendship begins by loving oneself and what is fitting to one's own nature.

Once again it is important that we not only have a good self-image, but that the image be authentic. Our self-image is authentic if we see ourselves in relation to God, the ultimate goal, and to others in human society as the natural condition of our existence. In this perspective, we can truly love others as ourselves without being egocentric as we see ourselves in others. Love begins, therefore, by a similarity between the lover and the beloved. Such similarity may be actual in the sense that both the lover and the beloved possess the same qualities and share the same interest. It is potential when one possesses what the other only desires. Aquinas sees a psychological effect of this distinction. It is only the first similarity that gives rise to love-of-friendship "as the affections of the one are bent upon the other as to himself." The second or potential similarity is more likely to give rise to love-of-desire, or a "friendship based on convenience or pleasure." It may, in fact, give rise to envy and hatred, if the other hinders our obtaining a thing we want. "That is why potters quarrel with each other, because one is a threat to the other's business."[7] "Mature love," writes Erich Fromm, "is union under the condition of preserving one's integrity, one's individuality. Love is an active power in man; a power which breaks through the walls which separate man from his fellow men, which unites him with others; love makes him overcome the sense of isolation and separateness, yet it permits him to be himself, to retain his integrity. In love, the paradox occurs that two beings become one and yet remain two."[8] Modern psychology agrees that similarity or seeing oneself in the other is the beginning of friendship. The initial attraction may have different origins, from a casual meeting and "love at first sight" to a discovery of common interest, sharing the same values, sometimes the

---

7. S.T. I–II, Q. 27, a. 3.
8. Fromm, *Art of Loving*, 20–21.

same adversary, physical attraction and complementarity like sexual difference, beauty, goodness, and similar causes. Psychology also points out that there is a process from such initial awareness of the other through a surface or interest contact to a true mutuality and an authentic love-of-friendship in which the whole person is involved. Extrinsic and surface motives may be a way to, but they are never a sound basis for, a lasting friendship.

Unity is the first effect of friendship. Such unity is different in love-of-desire and love-of-friendship. "When one has love-of-desire for a thing, one sees it as contributing in some way to one's well being. When one has love-of-friendship for a person, one wants good things for him as one does for himself; one therefore looks on him as another self, wishing him well in the same way as one does himself." Mutual indwelling, ecstasy, and jealousy are among other effects, to which modern psychology adds trust, intimacy, self-disclosure, security, spontaneity, and other effects. Mutual indwelling comprises both the cognitive and orectic effect of love: cognitive because the beloved is always present in the lover's thoughts; orectic because the knowledge passes into affection arousing pleasure when the loved one is present and desire when he is absent. Once again, the distinction between love-of-desire and love-of-friendship makes a difference.

In the love-of-desire, the lover seeks possession of the beloved. In the love-of-friendship, the lover dwells in the beloved as he looks on his friend's good or ill fortune as his own, his friend's will as his own will. "This love reaches its perfection when it is mutual, because in love-of-friendship love itself is reciprocal: friends love each other, and each desires and seeks good things for the other."[9] Ecstasy and jealousy are distinguished on the same basis, as love-of-desire becomes an obsession with oneself, and love-of-friendship an identity with the other. Similarly, jealousy in the love-of-desire becomes an antipathy to anything which stands in the way of obtaining and enjoying the loved object. "It is in this way that a man is said to be jealous about his wife: he fears that her associating with others may jeopardize the uniqueness of his own relationship with her; and an ambitious man feels antipathy to successful men as standing in the way of his own advancement." In the love-of-friendship "the object is the good of one's friend: when it is intense, therefore, it arouses in one an antipathy to anything prejudicial to that good. In this

9. S.T. I–II, Q. 28, aa. 1, 2.

way, a person is said to be jealous for his friend's interest. . . . In the same way, too, a person is said to be jealous for God's interests when he strives to the best of his power to prevent anything that goes against the honor or the will of God."[10]

Aquinas puts a final touch on his conception of love when he asks whether love as an emotion can do harm. "Love consists in the attachment of an orectic faculty to some good. Now a thing is never harmed by becoming attached to something appropriate; it is improved and enriched by it. Attachment to something inappropriate, however, causes deterioration and damage. A person is all the better, therefore, for love of a good which is appropriate to him; but he is worse off and indeed suffers harm, from love of a good which is, for him, inappropriate. It is therefore the love of God which enriches a man supremely, and he suffers greatest harm from the love of sin."[11]

Love is a force: a wound which kills and heals according to the goodness of the object and the measure of attraction to it. Since every agent always acts for a good which he desires and loves, love is the generator of all other emotions.

PLEASURE AND PAIN

All emotions begin in love and terminate in pleasure or pain. We want things which are in accord with our nature, delight in them when attained, and suffer when they turn against our wishes and expectations. Pleasure and pain are physical experiences in so far as sensibly or intellectually perceived. A pain that is not felt is not a pain. When the perception is through the exterior senses, we have pleasure and pain properly speaking; when the perception is interior through intellect or imagination, we have joy and sorrow on the intellectual level and emotions of pleasure and pain in the sensory. "Since the object of the rational orexis is something perceived as good, different sorts of perception involve different sorts of objects. There is, therefore, a distinction to be made between pleasures involving the mind, which are also called joys, and pleasure of the body, which are called simply pleasures." Moreover, "pleasure in the sensory orexis always involves some physiological reaction; pleasure in the intel-

---

10. S.T. I–II, Q. 28, a. 4.
11. S.T. I–II, Q. 28, a. 5.

lectual orexis involves nothing but a movement of the will."[12] Although the physical and mental experiences interact within the substantial oneness of the human person, the two experiences are, nevertheless, distinct: an authentic internal joy may coexist with a real physical pain and a true sorrow without physical pain, such as sadness for offending a friend or God.

Our attention will focus primarily on the sensory pleasure and pain in human life as more controversial in moral evaluation. "Pleasure is good" and "pleasure is bad" are two familiar ethical antitheses in the history of morals. In our contemporary society, they present even a more sensitive issue as more pleasures are available with fewer risks. This is particularly true in regard to sexual pleasure which, besides eating and drinking, is the most powerful human drive.

"Pleasure is a contentment arising from the attainment of a congenial good and the awareness of such an attainment." It is a repose rather than a movement, but an active repose: a way of experiencing contentment. Pain, on the contrary, is a union with some evil and awareness of that union. It is not just a failure to attain a good, a privation of pleasure, but a positive suffering of a real evil. As stated earlier, the perception of pleasure and pain is the condition of their experience. The kind of perception, intellectual or sensory, differentiates joy from pleasure and sorrow from pain and introduces into our moral consideration the question of their relationships and priorities.

PLEASURE

Pleasure or delight (*delectatio*) is one of the three goods traditionally distinguished in morals: the useful, the honorable, and the pleasurable. The useful is a means by which something tends toward another; the honorable is a thing towards which for its own sake the appetite tends; the pleasurable is that which terminates the movement of the appetite in the form of rest in the thing desired. Aspirin is useful; justice is honorable; an evening at the opera is pleasurable. Only the honorable (*bonum honestum*) and the pleasurable (*bonum delectabile*) are goods and ends in themselves. However, they are such on different levels: "A thing is said to be honest if it is desired for its own sake by the rational appetite, which

---

12. S.T. I-II, Q. 31, a. 3 ad 1; a. 4.

tends to that which is in accordance with reason; while a thing is said to be pleasant if it is desired for its own sake by the sensitive appetite."[13]

This means that sensory pleasure is a repose in a good, which may or may not be good in relation to reason. Consequently "as not every desired good is intrinsically and truly good so not every pleasure is intrinsically and truly good."[14] A point of clarification is called for in this regard. "Reason" as a criterion of authentic human pleasure must not be understood in a restricted "rationalistic" sense, but as the spokesman for the total human person. The contrast, therefore, between a "rational" and a "sensory" pleasure is not that one is human and the other is not, or that one is always good and the other always evil. The contrast is rather between what is natural to the human person as a whole and what is not. Some things may be very "rational," like a voluntary joy for another person's misfortune, yet entirely unnatural and inhuman from a moral point of view. Physical pleasures are not morally evil "any more than is sleep, when taken in accordance with reason, for reason itself demands that the exercise of reason be sometime discontinued."[15] The substantial unity of soul and body in the one human person must be kept in mind. "It pertains to the notion of this particular man to be composed of this soul, of this flesh, and of these bones."[16] Consequently, "since man is in fact composed of soul and body, whatever conduces to preserve the life of the body is of value to man, though it is not his supreme good, because he can abuse it."[17] Half an hour of jogging or swimming may sometimes be more rational than half an hour of meditation. Yet the sensory pleasure plays its own specific role in human life which can be both positive and negative; positive in the sense that sensory pleasure is not only a sign of a voluntary commitment to something, but that in fact reinforces such a commitment. Negative, because it can be destructive, not just of a rational judgment, but of the human person as a whole. Aquinas gives three reasons why physical pleasures may be destructive. "First they distract the reason . . . when we enjoy doing something we give it close attention, and of course when attention is absorbed in one thing it is partially or

13. S.T. II–II, Q. 145, a. 4 ad 1.
14. S.T. I–II, Q. 34, a. 2 ad 3.
15. S.T. I–II, Q. 34. a. 1.
16. S.T. I, Q. 75, a. 4.
17. S.T. I–II, Q. 59, a. 3.

even totally distracted from others . . . Second, physical pleasures can be contrary to the order of reason, especially when carried to excess . . . Third, physical pleasures can fetter the reason. For physical pleasure is accompanied by physiological reactions which are greater than in the case of other emotions, since the orexis is moved much more strongly by a thing that is present than by one that is absent."[18]

One does not need to be a mystic to see that rational and spiritual joys are more reliable, perfect, and lasting, not to mention honorable, than physical pleasures. But one must also be realistic enough to admit that relative to our human condition, the physical pleasures are more intense, more keenly felt, and to most people, more attractive. "More people seek physical pleasures because sense-goods are known better and more widely. Furthermore, people need pleasure as remedies for all sorts of grief and sorrow; and since most people are unable to achieve spiritual pleasures, which only the virtuous can do, they fall back on physical pleasures."[19] Let us face it: "no one can live entirely without any sensual or physical pleasure; the very man who teaches that all pleasure is evil is bound to be caught taking some pleasure: then people will be disposed towards pleasure more than ever by the example of what he does, ignoring what he says. For in matters of human activity and passion, where experience counts for so much, example carries more weight than words."[20]

Pursuing his thought along these lines, Aquinas concludes in the same article: "My own thesis, then, is this: some pleasures are good, and some are evil." Since pleasure is "that repose of the orexis in some loved good which comes at the end of some activity," every particular pleasure must be evaluated by the nature of the good achieved and by the morality of the action achieving it. If the good achieved is according to reason or connatural to the human person the pleasure is good; it is evil when the appetite comes to rest in something which is in disagreement with reason. "All things desire pleasure in the same way they desire good, for pleasure is desire come to rest in some good. But just as not every desired good is intrinsically and truly good, so not every pleasure is intrinsically and truly good."[21] Similarly the activity by which a pleasure is achieved must

---

18. S.T. I–II, Q. 33, a. 3.
19. S.T. I–II, Q. 31, a. 5.
20. S.T. I–II, Q. 34, a. 1.
21. S.T. I–II, Q. 34, a. 2 ad 3.

be good. Thus the joy of a thief over a successful robbery is evil because the robbery is evil. "A person is, therefore, judged good or evil chiefly in terms of what his will finds pleasurable: that person is good and virtuous who takes pleasure in good deeds; that person is evil whose pleasure lies in evil deeds."[22]

Here, however, we run into the familiar problem of subjective versus objective morality. Although some pleasures are natural to humans in virtue of their humanity (either specifically, like joy of moral integrity and contemplation of truth, or generically like food and sex), the fact is, nevertheless, that a particular person may feel differently on either the specific or generic level. An obvious example in the contemporary moral debate would be homosexuality. Aquinas does not discuss the subject in the present context, but he mentions it as an example of "non-natural" pleasure in an earlier question of this treatise, *Summa Theologiae*, I–II, Q. 31, a. 7. There he observes that a pleasure which is unnatural "absolutely speaking" may be natural "from a particular point of view." Pursuing the distinction, he attributes its causes to either ignorance or a particular pathological condition. "That which is not good by its very nature may be good in respect of a particular person in two ways: first, it may be that it is good for him because of his being at the moment in some abnormal condition: thus it is good for a leper to eat things which, for some in normal condition, are poisonous. Second, it may be that something which in fact is not good may be thought of as being so."[23] This is clear: but what do we do with people who find themselves in such a different condition or in ignorance? In evaluating such "particular natures" and their subsequent, related pleasures, we must recall our discussion on the meaning of objective morality and the role of conscience. The first distinction to be made is between a pathological and moral state of a person, because they call for different treatment and evaluation. Leaving the pathological state to medical and psychiatric competence, we must accept from our moral perspective the primacy of the agent or the personal conscience as the first, although not the ultimate, norm of such pleasure. As in the case of all human acts, a normal human person should be able to evaluate which pleasure fits and which does not, not only his immediate gratifications,

---

22. S.T. I–II, Q. 34, a. 4.
23. S.T. I–II, Q. 34, a. 2.

but his authentic human needs within the context of an ultimate goal and human fellowship.

PAIN AND SORROW

Pain and sorrow are common, if unfortunate, facts of life, from early childhood to death. In the Christian tradition, they are closely associated with the radical deficiency in human nature due to original sin and find their ultimate explanation in the suffering and death of Christ. Physical suffering is not the greatest evil and even may be voluntarily accepted in view of a greater moral or spiritual good. But neither is it something to be desired in itself, as the healing ministry of Christ in the gospel clearly indicates.

If pain and sorrow are facts of life, the question is how to take them psychologically and morally. Most of what we said about pleasure and joy applies also to pain and sorrow, although from a different angle, since pain is contrary to pleasure. The object of pain and sorrow is a present evil. A reaction to it must include a perception of it, which can be sensory and rational. Sensory perception results in the emotion of pain, which is followed by sorrow through the rational perception of evil. Sorrow may or may not coincide with physical pain. Such pain is said to be bodily because it is felt in the body. The actual emotion of pain, however, is still in the soul as the form of the body, and the body cannot feel unless the soul does so too. Aquinas believes that, in principle, pleasure is a stronger emotion than pain, because good is always more perfect and complete than evil, which is never absolute. Nevertheless, a person may more eagerly shun sorrow than seek pleasure, because sorrow may impede all other joys. Persons who are sad can hardly enjoy anything. Similarly, interior sorrow is stronger than physical pain, because the interior perception is more comprehensive, intense, and more difficult to control. But physical pain may be greater in the sense that it can increase interior sorrow and make the whole evil even more repugnant.

In evaluating pain and sorrow morally, Aquinas once again stresses the positiveness of the evil which causes them. Such evil is not just privation of a desired good, but a reality in its own way and shunned as such. In the physical world "privation is simply lack of the opposite good." In a perceiving mind, however, "even privations have some sort of ontological status; hence the expression an entity of mind (*ens rationis*)."[24] Such "entity of mind" must not be confused with "imaginary pain." For the mind the pain is real, although in the physical and metaphysical world it may be only a privation in what still remains essentially good. But the object of emotion is sensory good or evil which are particular. The difference, therefore, is significant for emotional reaction, which is not the same either psychologically or morally when we regret a lost good and when we suffer an occurring evil.

Pain and sorrow are always subjective, and so must be their treatment. In general, however, reactions to them may vary from hysteria to stoic endurance and even to the strange phenomenon of masochism. Aquinas' view is that in themselves, pain and sorrow are evil and that it would be unnatural to seek them in the way we seek pleasure and joy. Considering, however, what causes them and how all things must be judged in view of an ultimate goal, pain and sorrow can be good or bad. "Thus, given some saddening or painful object, it is a good thing a person feels sorrow and pain about it. For if he did not, it would have to be because he did not feel it, or did not look on it as unwelcome; and each of those attitudes would obviously be an evil. Given the presence of an evil, then, it is a good thing for sorrow or pain to arise from it." This holds for both physical pain and spiritual sorrow. For pain because it shows that "the senses recognize, and nature shrinks from what is harmful and causes pain"; for sorrow when the recognition of evil is "due to a correct judgment made by the reason, and the rejection of it to a will of such habitual goodness that it detests evil."[25] We cannot expect people to enjoy funerals either emotionally or rationally. Since moral goodness consists in right judgment and righteous will, the rational acceptance (endurance) of pain and sorrow for good reason is morally good. In this context, pain and sorrow serve a good purpose, helping the agent to grow morally and to avoid evil, especially sin. Given, moreover, the transcendent human goal, no physical pain or even sorrow is ever an absolute evil. Only total separation from what is truly and absolutely good is such an evil and we call it hell.

24. S.T. I–II, Q. 36, a. 1.
25. S.T. I–II, Q. 39, aa. 1–2.

Part V
Moral Formation

12

Dispositions

SO FAR WE HAVE DISCUSSED MORALITY ON THE LEVEL OF ACTIVITY, examining what constitutes a human act psychologically and morally as it proceeds from knowledge and will, supported or impaired by emotions. It may appear now that every human act is always a direct result of our cognitive and orectic faculties, so that between our capacity of doing something and actually doing it there is nothing but the doing itself. For example, it may appear that between our capacity of telling the truth or a lie and actually telling one or the other, or that between our capacity of loving and actual expressions of love, there is nothing but such expressions as they occur in our relationship.

This, according to Aquinas, is not the case. A concrete human act is itself the result of another, intermediary quality, which exists between the faculty or potency of act and particular acts, between the capacity of loving and the actual acts of love. We call this quality a disposition: a kind of moral ambiance predisposing the agent to act the way he does with consistency, promptness, ease, and joy. Dispositions are not seen; they are only experienced. We can say that a person has a certain disposition when we can predict his conduct in a given situation: "he always acts that way."

The study of moral dispositions is a preliminary, psychological investigation, leading to the study of moral virtues, which hold the central place in Aquinas' moral theology. They suggest that moral life, the *vita humana*, is not a succession of unrelated particular acts with no past or future, but that there is a moral continuity and that every human person has a moral history which becomes his character or personality. "How do we become the kind of persons we are," and "what kind of persons should we become" are important questions in what we generally call moral education. The more we emphasize the primacy of the agent or a personal response to values as the core of an authentic morality, the more important these questions become. Although specific methods of education vary and some, like political indoctrination of totalitarian regimes, must be rejected, the common aim of education has always been the development of the mental and affective potential of individuals and their social adjustment. The ideal is that the individuals make their own intelligent, free, and responsible moral decisions and find it easy to carry them out in spite of internal and external obstacles. Such intelligence, ease, and determination do not come automatically, but through learning and exercise: a long process of moral growth which combines natural endowment, personal effort, social support, and God's grace. It is in this way that we build our mental and emotional dispositions to meet difficult and contingent situations of life with freedom and consistency. In this process, the idea of human fulfillment and the ultimate goal must be kept in mind.

In the *Summa*, Aquinas discusses what we may continue to call moral formation or the formation of character under two sections: dispositions in general or the psychological basis of moral formation (I-II, QQ. 49-54), and dispositions in particular as they are good, or virtues (I-II, QQ. 55-67), and bad, or vices, in the treatise on sin (I-II, QQ. 71-80). After the treatise on law and grace which concludes the I-II of the *Summa*, the rest of Aquinas' moral theology continues as a systematic study of particular virtues and their contrary vices. The schema clearly confirms the centrality of virtues in morals. The following presentation of dispositions must therefore be viewed in anticipation of the discussion on virtues, and especially moral virtues and vices which make a person good or bad.

THE NATURE OF DISPOSITIONS

The nature of dispositions as a specifically moral phenomenon is only gradually developed in the *Summa Theologiae*, I-II, QQ. 49-54. The Latin term is *habitus*. The term is applied to a wide range of mental, sensory, and even organic states: from understanding the first principles to such character manifestations as kindness and shyness, and bodily states of health and beauty. The English translation of *habitus* as disposition seems to be more appropriate than the literal word "habit," which is also used.

The reason is that the word "habit," as we ordinarily understand it, misses the true meaning of Aquinas' *habitus*. Habit suggests a motor-reaction of an uncontrollable state, as when we say that someone has a habit of smoking. *Habitus*, or disposition as we shall call it, ultimately emerges as a morally significant quality of the mind, a consistency in deliberate activity: *habitus est quo quis utitur cum voluerit.*[1] Aquinas is very emphatic and persistent in this statement throughout his discussion of dispositions and later virtues. Habit is usually an impediment to freedom; disposition is a vehicle of the will to act freely yet steadfastly. Animals can be "habituated;" only humans are disposed.

In developing the notion of disposition, Aquinas' primary source is, of course, Aristotle and his medieval commentators. Disposition is, therefore, described as a quality, which is one of Aristotle's ten categories, indicating that a being is in a certain state. But there are four species of quality, and disposition is one of them. Other qualities mentioned are: form and figure, as having human appearance; capacity or incapacity for something, as being capable of laughing and incapable of flying; passivity and adaptability, as becoming warm or cold according to climate and temperature. Habitus or disposition is described as a "hard to change quality" of a being either in itself or its operation. Thus we can talk of such dispositions as health, sickness, beauty, toughness, and dispositions of activity as when some people are more perceptive, courageous, patient, etc., than others. This gives us the first important distinction between the *entitative* and the *operative* dispositions: the first being the dispositions of the body and the second of the mind as the principle of action. Operative disposition is defined as "a hard to change quality by which a person is disposed to act with ease, promptness and joy."[2] Since the way people act is more important than the way they look, and morality a specifically human phenomenon, it is obvious that operative dispositions become the center of our attention. To the distinction between the entitative and operative dispositions, we must add a further distinction between the

---

1. S.T. I–II, Q. 49, a. 3. Because different translators worked on the McGraw-Hill edition of the Summa, there is a certain inconsistency in terminology. Thus, the word *habitus* is translated as "disposition" in some and as "habit" in other volumes. In order to preserve our own preference and consistency, we substituted the word "disposition" or *habitus* for the word "habit" in our quotations.

2. S.T. I–II, Q. 49, a. 2, and throughout the treatise.

cognitive or *intellectual* and orectic or *moral* dispositions, corresponding to the cognitive and orectic faculties of the mind.

This initial understanding and classification of dispositions now opens a series of related questions helpful to further delineate the true meaning of moral dispositions. The first question is about the need of and conditions for the development of dispositions. The need of dispositions seems obvious from the indeterminateness of our rational faculties and their activities on the one hand and the need to act selectively and determinedly in view of our given goal. "Every faculty which can be exercised in more than one way needs a disposition to ensure that it is exercised in the right way."[3] We need dispositions to know better and to act easier. On the same ground, it is clear that dispositions are possible only in those faculties of the mind which are not naturally determined to one object or activity, but open to alternatives. Such are the reason and will. To be open to alternatives, however, is not enough: the alternatives must also be available. This means that true dispositions can develop only if the environment offers a choice, as we cannot get used to heat in a continuously cold climate. The conditions for dispositions are therefore indetermination and openness of the faculties on the one hand and the availability of different possibilities on the other hand. Fire can only heat, but we can act reasonably and unreasonably, choose one thing or another, unless we are psychologically programmed or forcibly deprived of freedom.

Implied in this is an important aspect of moral education. It suggests that a true and responsible moral formation can take place only in a free and pluralistic society, where values can be compared and freely integrated. The idea seems to have been espoused by the Vatican II *Declaration on Christian Education*. Unlike the rather frequent mentality of segregation and fear of contamination which characterized parochial and, not infrequently, seminary education in the past, the document sees the Christian education more in cooperation with the world as a whole and in an ecumenical setting. Such cooperation and freedom, however, must still be pursued within the boundaries of a given ultimate goal and the existential condition of human society, which are not optional. "For a true education aims at the formation of the human person with respect to his ultimate goal, and simultaneously with respect to the good of those societies of which, as a man, he is a member, and in whose responsibili-

---

3. S.T. I–II, Q. 50, a. 5.

ties, as an adult, he will share."[4] What makes the old Aquinas and the new Catholic concept of "liberal education" still different from the secular humanistic conceptions is not the psychological method of freedom and options, but the ethical acceptance or rejection of some ultimate goal. Contrary to such relativism, the concept of an ultimate goal or a vision of human fulfillment remains central to Aquinas' moral thinking. Without it psychology itself operates in a vacuum, as the critics of the college curricula and modern educational systems in general begin to point out.

The nature, need, and condition of dispositions are, in part, an answer to a second question concerning their subject or seat. Since being in potency for development, open to alternatives and environmental availability of alternatives are the conditions for dispositions, it is obvious that those faculties which are most undetermined in this regard are also the primary subjects of dispositions. Such are the faculties of the mind, in the first place the reason and will. The sensory faculties are included to the extent that they enjoy the same flexibility by being subject to the rational command. "The sensory faculties have two aspects: first, they act by natural instinct; secondly, they act at the command of reason. When they act by natural instinct, they are, like nature itself, capable only of a single activity. And therefore, just as there are no dispositions of natural capacities, so there are no dispositions of sensory faculties when these act by natural instinct. But when they act at the command of reason, they can be exercised in more than one activity. And so they can have various dispositions which make them well or ill adapted to various purposes."[5] All entitative dispositions are in the body and morally significant to the extent that the physical state of a person influences his mental activity. Theology, nevertheless, speaks of one entitative disposition of the soul, namely, the sanctifying grace which elevates the soul to a supernatural mode of being: a "new creation." Such elevation is then enriched by the corresponding, infused dispositions, the theological virtues of faith, hope, and charity.

ORIGIN, GROWTH, AND DECAY OF DISPOSITIONS

The origin of dispositions raises several important questions. One is philosophical, the question, namely, of how much we know by nature and how much by experience. In the history of philosophy this is known as

---

4. Vatican Council II, *Declaration on Christian Education*, n. 1.
5. S.T. I–II, Q. 50, a. 3.

the debate between the idealists advocating the innate ideas as the source of knowledge and the empiricists attributing all knowledge to sense experience. The second question is theological and concerns primarily the infused theological and moral virtues. Do baptism, confirmation, and other sacraments make a person wiser, more just, temperate, courageous? Finally there is a specifically moral and psychological question of how determined a person is or may become genetically or by technological means of mind control.

Aquinas takes the position of a multiple origin of dispositions: some are from nature, some partly from nature and partly from external agents; some are acquired, and some infused as God's gratuitous gifts. Dispositions which are from nature may be such either specifically, i.e., in virtue of being human, and individually, i.e., in virtue of being this particular person. This applies to both entitative and operative dispositions. Thus growing, aging, and reaction to infection are common entitative dispositions, although some, like healing, may also be reinforced by an external agent, e.g., medicaments. Individually, some people may be more resistant than others, and again reinforce their state by external agents. The origin of operative dispositions is a more complex issue because of two different operations: cognitive and orectic. There are some natural cognitive dispositions in both specific and individual nature. Thus the understanding of the first speculative principle (the principle of contradiction) is common to all humans. On the individual level, some people may be by nature more intelligent and imaginative than others. In the orectic faculty, there is a corresponding understanding of the first practical principle, that good is to be done and evil avoided. A rudimentary orectic disposition may also be particular to one person. Thus some people may by nature be more disposed to temperance, kindness, anger, etc.

Abstracting from a number of semantic and historically conditioned issues which Aquinas discusses in this context, the basic teaching is rather simple: except for abnormal and pathological cases, and some basic specific and individual natural inclinations, human beings can develop, change, and lose their natural endowments through their own activity. Activity or exercise of our faculties is the second and morally most important source of dispositions. Dispositions are acquired by repetitive acts. It may take time: one swallow does not make a summer. But time and effort pay. Infused dispositions are, of course, a theological issue and, indeed, a theological postulate. The reason is that on the one hand the ultimate goal (the beatific vision) transcends the natural human powers and dispositions, and on the other hand good acts are still required on our side. It is by the grace of God and our faith that such acts are supernaturally meritorious.

Finally there is the question of growth and decay of dispositions. If dispositions are qualities constituting a faculty (or a being) in its essence, then we cannot talk of growth or decline except metaphorically. Thus a person is human or not a person at all, although metaphorically a person can be more "human" than another. Those dispositions which do not constitute the essence of a faculty but only relate to it can grow and decay. Thus people can be healthier or sicker, more or less perceptive and intelligent, more or less temperate, sensitive, kind, etc. In this way we talk of intellectual development and moral and spiritual growth. The growth itself is of two sorts: one is in-depth or intensively; the other is extensively, covering new areas. In this regard, Aquinas makes a point, which will be important for understanding of moral virtues. The point is that only cognitive or intellectual dispositions can grow both intensively and extensively, in the sense that one can know better and one can know more. Moral dispositions can grow only intensively, on the assumption that one cannot really be disposed to temperance and kindness unless he is temperate in all things and kind to all people. One can, nevertheless, become more temperate and kind in the sense that he finds temperance and kindness ever easier.

A person can grow intellectually and morally, but he can also decay. This happens indirectly when the subject or faculty of a disposition corrupts biologically or psychologically: a brain tumor can affect one's thinking and willing. It happens directly by contrary acts or ceasing to act, as when one weakens and eventually loses his temperance by indulging in pleasures. Franz Schubert said that if he neglected his piano practice one day, he noticed it; if he neglected it two days, the audience noticed it. There is a bright side to such decay: if good dispositions can be lost so can bad dispositions too, and a sinner may still become a saint.

This somewhat technical analysis of dispositions contains a remarkable doctrine, telling us that we are basically self-perfecting and our moral and spiritual progress is in our hands. Although our basic capacities of understanding and willing are common to all and given to us, and there may be some rudimentary differences in our individual inclinations, we are, nevertheless, our own creators, free to decide our own way. In applying firmly, methodically, and constantly our mind to learning and our will to doing under the guidance of reason with social and religious support, we achieve an ever greater command and mastery in both understanding and conduct. Even the infused dispositions of faith, hope, and charity become in a sense our property, and we can increase them. We increase faith by applying it to new challenges, hope to new situations of despair, and charity by always doing more. Strictly speaking, we cannot give ourselves nor increase by ourselves the supernatural virtues; what we do is to increase our facility in applying them with promptness, steadfastness, and joy. This fits our concept of acting for the ultimate end, the vision of God, which, although a gratuitous gift, calls for a human response in good acts.

MODERN DEVELOPMENTS

Aquinas' treatise on dispositions is geared to his treatise on virtues which, in the context of the primacy of the agent or a conscience-oriented morality, becomes the focus of moral formation. Virtuous persons can be trusted. The history of morals is a complex subject when we think of all the ethical systems in it, making generalizations and classifications difficult. We believe, nevertheless, that most of them may be reduced to a distinction with which we are already familiar, namely, between a morality of law or act-oriented morality and a morality of virtues or person-oriented morality. The distinction is more a matter of emphasis than exclusiveness, since morality cannot permit a total suppression of either. But the emphasis makes a difference. Although a morality of virtues is humanly and theologically a more authentic conception of morality, the normative or a morality of law is pastorally and practically more expedient. This is particularly true in periods of missionary expansion and busy pastoral care, when teaching and learning of commandments is quicker and easier than an in-depth study of the network of virtues. But the switch from a morality of virtues as envisioned by Aquinas to the modern, manualistic preoccupation with commandments is due also to some more philosophical and theological changes, notably to nominalism. Bernard Häring summarizes this change and its consequences when he writes: "The fundamental intuition of Nominalism is the unique value of the singular, the individual. The only true reality is the individual. Only the particular man, the human individual, really exists. What characterizes the moral act of the individual is its absolute unprepossession, particularly in regard to the habit (this means what is already in possession, the basic attitude). Here we have a moral system of individual acts in contradiction to a morality of the Thomistic habits (the *habitus*, the permanent, constant, the pre-decided). A further characteristic is the typically biased concept of the good viewed as a conformity of action with will. This conception of the good paved the way for voluntarism and legalism."[6]

There is a difference in this regard between the Catholic and Protestant approach as well. Since all authentic virtues and human activity must ultimately be ordained to God who transcends our human capacities and offers himself gratuitously, yet good acts are required, the question is: how much comes from God and how much from the human agent, or how much is a person's character a gift of grace and how much the result of personal formation and environment? The emphasis on one or the other may have serious theological and moral consequences, diminishing human responsibility if we emphasize grace alone, or God's rightful and merciful role if we emphasize the human factor. While the Catholic theologians struggled to harmonize the natural and the supernatural in this regard, the Protestants took a more radical position of "faith alone," wary of any theological explanation of behavior that would give undue agency to man. This, of course, diminishes the role of moral virtues as permanent dispositions on which we can rely in making moral decisions. Moral decisions are rather existential responses to God's call and command, as spoken in the Scripture. The contemporary theological currents show a more reconciliatory trend. While the Catholic theology is moving away from the manualist legalism, the Protestants seem to be moving toward a more moderate position, seeking a reconciliation between an objective affirmation of God's action and man's subjective involvement.[7]

MODERN PSYCHOLOGY

Our survey of dispositions calls for a brief reference to modern psychology. Aquinas' own treatise on dispositions is a psychological groundwork for his treatise on virtues. Psychology is therefore an auxiliary science to morals. Modern psychology takes a more independent course, sometimes contrary to the traditional and theological tenets of freedom and responsibility. An example of such an extreme position is modern behav-

6. Häring, *The Law of Christ*, 14–15.
7. See Hauerwas, *Vision and Virtue*.

iorism. As a psychological and educational theory, behaviorism reflects the materialistic and mechanistic conception of the human person; a conception already implicit in Descartes' separation of mind and body. The British empiricists imprinted their own emphasis on human responses as purely mechanical and sensational. Sprung from such sources, modern behaviorism was inaugurated by John B. Watson in the United States and Ivan P. Pavlov in Russia at the beginning of the last century. Their research presents a shift from the study of mind to the study of observable behavior of organisms. The research was done on animals, dogs and white rats, under the assumption that the results are applicable to humans since the difference between animals and humans was considered to be only quantitative and not qualitative. Behaviorism has been re-articulated recently by B. F. Skinner. His methodical behaviorism is, in his own words, a psychological version of logical positivism. Skinner does not claim that behaviorism is a proven science. But in the line of logical positivism, he dismisses what he calls "mentalism" because mental data and operations are scientifically unverifiable. "No matter how defective a behavioral account may be, we must remember that mentalistic explanations explain nothing."[8] Skinner "questions," although in fact he denies, the possibility of free choice and the existence of mind: "no special kind of mind stuff is assumed" in his study. His theory of education is entirely biological: an interaction between organism and environment, guided by the twin principles of pleasure and pain. It is a system of manipulation to "reinforce," through pleasure and pain, those individual activities which evolution and social experience have determined to be "good" for both the individual and society. "All selves are the product of genetic and environmental histories."[9] While in the past such "product" has been evolutionary and at random, now we can make it selective: "until recently, species evolved because of random changes in genes and chromosomes, but the genetics may arrange conditions under which mutations are particularly likely to occur."[10]

Behaviorism draws legitimate attention to the bodily and environmental elements in education. But its mechanistic conception of the human person and its denial of creative freedom and self-determination are

---

8. Skinner, *About Behaviorism*, 246. See also "Behavior Control."
9. Ibid., 247.
10. Ibidem.

scientifically unfounded and morally unacceptable. As a psychological version of logical positivism, Skinner's behaviorism commits its own fallacy, identifying moral with scientific and scientific with empirical. The fact that a statement is not empirical does not mean that it is not rational and in its own way scientific. Skinner defends behaviorism against the "humanistic objections" (that it ignores consciousness, endowments, intention, creativity, self, etc.), but his basic rejection of the mind makes his defense futile. The basic objection to it, of course, is not scientific but philosophical and moral. The missing link is not in the sphere of "how" but in the sphere of "why." Reinforcement cannot be good just because it reinforces; it must have a purpose and worth which the technique alone cannot justify. As a theory without moral principles, behaviorism is even more threatening as new technology, psychosurgery, electric stimulation, and drugs become a reality with serious implications when applied in correctional institutions, clinical settings, and schools. "In the behavioristic view, man can now control his own destiny, because he knows what must be done and how to do it."[11] Man may know "how to do it," but "what must be done" and "why" are different questions, and disturbing ones if the know-how alone justifies the doing in psychology, physics, or any other empirical science. Skinner's behaviorism is offered as an "ideology" claiming not only to know how to teach virtues, but what virtue is. Responding to such a claim, Lawrence Kohlberg writes: "I know that science could teach me nothing as to what virtue is. Science could speak about causal relations, about the relations of means and ends, but it could not speak about ends or values themselves. If I could not define virtue or the ends of moral education could I really offer advice as to means by which virtue should be taught?"[12] This is already an echo of Aquinas' conception of moral formation and the nature of virtue, and could be his own objection to behaviorism. Virtue or a good disposition is meant to make a person good in view of an authentic (ultimate) human goal, which is beyond the empirical competence of positivistic science. To know how does not make a person good, because science and knowledge can be used and abused, as we well know.

Fortunately, there are other currents in contemporary psychology. From our perspective, we can welcome a return to a more introspec-

---

11. Ibid., 277.
12. Kohlberg, *The Philosophy of Moral Development*, 30.

tive and purpose-oriented psychology, as evidenced in the writings of such psychologists as Victor Frankl, Erich Fromm, Erik Erickson, Jean Piaget, and more recently Lawrence Kohlberg. It should be noted that most contemporary liberal education reflects in some way the classical and Christian tradition of a parallel development of knowledge and affection, social responsibility and democratic values, and assumes individual freedom. What is missing in these efforts is the constancy of values, since most of the contemporary liberal systems are based on probability and change rather than on certainty and ultimate principles. This was the defect of Dewey's progressive ideology, which Kohlberg proposes to correct by what he calls "developmental-philosophic strategy." The aim of this strategy is to clarify the meaning and purpose of development as related to both a formal psychological theory and an ethical theory of truth and worth. Kohlberg's study, like that of Piaget, has been mainly with children, since it is in childhood that the formative process begins, although the method has a broader application. Developmental psychology rests on the assumption that the human person is self-agent and capable of perfection. Moral education occurs in stages from an initial hit-and-miss (preconventional stage), through a gradually more patterned, law-and-order conduct (conventional stage) to a responsible and principled response to values in themselves (post-conventional stage). If the beginning, the first stage, is always an experience of values in physical consequences (reward and punishment), the subsequent stages, as the child grows into adolescent and adult, pass through assimilation of the accommodation to the environment, into a mature discernment of values in themselves beyond and above their physical, environmental, and authority support. Kohlberg asserts that the stages of moral development are common to all cultures and that each child goes through the same stages although at different speed. The development, however, can be blocked through lack of proper educational guidance at the earlier stages, so that a person may never reach the stage of moral maturity.

Kohlberg's developmental psychology has the advantage of delineating and interrelating the spheres of psychology and ethics, science, and ideology, so that "the formal standard of cognitive-developmental psychological theory is not itself ultimate but must be elaborated as a set of ethical and epistemological principles and justified by the method of philosophy and of ethics. The distinctive feature of the developmental-philosophic approach is that a philosophic conception of adequate principles is coordinated with a psychological theory of development and with the fact of development."[13] From our perspective, this is a welcome insight into the proper role of psychology in moral formation, as a science of working and development of the mind, not of their purpose. Equally welcome is the assertion of an extrinsic, moral purpose, a "why," as essential to the intrinsic, empirical research, the "how" of psychology. According to Kohlberg, it is the concept, not the content of causality that matters, so that "whether one starts from Kant, Mill, Hare, Ross or Rawls in defining morality, one gets similar research results."[14] The difference among philosophical conceptions of morality is minor, compared with having no principles at all. This, of course, is true for a better psychology; it does not diminish, much less eliminate the importance of having true philosophical principles as well. The distinction between psychological (empirical) research and the ethical principles (goal) is important to put Aquinas' thought into proper perspective. Psychology, its methods and results, are welcome as long as they are scientifically sound and do not usurp the ideological position of moral leadership which is not theirs. This belongs to the study of the ultimate goal of human life, which is the subject of moral science.

In conclusion, we feel that Aquinas' treatise on disposition has its place among the mainstream of contemporary psychology. There is a common assumption of genetic, self-formative, and environmental factors to be considered in the formation of individual character. The emphasis on one or the other varies, and if it becomes exclusive, it distorts the nature and goal of human life. This is true not only in regard to behavioristic emphasis on the environment (reinforcement), but in regard also to those romantic methods of education which take spontaneity and self-formation as sufficient means to true formation. We shall pursue this theme by turning now to the nature, origin, and role of those good dispositions which we call virtues and which make a human person not only competent, but also good.

---

13. Ibid., 85.
14. Ibid., 102.

13

Human Virtue

THERE ARE SEVERAL, BY NOW FAMILIAR, ASSERTIONS WHICH MAKE THE treatise on virtues in general (and subsequently, in the II–II of the *Summa* in particular) a sort of climax of the study of moral principles. The first such assertion is that moral life is the human life itself, unfolding from the natural capacities of understanding and willing into a free and responsible activity. We further asserted that such activity is always for some good and end, and that in the variety and hierarchy of goods and ends, we are naturally open and supernaturally called to an ultimate fulfillment in the vision of God. Although the vision of God is a gratuitous gift, good acts are required by God's providence as our human response to his offer of himself. In this schema, the particular human acts are morally good or bad (through their objects, motives, and circumstances) as they lead to or deviate from the ultimate goal. The proximate and in a sense the first norm for moral evaluation of particular acts in this light is each person's reason or conscience. But given the extrinsic ultimate goal and human sociability, fellowship, as the existential condition of our life and growth with, moreover, the obvious limitations of personal knowledge and will, the subjective reason is naturally subject to an objective moral order stemming from the natural law and ultimately to the wisdom of God or the eternal law as the supreme norm of morality.

Respecting therefore our subjectivity, but conscious of its limitations, we are called to a continuous self-objectification: the formation of conscience in truth and certainty and the will in rightful exercise. This is a long and arduous process, which we call moral growth or the formation of character. While we all possess the basic cognitive and orectic capacities for such a growth, the growth itself does not come instinctively, but through learning and practice. In this way, we create and develop in ourselves dispositions for better understanding and easier acting. It is here that virtues—the good dispositions of the mind—enter into our moral consideration as the final affirmation of the primacy of the agent within the reality of his human fellowship and the divine call.

THE NATURE OF VIRTUE

Etymologically virtue means strength or excellence. It is a disposition in a person. Consequently, what we said about dispositions will apply also to virtues. In fact, we cannot jump into the study of virtues without understanding the psychological and moral phenomenon of dispositions. Virtues, as dispositions, are not seen on a person but only experienced in conduct. Since people have different views of good or bad conduct, they also have different conceptions of virtues. In his book *After Virtue*, Alasdair MacIntyre sums up three different conceptions of virtues he finds in a historical survey from Homer's warriors to Benjamin Franklin's utilitarianism: "a virtue is a quality which enables an individual to discharge his or her social role (Homer); a virtue is a quality which enables an individual to move toward the achievement of the specifically human *telos*, whether natural or supernatural (Aristotle, the New Testament, and Aquinas); a virtue is a quality which has utility in achieving earthly and heavenly success (Franklin).[1] Because of such different accounts, the author states that "there is no single, central, core conception of the virtue which might make a claim for universal allegiance."[2] A similar critique of the conception of virtue, although from a different perspective, comes from Lawrence Kohlberg. He puts the issue between the "cultural transmission" or the "bag of virtues" conception and the "value clarification" approach which, he writes, is the modern equivalent of relativism. The author rejects the cultural transmission or the "bag of virtues" conception as a form of "indoctrination of conventional or social consensus morality," which begs the question, because to make virtues good, we would have to prove that such consensus itself is objectively good. He also rejects the "value clarification" approach (a method suggesting purely an explanation of students' own values) because this too does not question "the

1. MacIntyre, *After Virtue*, 173.
2. Ibidem.

intrinsic worth of these values."[3] Both writers recall Socrates' old question about "what virtue is" and "whether it can be taught," and both seek to uncover a conception of virtue which would guarantee its intrinsic value. This is also one of Aquinas' main purposes.

Unlike the treatise on emotions and dispositions which, in a sense, had to start from scratch, the treatise on virtues had a long tradition in pagan and Christian morality. But the frequent dichotomy between the Christian and pagan lists of virtues and their different conceptions of human values still presented a challenge in the search for a meaning of virtue which would be both human and Christian. There is no systematic treatment of virtues in the Old Testament. The Book of Wisdom enumerates what is known as the four cardinal virtues: "Wisdom . . . teaches temperance and prudence, justice and fortitude" (Wis. 8:7). But the meaning of virtue is implied in biblical thought, particularly in its emphasis on the morality of heart as distinct from external observance. "I will make a new covenant . . . not a covenant I made with their ancestors. Deep within them I will plant my law, writing it on their hearts . . . I will be their God and they will be my people . . . There will be no further need for neighbor to teach neighbor . . . they will all know me . . . (Jer. 31:32–33)." Such internalization of moral value and responsibility is the core of the New Testament, which definitely offers a morality of virtues, especially love (charity), that which gives life to all activity.

The pagan schema of the four cardinal virtues (prudence, justice, fortitude, and temperance) goes back to Aristotle and Plato and was known to the early Fathers of the Church. At the time of St. Ambrose it became an integral part of the Christian moral teaching. To these virtues were added three specifically Christian virtues of faith, hope, and charity, as listed by St. Paul in I Cor. 13:13. In the thirteenth century, they were given the name of theological virtues. These seven virtues provided a useful schema of the teaching of moral theology, especially in the Thomistic tradition.

In developing the concept of human virtue, Aquinas emphasizes three basic conditions: every virtue in order to be an authentically human quality must, at least implicitly, be ordained to the ultimate goal of human life; it must also have its own specific object or area of concern; it must be freely exercised, a *habitus* and not a "habit." Thus, to be just

---

3. Kohlberg, *Philosophy of Moral Development*, 1–3, 33–35.

means to practice justice in view of the total human fulfillment, in the area of a particular concern such as rendering what is due to another, and exercised by choice and not by feeling or instinct. Morality, as we have already indicated, must be total, specific, and free.

Aquinas begins with two definitions of virtue. One is from Aristotle, who calls virtue "that which makes its possessor good and his work good likewise." The second is from St. Augustine: "Virtue is a good quality of mind, by which one lives righteously, of which no one can make bad use, which God works in us without us." In regard to Augustine's definition, Aquinas makes two observations. The first observation suggests that although virtue is a quality, the term *habitus* or disposition (hard to change quality) may be more appropriate as the proximate genus of virtue; the second observation points out that the definition as it stands applies only to the infused virtues. However, if the last phrase, "which God works in us without us" is omitted, the definition applies to all virtues.

There is a very persistent and explicit emphasis throughout Aquinas' treatise on the specifically human quality of virtue: "we are talking about human virtue—*virtus humana*" which perfects specifically human powers and their activity for a specifically human goal. Not just any kind of strength or excellence is a human virtue. Consequently, the entitative dispositions are not true virtues because they are not specifically human and do not guarantee good use. Virtue must be an operative disposition and a good operative disposition, because it is by good acts that we achieve our ultimate goal. "Consequently, human virtue of which we are now speaking cannot belong to what is bodily, but only to what is proper to soul. Human virtue, therefore, does not imply relation to being, but rather to activity. Essentially, then, it is an operative *habitus*."[4]

Since virtues are good, operative qualities of mind, rendering the activity steady, prompt, and pleasurable, they are possible only in those faculties which are not naturally determined to one kind of function but open to alternatives. Such are the reason and will. The sensory faculties of the concupiscible and irascible are subjects of virtue to the extent that they "share in the life of reason which in man is what they are born to do." Two cardinal virtues, fortitude and temperance, are of this kind as "a certain habitual conformity of these powers to reason."

---

4. S.T. I–II, Q. 55, a. 2.

Virtues perfect the human agent acting for a goal, but they do so by perfecting the faculties through which the person acts. There is, therefore, a unity as well as diversity of virtues, reflecting the substantial union of soul and body in one person and different faculties of the soul. Because of such unity, there can be no authentic human virtue unless the person as a whole benefits from it. Although every virtue perfects a specific faculty in a specific area of concern, there is among virtues a unity which stems not only from their common ultimate goal, but also from a certain psychological interaction. This, according to Aquinas, happens in two ways: diffusively or by way of an overflow of perfection of one power into another, and dispositively or by way of preparation. A person, therefore, who is just will also find it easier to become temperate and courageous. Such psychological observation suggests, however, a more radical assertion, namely, that no one can really be virtuous unless he is virtuous in all.

As the substantial union of soul and body lays ground for the unity of virtues, so the diversity of operative faculties lays ground for their distinctiveness. Every virtue is a specific quality of a specific power in a specific area of concern. In practice, this means that morality cannot be vague; it is not enough to seek good and avoid evil in a general way, but such pursuit must be concrete and specific. Human acts are singular. Each power of the soul has its proper object or field of action, and thus every virtue is a specific perfection of that power. Moreover, since virtues perfect a power in all and each of its activities, it follows that wherever there is room for such perfection, there is room for a specific virtue. Thus the intellect must be perfected not only to understand better, but also to draw the right conclusions and make good practical judgments; similarly, the will must be disposed to love not only God, but also other people, parents, and country, and respect the rights of all. Courage and temperance cover the danger of death and the difficult areas of food and sex, but there are other demands to be met, demands of magnanimity, perseverance, tolerance, and modesty, each with its own glitter, yet all united in pursuit of the human good.

INTELLECTUAL VIRTUES

The traditional classification of virtues lists three major groups: the intellectual, the moral or cardinal, and the theological virtues, which are the gospel dimension to the classical and natural dispositions. Other classifications have been used as well, notably the distinction between the natural and supernatural or acquired and infused virtues, according as they are the result of voluntary exercise or bestowed by God's grace and ordained to a natural or supernatural end.

The intellectual virtues are of two kinds: those perfecting the speculative and those perfecting the practical intellect. Perfecting the speculative intellect are understanding, knowledge, and wisdom; perfecting the practical intellect are art and prudence. The distinction, of course, comes from Aristotle, embodied in the scholastic frame of mind. It makes sense, as we hope to show. We may know things for the sake of knowledge, and we may know in order to do something. The role of the speculative intellect is to know the truth. This comes to mind in two ways: grasping the principles, which is helped by understanding, and learning through inquiry and conclusions, which constitutes knowledge or science. Such inquiry may be in one or another area of interest, as for instance the science of physics or biology. It may also be done by going beyond the particular causes in search of an ultimate cause or principle of all existence, in view of an ultimate purpose which is the role of wisdom. One must have a metaphysical frame of mind to be comfortable with this schema. However, it does not take much to see that we would all feel more comfortable if our great physicists and biologists were also wise men.

Continuing his analysis, Aquinas focuses on another distinction important for the understanding of true human virtues, the distinction, namely, between the perfection of competence and that of use. "Since every virtue is ordained to some good . . ., a disposition . . . may be called a virtue for two reasons: first, because it gives the capability of functioning well; secondly, because together with this, it effectively ensures a right performance. This last condition . . . is realized only in those dispositions which affect the appetitive part of the soul, since it is the soul's appetitive power which brings to execution the intentions of all the powers and dispositions."[5] The virtues of speculative intellect provide competence, but they do not assure the good use of it and therefore fall short of perfect human virtue. In this regard Aquinas is critical of Socrates' position that knowledge is virtue and ignorance vice and would be equally critical of those modern educational theories which reduce morality to intelligence and consider knowledge as the sole factor in formation of character.

---

5. S.T. I–II, Q. 57, a. 1.

Reason, indeed, is the first principle for all human acts, and all other principles obey reason in some way. But the way they obey makes a difference. The members of the body, provided they are healthy, obey blindly, as I can move my hand any way I want. The appetitive faculties do not obey blindly, but with a certain contrariness. If all faculties obeyed the reason blindly, the intellectual virtues would suffice for all human activity. "This was the opinion of Socrates, who said every virtue is a kind of prudence" and "maintained that as long as a man possessed knowledge, he could not sin, and that everyone who sinned did so through ignorance."[6] This, writes Aquinas in the same article, is based on a false supposition of blind obedience and is contrary to moral experience: "For a man to act well, it is requisite that not only his reason be well disposed through a habitus of intellectual virtue, but also that his appetite be well disposed through a *habitus* of moral virtue."

ART AND PRUDENCE

The meaning of *virtus humana* is further illustrated by the distinction between art and prudence in the practical intellect. Art (the word must be taken in the broad sense of skill and craftsmanship) is a virtue, but a virtue of competence rather than good use as "an artist as such is not commendable for the will with which he makes a work, but for its quality."[7] Although a practical disposition, art is no different from speculative virtues." Art has the nature of a virtue in the same way as the speculative dispositions have. Namely, neither art nor a speculative disposition makes a good work with regard to a man's using it. The disposition, which is the distinctive function of a virtue perfecting the appetite, and again art, "falls short of the notion of perfect virtue, because it does not ensure the good use of what it produces, for which something further is required, although there cannot be a good use without a good art."[8] Knowledge, therefore, is a condition of human act, but not sufficient to ensure a morally good act. A person may be a skilled worker, a competent physician, or a brilliant writer, yet a bad person. We may say, therefore, that virtue in a true sense does not exist except when the will engages in the pursuit of true human good. This indicates, once again, that moral formation, no

6. S.T. I–II, Q. 58, a. 2.
7. S.T. I–II, Q. 57, a. 3.
8. S.T. I–II, Q. 57, a. 3 ad 1.

matter how progressive and psychologically sound, cannot avoid the issue of the ultimate meaning of human life.

If knowledge does not ensure moral goodness, can we say that goodness does not need knowledge? Can the simple and ignorant be good persons? We know that they can, according to the words of Jesus who blessed his Father "Lord of heaven and earth for hiding these things from the learned and the clever and revealing them to mere children" (Mt. 11:25). To be morally good, a person does not need to be learned. He must, however, have some knowledge, which is always a condition of human responsibility. Those who do not possess such knowledge by themselves should be wise to listen to the counsel of others: these "if they have grace, take counsel within themselves to the extent at least of recognizing their dependence, and of being able to discern good advice from bad."[9]

The use of competence is the concern of prudence, which for that reason is a true human virtue. The Scholastics distinguished between "producing" (*facere*) and "doing" (*agere*). "The reason for the difference is that art is right judgement about things to be made [*recta ratio factibilium*], while prudence is rectified judgement about things to be done [*recta ratio agibilium*].... Consequently, prudence, which is right reason about things to be done, requires that a man be rightly disposed with regard to ends; and this depends on the rightness of his appetite. Consequently, moral virtue, which makes the appetite right is a precondition of prudence." Art perfects the product; prudence perfects the agent. An artist can refuse to use his talents; a prudent man cannot refuse to be prudent. "Hence art does not presuppose rightness of appetite. As a consequence more praise is given to a craftsman who deliberately violates the rules of his craft than to one who does so unwillingly, whereas a willed mistake is more opposed to prudence than one unwilled."[10]

How free an artist is in his artistic creativity is an important moral and aesthetical question. On the one hand we must accept that art has a value in itself, the value of the beautiful, which we admire and enjoy. A good liturgy, a concert of spiritual music, a film of Christ's life and passion, can do as much and, perhaps, more good than reading a spiritual and theological discourse. On the other hand, the beautiful cannot be separated from the wholeness of the human person. The slogan "art for

9. S.T. II–II, Q. 47, a. 14 ad 2.
10. S.T. I–II, Q. 57, a. 4.

art's sake" is, therefore, valid only to a certain point. It is valid when it stands for the respect of the original contribution the art makes to human well-being and enjoyment; it loses such validity when it violates moral wholeness. In the last sentence the slogan "art for art's sake" may not be different from the slogan "physics for physics' sake," although we may be more liberal and indulgent to poets, sculptors, and movie producers than to the nuclear physicists in pursuing their skill. The principle is the same and it takes us back to the issue of indifferent acts.

Aquinas' morality is a morality of virtues, and among the virtues prudence has a leading role as the virtue of conscience. Its role is to mediate between the contingent means and a given end, not just by way of isolated, act-oriented decisions, but as a permanent disposition, making such decisions the result of a sound moral formation.

MORAL VIRTUES

Unlike the purely intellectual virtues which give competence but do not assure the good use of it, moral virtues are meant to assure the good use and thus the goodness of the agent and his work. Since prudence is such a virtue, and indeed, the underlying virtue of the entire moral life, at least on the natural level, it seems appropriate to begin our inquiry of moral virtues by expanding a little further our understanding of prudence. Aristotle defines prudence as "virtue of practical reason directing human activity according to the truth." Prudence is, therefore, an authentic human virtue because it assures a good use of intelligence in the pursuit of a true human goal, evaluating particular situations in the light of universal principles. It is a virtue because it stands for a permanent disposition to make such an evaluation as different situations arise and to make them with ease, promptness, and joy. As a virtue, it is the result not only of the natural understanding of the first principles common to all humans, such as that good is to be done and evil avoided, or even of individual intellectual endowment which may vary from person to person, but also of learning and experience and ultimately of God's gift of counsel. In the treatise on prudence (II–II, QQ. 47–56), which, as we already indicated, supplements the short consideration of conscience, Aquinas offers a comprehensive network of conditions, acts, and kinds of prudence. Conditions, also called integral parts of a virtue, are certain qualities which are necessary for the exercise of prudence. Such are memory of the past, learning from mistakes, insights into the principles, teachableness or docility (as one person cannot know everything), acumen, imagination and foresight, circumspection, and even caution "since the world is full of traps and hazards."

A person is prudent when he acts prudently. The principal act of prudence is the command that something be done. It is preceded by judgment and counsel or deliberation, since no reasonable command can be given without right judgment and due deliberation. Prudence implies all three acts, yet in practice people may be defective in one or all of them. There are people who take no time in deliberating and others who can never make up their minds or bring themselves to act. In moral formation, it is important to know where the problem lies. The three acts of prudence are so important that classical literature on the subject assigned them their own special dispositions called the potential parts of prudence. Potential parts or affiliated virtues are qualities in which the full and strict meaning of a cardinal virtue is not fulfilled. Such potential parts are in the case of prudence: *eubulia*, virtue of good counsel; *synesis*, the virtue of common sense, and *gnomen*, which stands for a sense of the exceptional or situations not covered by ordinary norm. It sometimes happens, writes Aquinas, "that something has to be done which is not covered by the ordinary rules of conduct, such as when we should not return a deposit entrusted to us by a would-be attacker of our country or some other such case. We ought, therefore, to judge matters of this kind by certain principles higher than the ordinary rules followed by sound judgement. They call for a corresponding superior virtue of judiciousness, and this is called gnomen, which implies a certain sharp-sightedness of judgement."[11]

Other ramifications of prudence are its subjective parts or kinds based on the fact that different responsibilities call for different kinds of prudence. Aristotle's list of lawmaking, executive, domestic, and military prudence is only a typology of a much greater variety. Indeed, "wherever in human affairs you find a special kind of ruling and commanding there also you find a special kind of prudence."[12] Consequently, there is not only a legislative, political, and military prudence, but also professional prudence of priests, doctors, educators, parents, and other professions, and prudence as required in some, as in adults, may not be so required

---

11. S.T. I–II, Q. 59, a. 5.
12. S.T. I–II, Q. 50, a. 1.

in teenagers. Yet in all these instances, prudence is always a virtue which makes a person good not as a specialist but as a human person. It is true that "the children of this world" may be "more astute in dealing with their own kind than are the children of light," but this is only in their own kind. Aquinas refers to this when he asks whether there can be prudence in sinners. There is a false prudence when a person "contrives fitting means to a wrong end," or even when the end is good yet "not the universal end for the whole human life, but the end for some specialized employment, as for instance, when a man versed in the method of commerce or navigation is called a prudent trader or sailor . . ." The genuine and complete prudence is the one which "with a view to the final good for the whole human life, rightly deliberates, decides and commands. This alone is prudence pure and simple, and in sinners it just cannot be."[13]

With this understanding of prudence, we may now speak of moral virtues in general. Whenever we talk of virtues, we ordinarily mean moral virtues and rightly so; the intellectual virtues, as we explained, perfect competence. Prudence perfects the application or the act of specification in commanding what is to be done. The act of exercise, the actual doing or not doing, remains the autonomous sphere of the will which, for that reason, needs its own perfection. This perfection comes from moral virtues as "dispositions of choosing the means appointed by reason as a prudent man would discern it." The purpose of moral virtues is to dispose the will in its function to move itself and other powers subject to it to do promptly, firmly, and joyfully what is specified by reason to be done against internal and external opposition. The perfection of moral virtues manifests itself in choosing the right means for the right end as "a prudent man" would discern it. We say "a prudent man" rather than "the prudent man" because prudence, as all other moral virtues, is open ended. We do not really know what to be absolutely prudent and just means; we only try to discern and decide the best we can in a given situation: how to best use the material wealth, pleasures, honors, and other things in view of our ultimate goal. A person who takes his chances on wealth, power, or a few moments of gratification is not a prudent person, but neither is the one who suppresses what one's body truly needs or his social status demands.

We already indicated that dispositions are different from emotions, although the distinction is not always easy to grasp. Yet, in the case of

13. S.T. I–II, Q. 47, a. 3.

virtues this becomes obvious. Emotions are movements of the sensory appetite; acts which come and go. Virtues are qualities of the mind which remain and are used at will. Emotions are in themselves morally neutral and good or bad only in terms of accord or discord with reason; virtues are always good or else they are not what we mean by virtue. To be virtuous, nevertheless, does not mean to be emotionless. Still, a distinction must be made between inordinate emotions, which impair the use of reason, and emotions which support it. Emotions are compatible with virtues and those virtues which, like courage and temperance, are concerned with passions, as their proper matter cannot exist apart from them. "The reason for this is that otherwise moral virtue would make the sensitive appetite idle. It is not, however, the function of virtue to deprive the powers subordinate to reason of their proper activities, but to have them execute the command of reason by exercising their proper acts." Even justice which is not concerned with passions is not necessarily emotionless. The joy of justice which results in the will "spreads through the fullness of justice . . . into the sensitive appetite. . . . By reason of this kind of overflow, therefore, the more perfect a virtue is, the more it causes passion."[14]

CARDINAL VIRTUES

In addition to being different from the intellectual virtues and emotions, moral virtues are also distinct among themselves. The distinction may best be introduced by the traditional list of four cardinal virtues: prudence, justice, fortitude, and temperance. Etymologically, the word *cardo* means a device on which a thing turns or moves, like the hinge of a door, suggesting that the four cardinal virtues are called so because the entire moral life hinges on them. Sometimes we hear objections to such preeminence of the cardinal virtues within the Christian context, arguing that Christian morality hinges rather on the theological virtues of faith, hope, and charity. This is quite true, but the theological virtues are of different order. "The theological virtues are above man. . . . Hence they should properly be called not human but superhuman or divine virtues."[15] Aquinas' observation suggests a distinction between "being in" and "getting in." Theological virtues unite us with God as being already in with

14. S.T. I–II, Q. 59, a. 5.
15. S.T. I–II, Q. 61, a. 1 ad 2.

him, since God becomes the direct object of our moral life. Unfortunately, most of us are still on the way, the "viatores," struggling to get in by overcoming our natural imperfections and obstacles. This gives the cardinal virtues their fundamental role.

There are two reasons why the traditional list of four cardinal virtues makes sense; both are based on the principle that virtue is a good quality which makes a person good and his work good as well. The first reason is that virtue perfects a power, and there are four principal powers of the soul's operation: reason, will, concupiscible, and irascible. "The formal principle of virtue of which we now speak is value in accord with reason. This can be considered in two ways. First, as lying in a judgment of reason; in this way, there is one principal virtue, called prudence. Secondly, according as reason puts its order into something else, either into what we do, and then we have justice, or into what we feel, and then we need two virtues. For the need to put the rule of reason into our emotions rises from their resistance to reason. This is twofold. They may incite us to something against reason, and so need a curb, which we name temperance. Or they may make us shirk a course of action to be steadfast and not run away from what is right: and for this courage is named."[16]

A second reason is that in every area of human activity, there is always one which is the most fundamental and most difficult. Thus, in regard to the specification of moral good, the most important and difficult is to give the right command which is the proper act of prudence. Deliberation and judgment, although integral parts of it, fall short of this fullness. In regard to justice, the most fundamental objective is to be just in a strict sense of duty on the basis of equality, without which we cannot claim to be generous, grateful, or charitable. There is a similar priority in temperance and courage. The most difficult areas of emotional control are the pleasure of touch (food and sex), the object of temperance, and the danger of death which is the proper object of courage.

CLASSIFICATION AND CHARACTERISTICS OF MORAL VIRTUES

Earlier in this chapter, we said that in developing the meaning of *virtus humana*, Aquinas stresses three basic conditions: every virtue must implicitly aim at the ultimate human goal; it must be specific, namely

16. S.T. I–II, Q. 61, a. 2.

perfecting a specific power and/or a specific area of concern; and it must be exercised freely as a *habitus* and not "habit." We summed up these conditions by stating that human morality must be total and specific and that wherever there is a special need or difficulty in human activity, there is room for a specific virtue. Although the human agent is one person in whom all virtues converge, and to be morally good one must be good in all, nevertheless, there are distinct powers and different areas of strength and weakness. This accounts for a comprehensive, although by no means exhaustive, network of moral virtues founded on the four cardinal virtues. The classification of virtues has its limits, but it may also have its usefulness, defining specific needs and priorities in moral formation. The network consists of four groups: the cardinal virtues and their integral, subjective, and potential parts. An example has already been given in the case of prudence. As a cardinal virtue, prudence deals with the most important act, which is the command. But to give the right command, or to be prudent, there are certain conditions which are called the integral parts of prudence, such as memory, foresight, docility, perceptibility, etc. We also saw that prudence may differ, according to different people and their responsibilities. This accounts for the subjective parts or kinds of prudence, such as parental, political, administrative, or professional prudence. Finally, there are dispositions perfecting one or another aspect of prudence, such as good counsel (*eubulia*) for deliberation, and good sense (*synesis*) and sense of exception (*gnomen*) for judgment.

We may illustrate the same network in regard to justice which, after prudence, is the leading moral virtue. Justice perfects the operation of the will, whose object is the human good. There is no need of disposition in pursuing one's own good, since this comes naturally, although a discernment of true good through prudence is always necessary. But to will the same good to another person and to share it within a community does not come naturally. It is the role of justice to perfect the will's sense of duty and equality in human society which, as we said many times, is the existential condition of human existence and progress. The meaning of the cardinal virtue of justice is to ensure social cooperation on the basis of equality and strict duty. To exercise justice, we need the mental preparation of doing good and avoiding evil, not as just a general moral principle, but as the basis of our social relations (the golden rule), which may properly be called the conditions of justice or its integral parts. The traditional morality speaks of three kinds of justice: commutative, distributive, and legal justice. Commutative justice deals with rights and duties among equal partners, e.g., contracts, work, and wages. Distributive justice regulates apportionment of burdens and benefits, equal rights, and a general protection of the individual in a society. Some new issues appeared in recent decades pertaining to distributive justice, especially in the area of limited resources, affirmative action, and organ transplants in hospitals. If only one kidney becomes available, who may receive it?

Among the kinds of justice, legal justice holds preeminence as the virtue which ordains the individual to the common good. "That justice which seeks the common good is a distinct virtue from the one which is directed to the private good of an individual; just as public law differs from private law."[17] It is unfortunate that legal justice which, in the mind of Aquinas is, we believe, an open-ended justice of the common good (*bene vivere humanum*) became identified subsequently with a legalistic or "state justice" and reduced to the issues of paying taxes and fulfilling similar obligations toward a government. In response to this limitation, as well as to new social and international demands of justice which cannot be met by our juridical structures nor left to charitable actions, the contemporary social encyclicals speak of "social justice" as the most excellent virtue of social relations, and a universal common good. In a debate which issued from the meaning of this new kind of justice in relation to the traditional triad, it is interesting to note that one author, Jeremiah Newman, argues that "social justice" is, in fact, a revival of Aquinas' legal justice, distorted in the era of absolutism, when the scholastic common good of Christendom became identified with the nation-state. The question of justice is, of course, a subject by itself, which we cannot expand in our present study.

Justice is a virtue which renders to each his due on the basis of equality. We know, however, that obligation and equality vary. The way we owe something in a business contract differs from the way we owe things in families and communities, and restitution for damage may differ from a thanks for a favor. There are, therefore, potential parts of justice: social virtues affiliated to justice, perfecting our relationship in areas where a strict justice does not apply for either a lack of equality or a strict obligation. Among these virtues we find religion (not as faith, but as a natural obligation of worship), piety and patriotism, obedience, gratitude, lib-

---

17. S.T. I-II, Q. 60, a. 3.

erality, friendliness, and equity. A similar set of virtues is affiliated with fortitude and temperance. The concern of the cardinal virtue of fortitude or courage is the danger of death. Since this is a very specific concern, it does not really call for subjective parts or kinds of courage. However, a series of virtues, such as confidence, magnificence, patience, and endurance may be considered both the integral parts of fortitude when they serve as a mental preparation in facing the death and affiliated virtues when concerned with their own specific difficulties, such as endurance in sickness and persecution, magnificence in donations, or patience in suffering. Temperance is concerned with pleasure of food and sex. Consequently, there are kinds of temperance, such as fasting, abstinence, sobriety, chastity, and conditions like the sense of honor and sensitivity to shame. There are also affiliated virtues dealing with other areas of pleasures and temptations, such as continence to keep sensory desires in check, humility to counteract ambitions, and clemency moderating our feelings of outrage and desire for punishment.

Some characteristics and questions concerning virtues in general have already been anticipated in our discussion of dispositions. The most important question is: how do we become virtuous? While there are some natural character predispositions, moral virtues, nevertheless, are mainly acquired by our actions, with the help of educators, Church, society, and God's grace. As dispositions, they grow extensively and intensively, although moral virtues grow primarily intensively, since as virtues they are meant to cover their entire field of concern. One cannot be truly just unless he is just to everyone, although he can become more just to all.

Virtues are also infused by God. Aquinas believes that this is true not only for theological virtues, but also for the natural virtues which we can strengthen by prayer and sacraments. The reason is that their final aim, too, is God as our ultimate goal and therefore must be proportionate to it. "The theological virtues are enough to shape us to our supernatural end as a start, that is to God himself immediately and to none other. Yet the soul needs also to be equipped by infused virtues in regard to created things, though as subordinate to God."[18]

Two characteristics of virtues may appropriately conclude our survey: the mean of virtues and their connection or unity. The mean of virtue is the balance between the extremes of too much or too little of things

18. S.T. I–II, Q. 63, a. 3 ad 2.

we need or want as determined by prudence (*medium rationis*). A suppression of all sensitive pleasure may be as harmful as overindulgence. Justice is a particular case, because the mean is not only rational but also factual (*medium rei*). The measure of restitution or just wage depends not only on our judgment, but also on what the rights and duties are. We may recall our discussion on the morality of external acts, which applies in this case.

The mean of virtue must not be confused with mediocrity. Perfection of the agent, which is the aim of virtues, is unfinished until, in the words of the gospel, we become perfect as our heavenly Father is perfect. With this in view, the rational mean (*medium rationis*) may be substituted by a higher norm, namely the law of love of God, in which case what may seem an extreme in human terms, e.g., perpetual virginity, becomes a more excellent virtue. On the other hand, however, one may be immoderate not only in regard to moral virtues, but in his intellectual ambitions, where truth is measured by the conformity to things and even in matters of theological virtues. This may happen not because we can ever believe in or love God too much, but by doing so in a wrong way. "There is nothing commendable," writes Aquinas, "in making public confession of one's faith, if it were to cause a disturbance among unbelievers without any benefit either to faith or the faithful."[19]

The connection or unity of virtues has been questioned as a convincing argument, as for instance, by Alasdair MacIntyre in his already quoted and excellent book, *After Virtue*. But the author puts his finger on the real problem, not only with regard to this particular question, but as to the meaning of virtue in general for the contemporary mind in two important reflections. He writes: "Any contemporary attempt to envisage each human life as a whole, as a unity, whose character provides the virtues with an adequate *telos* encounters two different kinds of obstacles: one is social and one philosophical"; social "from the way in which modernity partitions each human life into a variety of segments, each with its own norms and modes of behavior," and philosophical "from distinct tendencies, one chiefly, though not only, domesticated in analytical philosophy and one at home in both sociological theory and in existentialism."[20] In a second reflection, he states: "What is abundantly clear is that in everyday

19. S.T. II–II, Q. 3, a. 2 ad 3.
20. MacIntyre, *After Virtue*, 190.

life as in moral philosophy, the replacement of Aristotelian or Christian teleology by a definition of the virtues in terms of the passions is not so much or at all the replacement of one set of criteria by another, but rather a movement towards and into a situation where there are no longer any clear criteria."[21] To us this suggests that the problem, if there is one, with accepting Aquinas' conception of *virtus humana* is not its nature, definition, and characteristics, but the meaning and unity of the human life which virtues are meant to perfect. The fact is, indeed, that a person may be courageous to the point of sacrificing his life and lack every other good quality. But such courage is imperfect from the perspective of the totality of moral life, in view of the ultimate human goal. Isolated from other good qualities which are also needed, such courage alone cannot take us where we are supposed to go.

True and perfect virtues are therefore connected, not only by their moral interaction, since "there can be no prudence which is not temperate, just and brave," or justice which is not prudent, temperate, and brave, but also and primarily by charity "which directs man to his last end." Here is Aquinas' theological touch on moral virtues, and it is indispensable. It is analogous to his conception of imperfect and perfect happiness. As there is a natural, imperfect happiness, although people may argue about what it is, so also there are natural virtues, and a person may excel in one without having another. But besides these natural qualities, there are perfect virtues of those who have already achieved a likeness to God: "these are called the virtues of an already purified spirit. And then prudence sees only the things of God; temperance knows no earthly desires; courage is immune from passion; and justice, by imitating the divine mind, is united thereto in an everlasting covenant. Such are the virtues of the blessed, or, in this life, of those who are at the summit of perfection."[22]

---

21. Ibid., 219.
22. S.T. I–II, Q. 61, a. 5.

14

The Supernatural Dimension of Morality

IN THE BRIEF PROLOGUE TO *SUMMA THEOLOGIAE* I–II, QUESTION 55, ON virtues in general, Aquinas announces that he will now speak "of virtues and other matters connected with them, namely the Gifts, the Beatitudes and the Fruits of the Holy Spirit." These "other matters" connected with virtues are not just an appendix to the great moral themes which we discussed, but an integral part of the Christian moral life and an open invitation to every human being. Already in the treatise on virtues in general, we found a certain shift from a purely natural and rational to a more spiritual and supernatural basis of morality. Thus, the notion of virtue is more fully realized in the infused virtues, because God is more directly involved both as their immediate cause and their end. They are "more divine" than either the intellectual or the acquired moral virtues. Once again, the reason for this is the paramount role in human life of the ultimate goal and the fact that the ultimate goal is the vision of God: a gratuitous gift, yet naturally desired and humanly merited. At no time, therefore, do we renounce the natural power of reason and will; freedom is never threatened, and responsibility is never abandoned. Moreover, there is always a natural human goal: the "imperfect" humanistic and philosophic happiness, in principle within the intellectual and moral possibilities of man, although not without the help of God, the sovereign first cause of the natural order as well. But God proposes a new dimension of human goal, not in contradiction but in fulfillment of our natural aspirations. It is, nonetheless, a distinct goal, which puts our entire life on a different footing and transforms the natural goals themselves. The supernaturalness of this new moral opening does not make our natural powers automatically proportionate to it. To the act of creation God, therefore, added the act of sanctification through the redemption accomplished by Jesus Christ.

What gradually emerges from our analysis of moral principles is a disproportion between our natural powers by which we act and God giving himself as the ultimate object of our activity. No matter how great we become morally by ourselves, we still need God's own action to make us great in his eyes. It is because of such a disproportion, stated in our opening chapter on the ultimate end, that our thinking leads us towards a more spiritual and supernatural foundation of morality. In this regard, we begin to understand the place of prayer, worship and especially of the sacraments in our moral development. In discussing the Christian perspective on happiness, we suggested that Christian morality is not a sectarian ethical system, but an authentic call for and answer to the universal desire for a complete happiness. Concluding, as Aquinas does, the treatise on fundamental moral principles, with the infused theological virtues and the gifts of the Holy Spirit, he confirms once again his position by integrating what is sometimes called "the spiritual moral theology" into a normal moral progress open to all.

THEOLOGICAL VIRTUES

The theological tradition speaks of three specifically Christian virtues: faith, hope, and charity. In the *Summa*, as in the theological curricula, they enjoy a preeminence among the theological subjects; in the pastoral care, they are the core of preaching and ministry. A reemphasis in contemporary theology on such scriptural and spiritual foundation of morality is, therefore, a welcome development. From our perspective of the unity of human life, such development, however, is neither contrary to nor separate from the natural and rational components of morality. A good Christian must begin by being a good man or woman: faithful in small things before being entrusted with greater. Aquinas describes such unfolding of the natural into the supernatural, as follows:

> A person is perfected by virtues towards those actions by which he is directed towards happiness ... Yet man's happiness or felicity is twofold.... One is proportionate to human nature, and this he can reach through his own resources. The other, a happiness surpassing his nature, he can attain only by the power of God, by a kind

of participation of the Godhead; thus it is written that by Christ we are made partakers of the divine nature. Because such happiness goes beyond the reach of human nature, the inborn resources by which a man is able to act well according to his capacity are not adequate to direct him to it. And so, to be sent to this supernatural happiness, he must needs be divinely endowed with some additional sources of activity: their role is like that of his native capabilities which direct him, not, of course, without God's help, to his connatural end. Such sources of action are called theological virtues.[1]

Self-transcendence is an inborn human ambition whether it is expressed in technology, heroism, mysticism, or just a new record in sport and production. The greatest moral ambition offered in the gospel is to be perfect as God is perfect. The natural virtues help us to restore the image of God in us only partially; the theological virtues take us into his intimacy, transforming our human powers into a supernatural force. Although the natural virtues, too, must at least implicitly be related to the ultimate goal in order to be authentic human virtues, they do so through their own specific objects of being prudent, just, temperate, etc. "The object of theological virtues . . . is God himself, the last end of all things, as surpassing the knowledge of our reason, whereas the object of intellectual and moral virtues is something our reason can comprehend."[2] Faith and hope mark the beginning of a new relationship with God, a relationship of trust; charity complements both faith and hope. Faith is the first condition Christ expected to find; charity is the greatest commandment he gave. In charity, the lover is united with the Beloved. Faith and hope will cease, but charity remains. In order of value, therefore, "charity comes before faith and hope, because both faith and hope come alive through charity, and receive from charity their full stature as virtues." So does the entire moral life because "charity is the mother and the root of all the virtues, inasmuch as it is the form of them all."[3]

The theological virtues have most of the characteristics of the natural virtues: they are good dispositions which cannot be misused; they perfect the operation of the soul; they are freely exercised; they can increase and decrease, not in themselves, since they are a gift, but in their application

1. S.T. I–II, Q. 62, a. 1.
2. S.T. I–II, Q. 62, a. 2.
3. S.T. I–II, Q. 62, a. 4.

as our response to God's call. They are different from the natural virtues, in the sense that they give the possibility to act supernaturally, but not the dispositional facility on the natural level. Such facility is our response to grace in the words of 2 Peter, 1:4–8: "By his divine power, he has given to us all the things that we need for life and for true devotion, bringing us to know God himself, who has called us by his own glory and goodness. In making these gifts, he has given us the guarantee of something very great and wonderful to come: through them you will be able to share the divine nature and to escape corruption in a world that is sunk in vice. But to attain this, you will have to do your utmost yourselves, adding goodness to your understanding, patience to your self-control, true devotion to your patience, kindness towards your fellow man to your devotion, and to this kindness, love."

There is an important corollary to this "distinction in unity" of the natural and the supernatural morality. It tells us that through faith, hope, and charity our human efforts and commitments receive a new and formally distinct value and that a materially identical humanitarian and social action of a believer and unbeliever is still formally different. This, we believe, is the meaning of the Vatican II *Document on Laity*, when it states that the Christian "apostolate is carried on through the faith, hope and charity which the Holy Spirit diffuses in the hearts of all members of the Church."[4] Such an apostolate is not only a unique contribution to human welfare, but a supernatural cooperation in the redemption of the world.

THE GIFTS OF THE HOLY SPIRIT

A rather brief reference to the gifts of the Holy Spirit in this section of the Summa must not obscure Aquinas' deep attachment to the theology of the gifts and their profound significance as the concluding dimension of morality.[5] In salvation history, the Spirit is the Father's final redemptive gift given on the day of Pentecost: the principle of an entirely new relationship with God and with one another within our human fellowship. Prefigured in the Old Testament as the breath of life, the wind that blows,

---

4. Vatican Council II, *Decree on the Apostolate of the Laity*, n. 3.

5. Parallel texts may be consulted, especially Aquinas' *Commentary on Isaiah*, 2; *Commentary on Galatians*, 5: 6, and *Commentary on the Sentences*, L. 3, D. 34, q. 1, a. I. For the contemporary relevance of Aquinas' theology of the Gifts, see Kelly, "The Gifts of the Spirit."

the spirit that allowed the internalization of the law, the gift of the Holy Spirit is the fruit of Christ's promise and his resurrection.

There are at least two distinct references to the working of the Holy Spirit in the New Testament. One is a general presence of the Spirit in the faithful, the gift which makes us the adopted sons of God: "the Spirit that cries 'Abba, Father'" (Gal. 4: 6). Then there are the charismatic gifts St. Paul speaks of in 1 Cor. 12:4–11: "the gift of preaching and wisdom . . . preaching instruction . . . the gift of faith . . . healing . . . miracles . . . prophecy . . . the gift of recognizing spirits . . . the gift of tongues and the ability to interpret them. All these are the work of the one and the same Spirit, who distributes different gifts to different people just as he chooses." On the basis of such scriptural sources, the Fathers of the Church and early theologians developed the idea that the Spirit is the gift of God in us, as he is the substantial gift of the Father to the Son and of the Son to the Father in the Trinity. St. Augustine held that the Spirit proceeded by love as the Son does by intelligence, and Peter Lombard identified the gift of the Spirit with charity."[6] Aquinas accepts the idea but finds it incomplete. In his view, it is not enough that the Spirit be given; the recipient must also be adaptable to such giving. The infused virtues of faith, hope, and charity begin such adaptability, but they are not sufficient to bridge the gap between the human and the divine: they are still "our virtues" and causing "our activity." To be perfect as God is perfect, our activity, indeed life, must in a sense cease to be human and become divine in the words of St. Paul: "It is no longer I who live, but Christ who lives in me" (Gal. 2:20). The gifts of the Holy Spirit, according to Aquinas, make this change as "*habitus* by which man is perfected so as to obey the Holy Spirit readily."[7] He supports his theology from the text of Isaiah: "On him the Spirit of the Lord rests, a spirit of wisdom and insight, a spirit of counsel and power, a spirit of knowledge and of the fear of the Lord" (Is. 11: 2). He also sees a parallel in the Greek philosophical conception of enthusiasm, divine instinct, divine possession, and the heroic. The argument holds that in order to achieve the supernatural goal, we must not only be habitually disposed to do good, but disposed also to let God do good in us.

The gifts of the Holy Spirit are, therefore, dispositions, the character-forming qualities, yet distinct from other dispositions including the in-

---

6. Bouyer, "Gifts of the Holy Spirit."
7. S.T. I–II, Q. 68, a. 3.

fused virtues, however subtle such a distinction must remain. Without it, observes Aquinas, we could not explain why in the Scripture, fear is a gift but not a virtue. Other theological suggestions, such as that the gifts perfect the reason and virtues the will, or that gifts are against temptations and virtues to do good, are equally unacceptable to Aquinas. His position is that, first, there must be a distinction, fear being an argument in point, and second, that if there is a distinction, there must be a reason for it. The reason is given in the Scripture itself, which speaks not in terms of gifts but in terms of spirits, "in distinguishing the Gifts from the virtues, we ought to follow Scripture's own way of speaking. There they are spoken of as spirits rather than gifts" and the meaning of spirits is breath, life, movement, or a wind. They are a movement from without as the reason is a movement from within: the wind which blows where it wills (Jn. 3: 7). Here is how Aquinas develops his thought: "Now it is evident that whatever is moved must necessarily be proportionate to that which moves it. Moreover, the perfection of the mobile, in so far as it is mobile, is the disposition by which it is disposed to be moved well by that which moves it. Hence, the higher the mover, the more perfect must be the disposition by which the mobile is proportioned to it. Thus, a student needs to be more perfectly disposed in order to receive a more profound doctrine from his teacher. Now it is evident that the human virtues perfect man in so far as it is his nature to be moved by reason in the things he does, both interiorly and exteriorly. There must, therefore, be still higher perfection in man to dispose him to be moved by God. These perfections are called Gifts, not only because they are infused by God, but also because they dispose man to become readily mobile to divine inspiration, as is said in Isaiah, the Lord opened my ear; I do not contradict him, I did not pull back. Likewise, Aristotle says that it is not good for those who are moved by a divine prompting to take counsel according to human reason."[8]

This new possession of the lover by the Beloved is not limiting but liberating, since God does not destroy his creation. It is, to paraphrase Kohlberg's stages of development, the "post-human stage" of the human development. On this level, we become divinely prudent, "hungry for justice," courageous and temperate beyond all fear and temptation in the realization of our Christian vocation. It is characteristic that in discussing the virtues in particular Aquinas always concludes with their correspond-

8. S.T. I–II, Q. 68, a. 1.

ing gift, suggesting that when our resources are at an end, the Spirit takes over. We act no more *modo humano* but *modo divino*, by a divine instinct and feeling. Thus, it is not only the origin and object that are divine, as in the case of the infused virtues, but the way, the *modus operandi* as well: we not only cooperate with God's grace; the grace acts in us. We are finally efficiently free to embrace the only necessary good: God. Our deepest yearning to live "beyond our means" is fulfilled. We have reached the spiritual height of Christian morality: the "spiritual man" who finds God in faith and finding him he loves him, in loving him he relies on him and in relying on him, he gives himself entirely to him.

Yet this height of Christian morality is not a spiritual luxury reserved to a few mystics, although not all of us reach it. Unlike the charismatic gifts which are given for a particular service, the gifts of the Holy Spirit are "necessary for salvation." God perfects human reason with the natural light for a natural perfection; he further perfects it by the infused virtues. But neither of them is sufficient to receive God's full offer: "the case of the ultimate and supernatural end is different. Towards it man is moved by reason in so far as reason is formed by the theological virtues, which form it only after a fashion and imperfectly. And so the moving of reason is not sufficient to direct man to his ultimate and supernatural end without the prompting and moving of the Holy Spirit from above. Thus it is written, 'They that are led by the Spirit of God are sons of God and heirs'; and, 'Your good Spirit will lead me into a right land.'"[9]

The effects of such moral height are the Beatitudes (Mt. 5; Lk. 6): perfect and excellent operations of the blessed; and the fruits of the Holy Spirit, which are "love, joy, peace, patience, kindness, goodness, trustfulness, gentleness and self-control" (Gal. 5:22).

Beatitudes and the fruits of the Spirit are the manifestation of an authentic and mature Christian morality which begins in nature but ultimately becomes the work of God's grace, which is sufficiently given to all who open their minds and hearts to it.

---

9. S.T. I–II, Q. 68, a. 2.

Bibliography

Abbott, Walter, editor. *The Documents of Vatican II*. New York: Herder & Herder, 1966.
Arnold, Magda B., and J. A. Gasson, S.J., "Feelings and Emotions As Dynamic Factors in Personality Integration." In *The Nature of Emotion: Selected Readings*, edited by Magda B. Arnold. Harmonsworth: Penguin, 1968.
Baltazar, Eulalio R. *Teilhard and the Supernatural*. Baltimore: Helicon, 1966.
Bonaventure. *Commentarius in IV Libros Sententiarum*. Opera Omnia, 4. Quaracchi: Collegium S. Bonaventurae, 1889.
Bouyer, Louis. "Gifts of the Holy Spirit." *Dictionary of Theology*. Translated by Charles Underhill Quinn. Tournai: Desclée, 1963.
Claparede, E. "Feelings and Emotions." In *The Nature of Emotion: Selected Readings*, edited by Magda B. Arnold. Harmonsworth: Penguin, 1968.
Connery, John R., S.J. "Morality of Consequences: A Critical Appraisal." In *Readings in Moral Theology, No. 1*, edited by Charles E. Curran and Richard A. McCormick. New York: Paulist, 1979.
Curran, Charles E., and Richard A. McCormick, editor. *Readings in Moral Theology, No. 1*. New York: Paulist, 1979.
―――. *Readings in Moral Theology, No. 2*. New York: Paulist, 1980.
Fletcher, Joseph. *Situation Ethics: The New Morality*. Philadelphia: Westminster, 1966.
Frankl, Victor. *Man's Search for Meaning: An Introduction to Logotherapy*. Translated by Ilsa Lasch. Boston: Beacon, 1962.
Fromm, Erich. *The Art of Loving*. New York: Harper & Row, 1956
―――. *Escape from Freedom*. New York: Avon, 1965.
―――. *Man for Himself: An Inquiry into the Psychology of Ethics*. Greenwich, CT: Fawcett, 1965.
Fuchs, Joseph. *Human Values and Christian Morality*. Dublin: Gill and MacMillan, 1970.
Häring, Bernard. *Free and Faithful in Christ: Moral Theology for Clergy and Laity*. 3 vols. New York: Seabury, 1978.
―――. *The Law of Christ: Moral Theology for Priests and Laity*. 3 vols. Cork: Mercier, 1960.
Hauerwas, Stanley. *Vision and Virtue: Essays in Christian Ethical Reflection*. Notre Dame, IN: Fides, 1974.
James, W. "What is an Emotion." In *The Nature of Emotion: Selected Readings*, edited by Magda B. Arnold. Harmonsworth: Penguin, 1968.
Kelly, Anthony J. "The Gifts of the Spirit: Aquinas and the Modern Context." *The Thomist* 38 (1974) 193–231.

Knauer, Peter, S.J. "The Hermeneutic Function of the Principle of Double Effect." In *Readings in Moral Theology, No. 1*, edited by Charles E. Curran and Richard A. McCormick. New York: Paulist, 1979.

Kohlberg, Lawrence. *The Philosophy of Moral Development: Moral Stages and the Idea of Justice*. San Francisco: Harper & Row, 1981.

Liturgy of the Hours. New York: Catholic Book Publishing, 1975.

MacIntyre, Alasdair C. *After Virtue: A Study in Moral Theory*. Notre Dame, IN: University of Notre Dame Press, 1981.

May, Rollo. *Love and Will*. New York: Norton, 1966.

McCormick, Richard. *Notes on Moral Theology, 1965–1980*. Washington DC: University Press of America, 1981.

McCormick, Richard, and Paul Ramsey. *Doing Evil to Achieve Good: Moral Choice in Conflict Situations*. Chicago: Loyola University Press, 1978.

Moeller, Charles. *L'Élaboration du Schema XIII: L'Élgise dans le monde de ce temps*. Tournai: Casterman, 1968.

Newman, Jeremiah. *Foundations of Justice: A Historico-Critical Study in Thomism*. Cork: Cork University Press, 1954.

Prümmer, Dominicus M. *Manuale Theologiae Moralis secundum Principia S. Thomae Aquinatis in Usum Scolarum*. 3 vols. Barcelona: Herder, 1961.

Rahner, Karl. *A Rahner Reader*, edited by Gerald A. McCool. New York: Seabury, 1975.

Skinner, B. F. *About Behaviorism*. New York: Random House, 1976.

———. "Behavior Control." In *Encyclopedia of Bioethics*, edited by Warren T. Reich. New York: Free Press, 1978.

Thomas Aquinas. *Commentary on the Nicomachean Ethics*. 2 vols. Translated by C. I. Litzinger. Chicago: Regnery, 1964.

———. *Liber de Veritate Catholicae Fidei Contra Errores Infidelium seu Summa Contra Gentiles*. 2 vols. Turin: Marietti, 1961.

———. *Quaestiones Disputatae*. 2 vols. Turin: Marietti, 1953.

———. *Quaestiones Quodlibetales*. Turin: Marietti, 1956.

———. *Scriptum Super Libros Sententiarum*. 2. ed. Edited by Pierre Mandonnet. 4 vols. Paris: P. Lethielleux, 1929.

———. *Summa Theologiae: Latin text and English translation*. 60 vols. Mew York: McGraw-Hill, 1964–1981.

Tillich, Paul. *The Courage to Be*. New Haven: Yale University Press, 1952.

Van Der Poel, Cornelius J. "The Principle of Double Effect." In *Absolutes in Moral Theology*, edited by Charles E. Curran. Washington, DC: Corpus, 1968.

Weil, Simon. *Waiting for God*. Translated by Emma Craufurd. New York: Putnam, 1951.

White, Victor. *God and the Unconscious*. Cleveland: World, 1961.

www.ingramcontent.com/pod-product-compliance
Lightning Source LLC
Chambersburg PA
CBHW052102230426
43662CB00036B/1755